THE OLD WAY	THE NEW WAY
Dependency Training	*Assertiveness Training*

THE OLD WAY — Dependency Training

"A woman should know her place."

"Don't talk too much about yourself—be interested in *his* hobbies."

"Don't let him know how smart you are."

"You catch more flies with honey than with vinegar."

"A woman should be passive."

"A woman should be compliant."

THE NEW WAY — Assertiveness Training

"Assertive women give the feeling they're more confident of their femininity and sexuality."

"With an assertive woman, you don't have to play games—you're two adults."

"An assertive woman knows that femininity is not passivity."

"Men don't want relationships with frail baby-dolls—they want the excitement of a fully-grown woman."

Learn how to get where and what you want in bed, at work, on the social scene, and at home—

**HOW TO BE AN ASSERTIVE
(NOT AGGRESSIVE) WOMAN IN LIFE,
IN LOVE, AND ON THE JOB**
A Total Guide to Self-Assertiveness

How to Be an Assertive (Not Aggressive) Woman in Life, in Love, and on the Job

A Total Guide to Self-Assertiveness

by
Jean Baer

A SIGNET BOOK

SIGNET
Published by the Penguin Group
Penguin Books USA Inc., 375 Hudson Street,
New York, New York 10014, U.S.A.
Penguin Books Ltd, 27 Wrights Lane,
London W8 5TZ, England
Penguin Books Australia Ltd, Ringwood,
Victoria, Australia
Penguin Books Canada Ltd, 10 Alcorn Avenue,
Toronto, Ontario, Canada M4V 3B2
Penguin Books (N.Z.) Ltd, 182–190 Wairau Road,
Auckland 10, New Zealand

Penguin Books Ltd, Registered Offices:
Harmondsworth, Middlesex, England

Published by Signet, an imprint of Dutton Signet,
a division of Penguin Books USA Inc.

A hardcover edition is published by Rawson Associates.

First Signet Printing, October, 1976
23   22   21   20   19

*For Herb,
who changed my life
in every way*

Acknowledgments

The material presented here comes from 150 interviews, personal observation and experience, the published literature about behavior therapy and Assertiveness Training, participation in many Assertiveness Training groups for women, and my own work as co-leader of a pilot study group at the Payne Whitney Clinic, The New York Hospital.

A great many people deserve thanks for making this book possible—so many that I cannot list them all and I must ask the forgiveness of those who are omitted.

First and foremost, I am indebted to the more than a hundred women who told me all about their assertive problems—in professional, social, emotional, and sexual situations—via in-depth interviews. Most of these interviews lasted two to three hours. Some extended over several sessions and totaled as many as twelve hours. I want to express my special appreciation to the members of my Payne Whitney group who spoke so freely and at such length with me.

A special word of thanks to the seven well-known women who took time out from their busy schedules to talk frankly with me about their personal assertiveness difficulties. They are: actress Elizabeth Ashley; literary agent Ann Buchwald; Pat Carbine, editor-in-chief and publisher, *Ms.;* Lenore Hershey, editor-in-chief, *Ladies' Home Journal;* Dr. Helen S. Kaplan, clinical associate professor of psychiatry, Cornell University Medical College (Dr. Kaplan was also extremely helpful as a professional source for my sex chapter); lawyer Jill Wine Volner; and TV star Barbara Walters.

Some of the nation's leading behavior therapists were helpful in providing counsel and case histories that I might pass on to readers. These include: Dr. Eileen D. Gambrill, lecturer, School of Social Welfare, University of California at Berkeley; Dr. Alan Goldstein, associate professor of psychology and psychiatry at Temple University School of Medicine; Dr. Arnold A. Lazarus, professor of psychology, Rutgers University, New Brunswick, New Jersey; Andrew Salter, the noted psychologist and author; and Dr. Richard B. Stuart, past president, Association for the Advancement of Behavior Therapy.

I would also like to thank Dr. Sandra Lipsitz Bem, assistant professor of psychology, Stanford University; Dr. Beverly Hotchner, executive director of the Center for Human Concerns, St. Louis, Missouri; Dr. Barbara Hogan of the Human Sexuality Program at the Mount Sinai School of Medicine, New York; Drs. Barry Lubetkin and Steven Fishman of the Institute for Behavior Therapy, New York; Dr. Elizabeth Mintz of New York City; Ms. Debora Phillips, director, Child Therapy Program, Temple University School of Medicine; Dr. Lee Salk, professor of psychology and pediatrics, Cornell University Medical College.

And a special word of thanks to Sharon Bower of Stanford University's Institute for Behavioral Counseling, management expert David McLaughlin of McKinsey & Co., and sex therapist Freida Stuart, who gave so generously of her time and whose book *Marital Pre-Counseling Inventory* (co-authored with husband Richard B. Stuart) was so helpful in the preparation of this book.

And most of all I want to express my appreciation to my husband, Dr. Herbert Fensterheim, clinical associate professor of psychology in psychiatry, Cornell University Medical College, and head of Behavior Therapy Treatment and Study, The New York Hospital, Payne Whitney Clinic, for his assistance, encouragement, support, and tolerance of my 6 A.M. sessions at the typewriter.

Author's Note

Throughout this book I refer to my husband in two different ways. When I quote him as an authority on Assertiveness Training, I use his professional title: Dr. Herbert Fensterheim, clinical associate professor, Cornell University Medical College. When I refer to him in a personal sense, he is simply "Herb."

Contents

How to Be an Assertive (Not Aggressive) Woman in Life, in Love, and on the Job

A Total Guide to Self-Assertiveness

Introduction

The Salespeople
Always Called Me Jean

Whether you're young or old, black or white, rich, middle class, or poor, single or married, extrovert or introvert, *you can learn to be an assertive woman.* In my own case, I managed the switch from the mouse I was to the *me* I had always dreamed of being—but never dared to try—when I was over forty, had spent twenty-one years in the same job, and a lifetime of rationalizing "If I do this, he/she won't like me."

My particular history of "patsyism" stemmed from childhood. My mother brainwashed me. She brought me up on fairy stories where heroines neither toiled nor spun but were coveted by handsome princes. Her particular favorite was Lewis Carroll's classic *Sylvie and Bruno,* in which Sylvie feels she must choose between "All must love Sylvie" and "Sylvie will love all." So I grew up feeling that I must love everyone and that everyone must love me.

Mother had certain inviolate ideas which she dinned into me. Girls were supposed to be ladylike, turn the other cheek whenever conflict occurred, "not be selfish," and work toward three objectives: popularity, a college degree, marriage. Another dictum was "Please men." That meant never showing you were "too intelligent" or "too strong." If you did, you

1

merited the label "unfeminine." A career was "a temporary thing until you settle down." And naturally, once you acquired that solid gold band on your third finger, left hand, your husband's needs and desires always came before yours.

I outfoxed her on two scores. I did *not* marry young and I *did* have a career, but her thinking, compounded by similar precepts from teachers and society, had a severe effect on me. It set up a pattern of unassertiveness, manipulation (I'd try to maneuver circumstances in an indirect way lest friends, dates, or bosses consider me "aggressive"), and constant cover-up of my real feelings (I'd express what I *thought* I should be feeling, not what I actually felt. After all, who would be interested in my true reactions? What man would want me if I showed I had brains?).

Socially, in my quest to gain that popularity goal, I rarely refused a request, no matter how unreasonable, and spent almost all my spare time doing favors for others (if anyone got sick, there I soon was with the container of chicken soup). When single, I went out with any man who asked me; it never occurred to me that I had the right to turn down an unattractive specimen ("You never know who you can meet through someone" had been another of my mother's dictums). On one occasion a female friend decided to give a party, told me about it, hired my cleaning woman to serve, and did not invite me. The night of the event, after everyone left, she called me up to "come over and eat leftover ham." *And I went.*

I wasn't a complete mouse. While I could not be assertive for myself, at work I could be very assertive for others. So naturally I went into the public relations profession. As a publicist, I brought others—with less ability—to national prominence while I remained in the background, saying, "One more shot, please" to the photographer. I freely gave away my ideas to others. For instance, on one occasion, while lunching with a representative of a news syndicate, I came up with the suggestion of a specialized teen-age column.

"You do it," he said.

"Oh, no," I responded. "I'll write it, and my boss can sign it." That's how we handled it. Eventually the column appeared under her by-line in some one hundred newspapers. She also got the profits, from which she paid me a small fee for doing *all* the work. It never occurred to me to question the justice of this.

Instead of making a decision or taking an active role in my own life, I sat back and waited for things to happen—a new job, that knight on a white charger. Even with my passivity, good things did happen. A college friend who held the post of public relations director at *Seventeen* magazine quit to marry a Boston internist and wangled the job for me. I stayed in it for twenty-one years, always trying to please the boss, never thinking in terms of my own advancement, and expecting constantly to be fired, even though I won numerous professional awards.

My career as an author was completely someone else's idea. A woman friend, who happens to be a literary agent, said to me, "You should write a book on your travels." Even though I spent my days writing articles (to be by-lined by others) and harboring occasional thoughts of writing my own book, left to my own devices I would never have done anything about it. But the agent set up a luncheon with an editor at a publishing house, and, spurred on by her, I dutifully recounted various anecdotes about my experiences in foreign lands. The editor said, "There's a book in this." Suddenly, there I was with a contract couched in very legal language and complete with deadline. I was very insecure about doing the book, but I was also afraid I'd go to jail if I didn't meet the deadline. So I wrote the book. Subsequent books stemmed from what other people told me I should write.

Then a lucky thing happened to me. I married Dr. Herbert Fensterheim, a very special man. I asked once how I came to marry him when I'd always eluded wedlock with anyone else, and he said, "Oh, I never asked you. It was obvious you had problems with decisions, and if I asked you, you would have said no. So I just kept announcing, 'We are getting married,' and eventually I changed this to, 'We are getting married in June.'" His theory was so right. I think I loved Herb from the day we met, but my inability to make decisions was so strong that if he had said, "Will you marry me?" I would have refused from sheer habit. He made the decision for me. I went along.

In addition to his numerous attractive personal characteristics, the special thing about Herb is that in his professional work at Cornell University Medical College—The New York Hospital Center, he specializes in behavior therapy (BT), which includes Assertiveness Training (AT). He saw my assertive difficulties and offered help.

He gave me a private course in Assertiveness Training. He taught me how to set long-range goals and sub-goals, how to take chances, and express resentments instead of keeping them to myself. He asked leading questions like, "Why have you been the good little girl on the job all these years? Where were you when the executive editor quit and everyone else was jockeying for promotions?" (I was on the West Coast working from 6:00 A.M. to midnight on some publicity stunt.) . . . "What could you do to make your present job better?" . . . "Where do you want to be five years from now?" . . . "Why do you always keep quiet when friends put you down, and then come home and cry? Try speaking up and see what happens."

Under his tutelage I learned to utter such statements as "I want" . . . "I will" . . . "I won't" . . . "I don't like what you've said." And I learned not to confuse the goal of being liked with the goal of being respected. In short, he trained me in the whole roster of assertive actions I am going to take up in this book, and I applied them to my life as a woman in the 1970s. Suddenly, and without any probing into the past as in Freudian analysis, my whole life began to change. Assertiveness Training had succeeded in enabling me to stand up for myself socially, professionally, and emotionally where seven years of traditional analysis had failed. As a result of AT:

I thought through my job situation. My job at *Seventeen* was sheer misery for me. There had been a series of new regimes and concomitant firings. Obviously, as a member of the "old guard," I, too, was slated for the axe. I made the deliberate choice to wait it out in order to get the considerable severance pay. Meanwhile I laid the groundwork for a future career as a free-lance writer. On the day I did get fired (the phrase used by management was "disbanding your department"), I was the world's happiest woman. If this had happened to me before Assertiveness Training, I would have been a candidate for a mental ward. Incidentally, I had always thought that without the prestige of my glamorous job, no one would ever come to the phone when I called. I was amazed when one book reviewer commented, "So you finally left. That job always held you back so."

I made progress in making requests of other people. For instance, I was writing a three-part series for a newspaper syndicate. It was due on Tuesday, and the preceding Saturday, I could see that if I had to keep on with all the household chores, I couldn't meet the deadline. At the same time, I could hear my mother saying, "It's a woman's duty." But this time the duty didn't seem as important as the deadline. I walked into the dining room, where Herb sat watching a hockey game at 2:00 P.M. on Saturday, and stated calmly, "I'm on a deadline and I'm frantic. I want you to cook tonight's dinner—and tomorrow's and Monday's. I just can't."

Said Herb, "Fine."

I was dumbfounded. "You will?"

"Sure," he said.

"But you've never done it before."

He said calmly, "You never asked me."

Now he makes dinner twice a week. My speaking up started a change in household roles, and, furthermore, my mother's voice hasn't returned to haunt me.

When something bothers me, I say so. For instance, some years ago my agent, a lovely, kind woman who also has problems with assertion, took on a client who wrote a book similar to one I had written. It was brought out by the same publisher, thereby affecting sales, advertising and promotion for both of us. I was furious. Did I tell the agent why? No, I couldn't be that direct. Instead I delivered a tearful speech about how "close friends shouldn't work together" and left her for another agent. The latter didn't work out, and subsequently I asked agent number one to take me back, which she did. Then when she again told me about a writer who had come to her with an idea similar to one I had in the works, I had learned my lesson well.

"Jane," I said deliberately, "it's going to be a repetition of what happened before. If you handle me, you shouldn't handle that book."

She listened and said she'd get back to me. The next day she telephoned, saying, "I've decided not to take that book."

Confrontation, inner turmoil, tears, bad consequences—all avoided by being direct.

I can say no, both to unreasonable requests and things I just don't want to do. Because I was always unable to refuse any invitation and used to call up at the last minute with the excuse "I'm sick," I used to spend a great many Saturday nights chained to the house (if I went out, someone would be bound to see me and tattletale to the hostess). Now, because I say no in the first place, I have a great deal more free time to do the things I want to do.

I can respond to put-downs. In my preassertive days, it seemed to me that the whole world constantly put me down with such cracks as "You shouldn't wear that color" ... "How tired you look" (when I had just returned from three weeks in Maine) ... "Why do you write such junk?" I made a deliberate attempt to master the art of response to put-downs and it must have worked. In the past six months no one has tried!

As a result of these various experiences, I, who had always seemed so assertive on the outside, became truly confident inside. This new self-concept had a number of results. I demand higher fees for my work and get them. I can walk out from no-win situations and not stay in them for years, dithering obsessively. I can take on challenges. I had always thought of myself as completely nonintellectual. After AT, I wrote with my husband, in what was a full collaborative effort, the book *Don't Say Yes When You Want to Say No* on Assertiveness Training, which not only became a best-seller but won an award from the American Psychological Association for "noteworthy contribution to the public's understanding of psychology." When I finish this book I, who remained twenty-one years in the same job because I was afraid of getting fired, am going to try to write a novel. I say to myself, "You may fail." And then I answer myself, "So what? At least you will have tried. It will be more of a failure if you don't try at all."

People treat me differently now. Even though I am a middle-aged woman, salesclerks had always—from teen-age years on—called me Jean. Whether at Macy's, Bloomingdale's, or Bergdorf's, I would sign my name to the check and invariably hear, "Thanks, Jean. You'll enjoy the dress, I'm sure." It annoyed me, but I never spoke up. Suddenly the first-name calling stopped and was replaced by Ms., Mrs. or occasionally Madame. Without my uttering a word, my new attitude of self-respect had produced more respect from others.

Many women of the 1970s are like me. As they fight to change the roles thrust upon them by family training and societal pressures, they still feel anxious and insecure. They know different options are there, but fears keep them from acting on them. Instead of doing, they dream and drift. They feel "All must love Sylvie" and "Sylvie will love all"— "All must love me" and "I must love all."

But you don't have to love everybody, and everybody doesn't have to love you. You do have to like and respect yourself. Act assertively—and you'll find that this will happen—and others will like and respect you too.

Just as I learned to be an assertive *me*, you can become an assertive—not aggressive—*you*.

Chapter 1

Assertiveness Training—
And Why Women
Particularly Need It

Jane and Bill play tennis. She's the better player but can't let herself win. "If I do," she explains, "he may not ask me out again."

Pat, married and mother of three, works as a decorator out of her home. One day her long-lost California cousin telephones, announcing, "I'm coming East. Can I stay with you for two weeks?" It couldn't be a more inconvenient time and there's no spare room, but Pat can't say no. "If I do, she'll be angry," Pat reasons.

Alice dates a lot, earns a high income at a demanding job, and loves her free-wheeling life. But her mother can't adjust to an unmarried twenty-six-year-old daughter and constantly reiterates, "Oh, darling, if only you were married." When Mother says this, Alice forgets all the rewards of her existence, feels defensive, and becomes tongue-tied.

New on her executive job, Lucy inherited an assistant from the previous regime who usually shows up late and rarely turns in assignments on time. Lucy hesitates to use her authority. Instead she comes in early to finish the assistant's work, thus incurring the resentment of other subordinates and failing to fulfill her own responsibilities as boss.

Jane, Pat, Alice, and Lucy differ in age, appearance and economic circumstances, but they share one quality in common: They are unassertive. They kowtow to others, can't refuse unjustified requests, fail to express their real feelings, fear success, essentially let others control their existence, and continually feel like the victims of circumstance.

This kind of behavior produces sad and severe consequences: You don't know who you are, what you want, or how to get it. You go along rationalizing, "If I do this, I won't get promoted ... will lose a friend ... job ... husband." You have a whole series of misconceptions: it is better to please other people than to please yourself ... if you constantly go out of your way to please other people, they will like and respect you ... by always putting other people's needs before your own, you will be able to count on these same other people when you need them ... if you do not please other people, you hurt your own chances for happiness.

But if you try to please everybody, you end up by being nothing to yourself. When you are nothing to yourself, how can you be important to someone else?

Why is it so difficult for many—if not most—women to act assertively?

What is Assertiveness Training?

How does assertiveness differ from aggressiveness?

What changes can come about from Assertiveness Training?

WHY WOMEN PARTICULARLY LACK ASSERTIVENESS

Psychoanalysts and parents, teachers and television, writers and business executives have all done their part to make women think "Assertive women finish last"—in relationships, on the job, in bed.

Read the Bible and you get the idea of how long ago women were trained to "know their place." According to Genesis, "In the beginning God created the heaven and the earth. . . . And God said, Let us make man in our image, after our likeness; and let them have dominion over the fish of the sea, and over the fowl of the air, and over the cattle, and over all the earth. . . . And the rib, which the Lord God had taken from man, made he a woman and brought her unto the man. . . . And the Lord God said unto the woman, What is this that thou hast done? And the woman said. The serpent beguiled me, and I did eat. . . . Unto the woman He said, I will greatly multiply thy sorrow and thy conception; in sorrow thou shalt bring forth children; and thy desire shall be to thy husband and he shall rule over thee."

Ever since biblical times literary figures have constantly put women down. In *Justine* Lawrence Durrell wrote, "There are only three things to be done with a woman. You can love her, suffer for her or turn her into literature." Penned Emerson, "A woman's strength is the irresistible might of weakness." The negative feelings and consequences of a girl beating a boy in intellectual competition are poetically summarized by Whittier in his poem "The School Days." Having outperformed the boy in a spelling match, the girl says:

> "I'm sorry that I spelt the word;
> I hate to go above you,
> Because,"—the brown eyes lower fell—
> "Because, you see, I love you."

Freud regarded women as essentially inferior to men and believed they were preoccupied with penis envy, a misery which a woman could alleviate only by giving birth to a son. In her two-volume *Psychology of Women,* Dr. Helene Deutsch emphasized submissiveness and masochism as natural feminine characteristics. A leading female therapist confessed to me recently, "The voice of my first great teacher, Theodor Reik, comes down through the years, saying, 'A woman should be passive.' "

This ideology is not a thing of the past. It still exists because in our culture the idea of what it means to be female inevitably suggests some kind of submissive role. This nonconscious assumption is at least as prevalent among women as men. It starts with the "dependency training" women receive as children and is reinforced by schools. If independence, assertiveness, and serious intellectual thought are desirable human characteristics, they are then desirable for women as well as men. Unfortunately and unwittingly many parents don't see it that way.

Many mothers and fathers make it impossible for their daughters to grow up into assertive human beings. From the very first they begin to raise their children in accordance with the popular stereotypes; they encourage their sons to be aggressive, competitive and independent; their daughters are rewarded for being passive and dependent. A recent study showed that six-month-old girls were already being touched and spoken to more by their mothers than were infant boys. By thirteen months these same girls showed greater reluctance to leave their mothers than the boys. When a physical barrier was placed between the girls and their mothers, the girls cried and motioned for help while the boys made active attempts to get around the barrier.

Parents also teach daughters a self-derogatory way of thinking. Other studies reveal that when little boys boast or ask, "Didn't I do that well?" they receive praise in answer to the question. The girls, who pose the same query, receive much less positive reinforcement—boasting, for little girls, is considered unfeminine. Thus, early on, girls get discouraged from self-praise. Instead of thinking, "I really did that well," they often learn to react, "Gee, I'm really dumb."

In later years parents often keep a closer watch on their female offspring than on their male. Daughter may have a curfew, but son does not. Son's friends aren't questioned, but mother will often say to her daughter, "She doesn't seem quite the right friend for you." Parents may also permit the sixteen-year-old son to use the family car more often than his seventeen-year-old sister. In the dating years men still take the initiative, and most girls (with some progressive exceptions) still sit and wait for the phone to ring. Mothers, magazines, and *The Total Woman* still advise, "Be interested in *his* hobbies" ... "Don't talk too much about yourself" ... "You catch more flies with honey than with vinegar."

Parents also try to force children into stereotyped ideas about work and career choices. If a young boy gets all excited by biology, he is almost certain to be encouraged to be a physician. A girl with the same enthusiasm is usually told to consider nurse's training.

There's still a double standard in school which has its influence on the growth and development of children. As early as nursery school, boys are encouraged to work on their own; girls receive assistance and attention but they are not sent off to work on their own. The result: boys learn to be independent and girls learn to depend on other people for assistance and approval. This dependency training exacts a high toll from young girls' motivation to succeed, to search for new ways of doing things, to take risks. One study showed that elementary school girls were more likely to try solving a puzzle by imitating an adult whereas the boys were more likely to search for a novel solution not provided by the adult.

The formative years and societal thinking affect both men and women. Men have been conditioned to think they must speak up, take the initiative. They depend less on others for approval. Meanwhile women don't think of themselves as equal to men so they don't act equal; consequently men, employers, relatives, society do not treat them as equal. Both men and women learn to suppress any behavior that might be considered inappropriate for their sex. Men are reluctant to be gentle, and women are afraid to be assertive.

Instead women learn and maintain behaviors which they have been trained to regard as feminine. They try to please others. They have the idea "I'm just here to make you happy. What I want doesn't matter." If challenged, they don't defend their ideas. Feeling their intellectual ideas don't matter any more than do their emotional needs, they hesitate to speak up about what they really feel or think. They use phrases like "I sort of think" or "I sort of feel" instead of straight talk.

So as not to be called "unfeminine," "castrating" or "bitch," they learn to accomplish what they want in indirect, manipulative ways. I still say, "It's cold in here" and wait for someone to close the window. Before Assertiveness Training I used to ask my husband, "Will you be going by Thirty-sixth Street and Third Avenue today?" instead of the direct, "Would you be able to pick up some masking tape at the hardware store?" If I could somehow get him to volunteer to buy the masking tape, I reasoned, then he couldn't call me a lazy wife.

Many women still cling to Mother's verbal legacies from another day and age. For instance, one woman in an AT group I co-led at Payne Whitney Clinic was always told by her mother, "If you're not with your husband twenty-four hours a day, you will lose him." She was told this from the age of eight on. Now, at thirty-four, she is a working mother, and recently her husband bought a Wednesday night series for the Metropolitan Opera. She has a class she wants to take on Wednesdays. Her husband volunteered to attend the opera with a male friend. But she still says, "I hate the opera. I want to take the class. But I'll go to the opera. I can still hear my mother saying, 'Don't let him go places without you.'"

Because of conditioning in the formative years, most women meekly accept certain societal assumptions. Dr. Elizabeth E. Mintz, a New York psychologist, points out four major ones in a paper on "What Do We Owe Today's Woman?"

Assumption One: It is natural for a woman to want to get married. If she does not wish to get married, she is anxious about sex, or unfeminine or in some way "unnatural."

Assumption Two: It is natural for a woman to wish to have children. If she does not wish to have children, she is in psychological trouble.

Assumption Three: Lack of ambition is a psychological problem in a man but is normal and therefore healthy in a woman.

Assumption Four: It is natural for a man to take the initiative in seeking a relationship with a woman. If *she* makes the overture, she should at least conceal her interest partially by finding some suitable excuse for calling. The man should certainly make the first sexual overture. If a woman makes it, she usurps his role.

There are other assumptions which are, in actuality, myths: women are less competitive than men, more passive, have lower self-esteem, lack motivation to achieve.

In *The Psychology of Sex Differences*, Eleanor Emmons Maccoby and Carol Nagy Jacklin write, "From our survey of all the data, many popular beliefs about the psychological characteristics of the two sexes have little or no basis in fact." But fact or not, the effect is there.

Becoming Androgynous

According to *Webster's New Third International Dictionary*, the word bipolar means "having or marked by two mutually repellent forces or two diametrically opposed natures, qualities or views." In American society we usually think of men and women as polar opposites. At one end of the pole is masculinity, at the other end, femininity. Men are supposed to be masculine, women are supposed to be feminine, and neither sex is supposed to be much like the other. With this notion, if you acquire such male-associated qualities as ambition or independence, you move toward the masculinity end of the pole, in the process becoming less feminine.

Dr. Sandra Lipsitz Bem, assistant professor of psychology at Stanford University, makes the point that this is not so. She feels that behavior should have no gender, that masculinity and femininity are complementary characteristics, that it is possible for an individual to be both masculine and feminine. A woman can acquire such traditional male characteristics as "self-reliance" and "willingness to take a stand" without giving up her femininity.

Dr. Bem feels we "need a new standard of psychological health for the sexes, one that removes the burden of stereotypes and allows people to feel free to express the best traits of men and women ... allowing them to be *androgynous*" [from *andro*, male, and *gyne*, female, and meaning having the characteristics of both sexes and not being typed as either masculine or feminine]. Says Dr. Bem, "Androgynous people are not limited by labels. They are able to do whatever they want, both in their behavior and their feelings."

When Dr. Bem and her colleagues studied the effect that rigid sex roles can have on behavior, they utilized the Bem Sex Role Inventory (BSRI), which consists of a list of 60 personality characteristics: 20 traditionally masculine (ambitious, self-reliant, independent, assertive), 20 traditionally feminine (affectionate, gentle, understanding, sensitive to the needs of others), and 20 neutral (truthful, friendly, likable). The psychologists made up this inventory from a list of 400 such traits that they had given to undergraduates, asking them to rate the desirability of each characteristic "for a man," "for a woman." With BSRI in hand, they conducted a series of experiments to test their tenet: that sex-typed people would do well only when the behavior was traditionally considered appropriate for his or her sex, whereas those who were androgynous would do well regardless of the sex-role stereotype attached to the particular action.

The psychologists studied assertiveness, predicting that "feminine" women would find it harder to be assertive than anyone else. For example, students were called on the phone with an unreasonable request: When would they be willing to spend over two hours, without pay, to fill out a questionnaire about their reactions to various insurance policies for students? The caller did not ask whether the people would be willing to participate but simply to indicate when they would be available.

In this situation, agreeing would cost a person time, effort, and inconvenience, but refusing required the student to assert his or her preferences over those of the caller. The results showed that women who scored "feminine" on the BSRI would find it harder to speak up and turn the caller down— 67 percent of the "feminine" women said they found it very difficult as compared to only 28 percent of the "masculine" men and androgynous students of either sex.

Says Dr. Bem, "This research persuades me that traditional concepts of masculinity and femininity do restrict a person's behavior in important ways. In a modern, complex society like ours, an adult has to be assertive, independent and self-reliant, but traditional femininity makes many women unable to behave in these ways. Androgyny, in contrast, allows an individual to be both independent and tender, assertive and yielding, masculine and feminine. Thus androgyny greatly expands the range of behavior open to everyone, permitting people to cope more effectively with diverse situations."

Are you sexually stereotyped—or androgynous? The following exercise may help you to describe yourself and identify behaviors you want to change.

TEST YOUR ANDROGYNY QUOTIENT

STEP ONE: Buy a good-sized workbook. This will serve as your Female Assertiveness Notebook (FAN), and you can use it for this exercise and others throughout the book.

STEP TWO: The following table* gives the masculine and feminine items on the BSRI. Copy them into FAN.

Masculine	*Feminine*
Acts as a leader	Affectionate
Aggressive	Cheerful
Ambitious	Childlike
Analytical	Compassionate
Assertive	Does not use harsh language
Athletic	Eager to soothe hurt feelings
Competitive	Feminine
Defends own beliefs	Flatterable
Dominant	Gentle
Forceful	Gullible
Has leadership abilities	Loves children
Independent	Loyal
Individualistic	Sensitive to needs of others
Makes decisions easily	Shy
Masculine	Soft-spoken
Self-reliant	Sympathetic
Self-sufficient	Tender
Strong personality	Understanding
Willing to take a stand	Warm
Willing to take risks	Yielding

STEP THREE: Use these characteristics to describe yourself. Indicate on a scale from 1 to 7 how true of you these various characteristics are:

*From "Beyond Androgyny: Some Presumptuous Prescriptions for a Liberated Sexual Identity," by Sandra Lipsitz Bem, Stanford University. To be published in J. Sherman and F. Denmark (eds.), *Psychology of Women: Future Directions of Research,* Psychological Dimensions, in press.

Example: shy

Mark a 1 if it is *never* or *almost never true* that you are shy.

Mark a 2 if it is *usually not true* that you are shy.

Mark a 3 if it is *sometimes* but *infrequently true* that you are shy.

Mark a 4 if it is *occasionally true* that you are shy.

Mark a 5 if it is *often true* that you are shy.

Mark a 6 if it is *usually true* that you are shy.

Mark a 7 if it is *always* or *almost always true* that you are shy.

Then total your separate scores on both the masculine items and the feminine items and divide each by 20. You must score 4½ or more on *each* to be called androgynous.

The women's movement has certainly questioned the feminine legacy of passivity, self-effacement, coyness, dependency, and the subordination of one's own needs to those of others. But societal change is slow. The old feminine conditioning lingers on. Women need techniques to achieve the roles they want. For many the answer lies in Assertiveness Training.

THE ASSERTIVENESS TRAINING METHOD —A TOOL FOR CHANGE

Assertiveness Training is based on the idea that by changing your actions, you change your attitudes and feelings about yourself. The goal: a new feeling of self-esteem: "I like me . . . I like the me I am." The premise: You have learned kinds of behavior that make you feel helpless, depressed, and unsatisfied, unable to stand up to others, fearful of rejection and emotional situations. But what you learned from parents, schoolteachers, playmates can be unlearned or modified. By learning how to act differently, you can change your behavior so that you can achieve what you want to do and become what you want to become. Just as you have trained yourself (or have been trained) to be a mouse, you can teach yourself to be a tiger (nonkilling variety).

Traditional psychotherapy, stemming mostly from Freud, Adler, Jung, Horney, Sullivan, and such, concentrates on the "why" that makes you the way you are today. This "why" emphasizes your unresolved childhood fantasies, conflicts, and traumas. Some twenty-seven years ago the new therapeutic technique of behavior therapy came into use. Rather than concentrating on the unconscious and the past, behavior therapy works on the current you. It focuses on observable behavior (the way you talk, move, react to others) rather than on father fixations, too much mother love, or the unconscious drive to fail. It says that what you do right now influences your personality and self-concept. By changing the way you act in the present, you change your personality structure, the way you act toward others, the way you feel about yourself, and the way others feel about you. The area of behavior therapy that concerns the skills of relating to people and the world around you is called Assertiveness Training.

Assertiveness Training (AT) goes far beyond consciousness-raising groups. It teaches you not merely how to realize and talk about your problems but how to *do* something about them. It teaches a specific series of behaviors of varying complexity. Some are elementary—like assertive body use (looking people in the eye, standing proud) and speaking in a firm voice rather than in a wishy-washy whisper. Some involve learnable skills—how to say no when you want to say no and yes when you want to say yes; how to initiate, maintain, and end conversations; how to be able to accept compliments, respond to put-downs, make requests. Still others involve more complex interactions—learning how to behave adaptively in difficult job situations; to accomplish goals, develop a more satisfactory social life; to achieve close relationships, express angry and tender feelings.

The change of one simple behavior can affect other behaviors and thus change many things. The breakthrough for me in Assertiveness Training came the night I was able to say, "I don't want to do that" to my husband. One of my mother's dictums stressed the necessity of giving your husband a good dinner. And I always did, even though I got up at six, worked all day at a very demanding job, and usually came home wanting a little French maid to bring me dinner in bed. The only French maid available was named Jean (me), and she felt she had to serve her husband the gourmet food Mama had brought her up to feel was proper fare for a hard-working man at the end of a long day. No hamburgers for me.

One Friday I came home after a particularly taxing day, took one look at that mangy chicken in the refrigerator, went upstairs, took a bubble bath, and retired to bed with a highball and a good spy story. Herb arrived some time later, took a look at me, and inquired with concern, "Are you sick?"

I answered, "I feel fine. I just don't want to cook tonight. You have a choice. There's a chicken. You can cook it. You can order in. Or we can go out. I'm not doing anything."

He applauded ("Thank God you're not playing martyr again!") and took me out to dinner. Furthermore, I found that once I said "I don't want to do that" to my husband, I could say "I can't take care of the dog while you're on vacation" to my stepmother and "I want x-y-z provisions in the contract" to my agent.

Many people have different concepts of assertion. Webster's defines the verb "assert" as "to state or affirm positively, assuredly, plainly, or strongly."

That's a very limited explanation. Dr. Arnold A Lazarus, professor of psychology at Rutgers University, considers assertive behavior as that aspect of "emotional freedom" that concerns standing up for your rights. This involves knowing your rights, doing something about them, and accomplishing this within the framework of striving for emotional freedom.

Andrew Salter, a leading New York psychologist who is considered the father of modern behavior therapy, prefers the word "excitation" to assertiveness ("Assertiveness has aggressive connotations"). He contrasts "inhibitory" people with "excitatory" people. "The inhibitory try to be everything to everybody, and end up by being nothing to themselves. They are chameleons trying to please the people they are with. They express everything but what they feel. They find it difficult to say no. They are always doing things they don't want to do."

In contrast the excitatory person "is direct. He responds outwardly to his environment. When he is confronted with a problem, he takes immediate constructive action. He sincerely likes people, but he does not care what they may think. He makes rapid decisions and likes responsibility. Above all, the excitatory person is free of anxiety."

For Dr. Herbert Fensterheim, clinical associate professor, Cornell University Medical College, the assertive woman has four characteristics:

1. She feels free to state what she thinks, feels, and wants. If doing this causes argument, she can cope and not go to pieces, harbor resentments, or attack wildly.

2. She can communicate in an honest, appropriate, and direct way (as opposed to dishonest and manipulative) with other people—salespeople, co-workers, subordinates, bosses, friends, and family.

3. She goes after what she wants in life. She does not wait for the perfect job to fall into her lap or the knight in shining armor to ride along on a white charger.

4. She acts in a way that makes her respect herself. For again the goal of Assertiveness Training is self-esteem. Assertiveness doesn't involve only your behaviors with others but your own self-regulatory behaviors as well. When you procrastinate, eat too much, or perform any act that causes you to lose respect for yourself, your self-esteem dips. To be truly assertive you must be in command of yourself. The idea is that you'll look in the mirror one day and say "Mary, you are a happy, fairly bright, increasingly mature, growingly efficient person. I am really getting to like you."

ASSERTION VS. AGGRESSION

Far too many people confuse assertion with aggression. Nonassertiveness is self-denying, inhibited behavior where you allow others to choose for you. Assertiveness is making your own choices, standing up for yourself appropriately, and having an active orientation to life. You stand up for your legitimate rights in such a way that the rights of others are not violated. In the process, you may hurt someone, but that is not your intent. Aggressiveness is an act against others that minimizes their worth as people, where you enhance yourself at the expense of another person, stand up for your rights in such a way that the rights of others are violated, and achieve by inflicting deliberate hurt. The purpose of the aggressive behavior is to humiliate, dominate, or put the other person down rather than to simply express your honest emotions or thoughts. You attack the person rather than his/her behavior. Frequently aggressive behavior may take the form of an outburst that stems from past pent-up anger. Letting someone else know your angry feelings at the time they occur can be assertive behavior.

As Mr. Salter says, "Excitation (or assertiveness) is a two-way street. Aggressiveness is a one-way street which pays no attention to the wishes of the other person. It is nonadaptive."

Because they have been socialized to be submissive, women particularly get confused when they want to speak up. They see the alternative to keeping quiet as aggressiveness—and that's "unfeminine." But the AT goal is to be effective in an appropriate way.

Let's take some situations common to women and show what possible nonassertive, aggressive, and assertive responses might be.

SITUATION ONE: Recently you met a new man at a ski resort. He volunteered to drive you back home and en route you stopped for dinner. When the check came he discovered he had little cash and no credit card. You volunteered to lend him the money and forked over $25. That was a month ago and you haven't heard from him since. You want your money back.

SITUATION TWO: You're in line at the supermarket counter with a shopping cart full of groceries. The quick checkout counter is closed. You've already been Nice Nellie and let one woman with a few items go ahead of you. Now, a second woman asks, "Can I go through?"

SITUATION THREE: You have a very dependent and talkative friend who calls every day at six o'clock just when you're preparing dinner. You can never get her off the phone.

SITUATION FOUR: You and your husband go to a party where most of the guests are your friends. You make the mistake of leaving him to his own devices. Because he knows so few people, he doesn't enjoy the party. The next day he loses his temper and calls you an "inconsiderate bitch." You know you did wrong but are furious at the way he spoke to you.

These are all situations that call for an assertive response. Decide how you would handle them.

Here are the answers:

SITUATION ONE: The man who owes you money.

Unassertive: You do nothing, wait for him to call, and hope someday you'll find that $25 check in the mail.

Aggressive: You call him and say, "Listen, what kind of person are you? You owe me money and you don't even have the decency to pay it back—or even to get in touch with me. I have the feeling you'll never pay it back."

Assertive: You call and explain, "I'm calling about the money situation. Perhaps you've forgotten the $25 you owe me. Can you send me a check for it?" And if he says, "I don't have it now," you counter with, "What do you think we should do about it? I need the money."

SITUATION TWO: In line at the supermarket counter.

Unassertive: You let the second woman get ahead of you and inside you seethe at your own passivity. That night you take your anger out on yourself or your family.

Aggressive: You berate the woman with some crack like "Don't be so pushy."

Assertive: You say, "Sorry, I was here first" and start getting your money ready for the clerk.

SITUATION THREE: The friend who is a compulsive telephone talker.

Unassertive: Day after day you continue to listen, following your familiar pattern of putting her needs ahead of yours.

Aggressive: "Listen, other people have problems too, only you never seem to think so. I'm getting pretty tired of listening to you say the same things over and over."

Assertive: "Look, I'm glad to talk to you but this is always a bad time for me. Let me call you back after dinner when my mind will be clear to concentrate."

SITUATION FOUR: You and your husband fight over your behavior at the party.

Unassertive: Knowing you're guilty of inconsiderate behavior, you attempt to bribe your husband by offering to make him his favorite dinner—a complicated stew which takes some fifty ingredients and five hours to cook. This makes you feel more put-down.

Aggressive: You yell back at your husband and bring up a long list of his faults. Sample accusation: "Five years ago you flirted with your old girlfriend at a party and I didn't behave to you the way you acted to me." You have a terrible fight and the ensuing silence lasts for days.

Assertive: You admit, "I was inconsiderate. I won't do it again, but I don't like the way you spoke to me. There was no need to yell like that. You may be right, but there is a proper way to behave."

In their anxiety about producing interpersonal conflicts that often prevent them from taking stances and expressing their true feelings, beliefs and opinions, women manifest unassertive behaviors in a number of ways. If you're the patsy type you may say it with silence, lack of action or a manner that begs "Don't take poor little me seriously." If you're openly aggressive, you use sarcasm, curtness, rudeness, hostility as weapons. You may be a concealed aggressive; you come on oh-so-sweet and appear to interact so well but inside that velvet glove you've got your steel knuckle ready for use. Whatever unassertive or aggressive tactic you use, it will not enable you to really like yourself. Assertiveness will.

WHAT HAPPENS IN ASSERTIVENESS TRAINING

The important thing about Assertiveness Training is that it works. To make it work, you must first realize it is *you* who are going to change your own behavior. As a result others' behavior toward you may also change, but *the intent is to change you*. In many instances Assertiveness Training gives you the problem-solving skills that men had developed in them as toddlers.

What can happen to you as a result of effective Assertiveness Training? Let me give you four examples from the group in which I served as co-leader at the Payne Whitney Clinic of The New York Hospital.

CASE

In the group Amy Wright, an executive secretary, found out that her major problems in being assertive emerged in close relationships. She said, "I always had the idea in my head that I must be a good woman. That meant being agreeable, and catering to a man." As a result, in her relationships, Amy found that she always took over any errands that had to be done. At one session, she told the women's AT group, "My fiancé is a student, studying medical lab work. He always asks me to do research and never says thank you."

In the group Amy practiced what she should say to improve the situation, and the next week she proudly reported back. The dialogue between Amy and her fiancé went like this:

AMY: Look, we have a problem. I know you have good feelings toward me. But I do all these things for you, and you never say thank you. It took me seven hours to do all that research. I'd feel much better if you could thank me.
FIANCÉ: You know I mean it.
AMY: I'm not a mind reader. Your not thanking me hurts me.

Amy says, "My speaking up has helped make him more aware of my needs. He's more considerate now. There's a real change in our relationship."

CASE

Betty, an almost model-pretty woman of twenty-eight, felt she always had had assertive difficulties. Daughter of a physician father and housewife mother, she says, "I always had a bad self-image. I didn't ask for things. I didn't think I was worth it. I wasn't encouraged to be demanding or ambitious. My brother was encouraged to be the professional, I the nurse." After graduation from college, Betty decided to become an occupational therapist ("more creative than nursing"). As a result of Assertiveness Training she thought through her job goals and began to think "What would I like?" She considered getting a Ph.D. in clinical psychology, eliminated that as "being too financially difficult," and finally decided on a two-year course leading to a master's degree in social work.

This decision brought up the matter of money. Betty had some savings but not enough to cover tuition, rent, food, clothes, and other life necessities. She also had two elderly aunts, who had never married and now felt marriage would have solved all their problems. Through the years they had put away money for Betty's marriage. They constantly asked her, "Why aren't you married?" ... "How's your social life?" ... "What are you *not* doing that you can't get yourself a man?" The decision to go to social-work school triggered new attacks: "Are you going to be a hermit now? You'll never meet anyone but women at that school. You should be going out—not going back to school at your age."

Betty wanted to finance her graduate work with the money the aunts had in escrow. With that idea in her head, and hoping she would be able to summon up the courage to ask for it, she went to the aunts' house for dinner. There she revealed her new professional ambitions, saying, "I do want to meet someone, and, of course, someday I want to get married. But right now I'm so proud of my decision to go to social-work school. It will mean such advancement for me. And I can pay for my own tuition." She didn't even have to ask for the money; the aunts volunteered it! Says Betty, "If they hadn't, I think I would have had the guts to ask. I had my sentence all ready: 'When I get married, I won't need the money. I need it now.'"

CASE

In the group, Debbie, a pert copywriter of twenty-eight, never spoke of any sexual difficulties. She talked a great deal of the "shoulds" with which she had been brought up ("A man should have a more demanding job" ... "A man should ask you out"). As a result of her Assertiveness Training Debbie is now in line for a promotion, able to question "Why?" if a superior makes a demand which she considers unprofessional, and to call a man without waiting for him to call her. But she has learned something even more important: She has changed a ten-year pattern of promiscuity.

Privately, after group training, she told me, "I went to bed a lot of times because I couldn't say no. There must have been twenty million instances. I always said yes, even at times of the day when I didn't feel like it. I was afraid of rejection. I've had a lot. And always after one or two sex sessions, the men just dropped me. If I had said no straight off a couple of times, the whole relationship wouldn't have been as tense as it became with immediate involvement. The men might not have dropped me." So Debbie started saying no. She says, "Now I have sex when I want to—not because I'm afraid to say no. And my relationships are much better."

CASE

Me. Since childhood I had had a love-hate relationship with a girl named Tess. She continually picked on me, and I put up with it. I went further than that. I got her seventy-two dates (once I was so angry with her that I totaled them up, and I'm sure I forgot some), toted her along to countless parties when I was single, wrote her résumé when she went job hunting, and freely provided introductions to professional contacts who might help her. Once I asked Tess, "Why don't you ever do anything for me?"

She answered, "But I do. I listen to you!"

In my neurotic need to somehow get her to like me and behave the way I thought she should (get *me* dates, take *me* to parties, introduce *me* to interesting people), I kept right on in the face of insufferable put-downs. Two instances:

• My first book, *Follow Me!*, came out and my agent threw a party for me. The guest list included innumerable available men, so I begged the hostess to invite Tess ("She hasn't got a man in her life at the moment"). The hostess did. The day of the party I walked into the room and everyone exclaimed, "Author, author!" Then I heard Tess's voice saying, "I went over all the anecdotes you got from me and rewrote them in my copy of the book just to show how much better they could have been written." I was speechless. The crack and my inability to reply ruined the party for me.

• After a particularly hectic workweek which included a fashion show for blind teens in Washington and a speech to a cosmetic industry conference in New York, I was about to finish off the frantic schedule with a talk to high school newspaper editors on Friday. Early that morning Tess called, saying, "I feel depressed." Despite my fatigue, I promptly invited her to dinner and managed to find time to buy astronomically priced lobsters. She never showed up. I left several messages with her answering service. She never had the decency to call until two days later. When I asked, "What happened to you?" she blithely said, "I forgot."

These are just two isolated instances. There were many others. In all the years I never evaluated "What am I getting out of this relationship?" I thought only "It must be my failure. There must be something I can do to change her." Again I said the refrain to myself: "I must love everyone—everyone must love me."

Then I married and subsequently started Assertiveness Training. The next time Tess pulled one of her put-downs (It was something like, "I'd be ashamed to write those man-catching articles you do for the women's magazines"—this from a woman who had never sold an article or book, even though she had tried), I was able to speak up. I said, "Look, Tess, when you say something like that, it makes me feel very bad. You've mistreated me for years and I don't like it. If we are to maintain our friendship, you have to try to change, and I have to stand up for myself if you don't change."

She listened. I hoped the statement would have some results.

Shortly after, she became engaged and called to ask me to hold open a certain date for an engagement reception. "You'll get an invitation," she said. My husband was reluctant to go ("How can you go after the way she has treated you?"), but I was full of curiosity about her fiancé. Herb consented to please me and even canceled his attendance at an important professional conference. No invitation ever arrived. The day of the event passed. From a mutual friend I heard that the party had taken place.

This time I finally was assertive. I telephoned Tess, made a luncheon date, and over a cheese omelet asked, "What happened this time?"

She answered, "Oh, did I invite you? *I forgot.*"

At that point I realized I had a decision to make. Clearly she was not going to change. I could (a) break off the friendship or (b) turn it into a very superficial relationship where we saw each other once or twice a year. I opted to make the deliberate choice to break it off completely. Ending this thirty-year relationship did a lot for me. I freed my life from the pressure of someone who constantly put me down. I also saw that perhaps it was time to end other relationships that existed from grammar school days—and I did. I could never have done this without Assertiveness Training.

WHAT PEOPLE WANT TO KNOW ABOUT ASSERTIVENESS TRAINING

Many people intrigued by Assertiveness Training have questions to ask.

How can you tell if you need Assertiveness Training? First, systematically survey the problems you face, the things that make you feel bad, the situations that make you frustrated, the things that you'd like to have different about yourself and your life situation. Do these relate to the area of assertiveness? Second, in addition to thinking about yourself and any difficulties you experience in being an assertive woman, read about it. Several excellent books exist on the subject; consult the Bibliography of this book. Answer the questions in the two quizzes in Chapter 3. If you have a great deal of discomfort in situations that call for assertive actions, or if you have specific assertive blocks (like the inability to say no), Assertiveness Training may be of enormous help.

Sometimes you can't make the decision about your need for Assertiveness Training by yourself. Some of the signs which often, but not always, indicate professional Assertiveness Training may be of help are (a) *unwanted feelings*—depression, frequent outbursts of anger, frequent feelings of helplessness, frustration, and of being pushed by others: (b) *inadequate life situations*—you lack a social network, close relationships, the sense of movement professionally.

Most of the Assertiveness Training courses are short—a matter of weeks rather than the years of traditional analysis. How can I learn much with such short-term treatment? Increasing evidence from studies done at major universities shows that such short-term courses do bring about behavioral change. At this point behavior therapists have only one- and two-year follow-up data on the effectiveness of Assertiveness Training, but they indicate that the changes do last. However, the main function of these AT sessions—whether they are individual or group—is to get you started. When you get the basic concept, which is learning and practicing specific assertive behaviors, you may begin to apply them in a variety of areas (at home, work, or with friends) and thus begin a lifetime process of becoming more like the person you are capable of becoming and want to be.

It is a lifetime learning process because as you begin to act differently you have a whole series of new experiences. You may learn to form close relationships more easily and so you have them. And this leads to new reality problems of living with and loving another person. You never reach a point where you can say "I'm through." There is always one new step to take.

Won't Assertiveness Training turn me into a pushy person? The very need to raise that question indicates your fears about being assertive and your lack of understanding of what assertiveness is. Pushiness implies behavior that isn't appropriate. Since part of the definition of assertiveness is to be appropriate, pushiness is not assertiveness; it is aggressiveness. Most people with problems in assertion don't have to worry about coming on too strong. There are a few people who do go through a phase where this happens. But it's usually a short phase and rather quickly brought under control.

It is interesting to note the different motivations which lead men and women to seek Assertiveness Training. Men often feel they express hostility in relationships with others and want to learn more effective, less aggressive ways to reach out to others. Women most often come from a submissive position and want to learn how to stop being controlled by other people.

I'm in traditional analysis now. Should I switch to Assertiveness Training? The basic philosophies are quite different. AT says, "Change what you do and you'll change yourself as a person." Traditional treatment concentrates on your unconscious and says, "You must first change yourself as a person and the consequence will be that you'll change what you do." If you're currently in traditional treatment and have doubts of which approach would be best, do two things:

1. Consult with a behavior therapist and just listen to what he/she has to say about you and possible treatment.

2. Discuss the problem with your current therapist and listen to what he/she has to say. There may be some very good reasons for changing or not changing at this time.

Remember, the basic decision is yours. You listen. You decide. The ethical principle involved is that the patient has the right to choose her own form of treatment. The assertive principle involved is that after taking everything into consideration you do what you will most respect yourself for doing. In some cases you can combine treatment, and this is something you might take up in the discussions with your own therapist and the behavior therapist.

How do I find a good Assertiveness Training practitioner? There are two kinds of Assertiveness Training:

1. Primarily educational. These are essentially AT courses given at schools, Y's, etc., that aim to give you the basic concepts in relatively limited areas—finding a job, social behavior, the special problems of women.

2. Primarily therapeutic. To help you through your specific assertive problems of bad feelings about yourself, not in an AT lecture course but in group or individual sessions.

If you feel you could benefit more from therapy than by attending a brief lecture series, be sure you choose a well-qualified professional. Someone may be qualified to teach job strategy, weight reduction, or the art of winning friends and influencing people, but that does not mean he/she has the background to teach Assertiveness Training. While researching this book, I read an ad headlined "Assertiveness Training" in a national publication which offered a phone number. When I checked it out, I learned that the gentleman who answered the phone provided a three-week course in "positive thinking." He had no Ph.D. nor even an M.A., and when I asked him his qualifications, he answered, "A background of success, starting from the time I was president of my grade school class." I wouldn't let him teach me anything!

Unfortunately, AT is becoming a fad and as such it is attracting some dishonest and unqualified practitioners. If you want help of the therapeutic variety, follow the same principles you would in choosing any doctor. Check out his/her professional qualifications; make sure he has been trained in the areas you want to work on.

You can check your local university (write to the head of the psychology department) or medical college for names. If you want a roster of behavior therapists, write for a list of the Clinical Fellows of the Behavior Therapy and Research Society, c/o Eastern Pennsylvania Psychiatric Institute, 3300 Henry Avenue, Philadelphia, Pennsylvania 19129. Go only to someone who has had intensive training—that means he/she has an M.D., Ph.D., or M.S.W. and has studied Assertiveness Training.

In my opinion, there are four top therapists in the field—unfortunately all men. They are (in alphabetical order), Dr. Herbert Fensterheim; Dr. Arnold Lazarus; Andrew Salter; and Dr. Joseph Wolpe, director of the behavior therapy unit at Temple University School of Medicine. They will probably kill me for offering this advice, but if I wanted the name of a competent therapist, I would write to any one of them and request a referral. These four leaders train the professionals. Besides, it's a good assertive exercise to go right to the top.

To the uninitiated and the novice Assertiveness Training looks easy. It is not. It is a highly technical and professional branch of behavior therapy.

If you change from Assertiveness Training, can't you upset the status quo in your own life? Your new assertive actions may lead you to change, quit, or possibly lose your job. They may temporarily disrupt your marriage or even end it (you may decide "I'm tired of my husband always walking over me"). Or they may improve it. Your husband may say, "What a relief to see you a mature person instead of that forty-year-old little girl!" You may win some new friends, lose old ones, as I did, and even decide on a whole new set of life goals. Remember, AT does not promise the easy way; it promises a chance at the fulfilling way.

Should I go to a male or female therapist for Assertiveness Training? If you get involved with the kind of AT which is primarily educational, I feel your best bet would be equal co-leaders: one male, one female. If you take Assertiveness Training for therapeutic reasons, the sex of the therapist isn't as important as the kind of person he/she is. In their book *I Can If I Want To,* Drs. Arnold Lazarus and Allen Fay offer a therapist selection questionnaire. Here are some of the feelings you should have if you've selected the right kind of person.

1. I feel comfortable with the therapist (T).

2. T does not treat me as if I am sick, defective, and about to fall apart.

3. T is willing to tell me how she/he feels about me.

4. T admits limitations and does not pretend to know things he/she doesn't know.

5. T answers direct questions rather than simply asking me what I think.

6. T encourages the feeling that I am as good as he/she is.

7. T acts as if he/she is my consultant rather than the manager of my life.

8. T encourages differences of opinion rather than telling me that I am resisting if I disagree with him or her.

9. T is interested in seeing people who share my life (or at least is willing to do so). This would include family, friends, lovers, work associates, or any other significant people in my environment.

10. The things that T says make sense to me.

11. In general, my contacts with the therapist lead to my feeling more hopeful and having higher self-esteem.

Will men be threatened by my new assertiveness? Some may. Are they the kind you want? My husband told me, "Assertive women generally give me the feeling that they're more confident of their femininity and sexuality. With them, you don't play games. You're two adults. I don't want to relate to a frail little girl. I want to relate to a woman. I have two daughters as is. I don't want another one."

Chapter 2

Just Like You
and Me

Many people picture the typical female celebrity as confident, organized, strong in personality and inner psyche, fearless, able to do anything she wants to do—in short, assertive. "After all," reasons the average Ms., Miss, or Mrs., "X's name appears constantly in the paper, in lights, on contracts for fabulous amounts of money. Look at all she has accomplished. Everyone thinks she's wonderful. She must think so too."

Not true. Like their counterparts on Main Street, celebrities also worry about going places alone, handling criticism, coping with "too much to do," their inability to be direct with people close to them, hurting others when they flare up in anger, being thought "too tough" by men and coming on too strong. In short, they're just like you and me. They, too, have problems in asserting themselves appropriately.

For this book I have interviewed the following highly talented women.

1. Pat Carbine, editor-in-chief and publisher of *Ms.*
2. Lenore Hershey, editor-in-chief, *Ladies' Home Journal*
3. Helen S. Kaplan, M.D., Ph.D., clinical associate profes-

sor, Cornell University Medical College, internationally known sex therapist

4. Ann Buchwald, literary agent and author
5. Elizabeth Ashley, stage and screen star
6. Jill Wine Volner, Washington lawyer, star of Watergate
7. Barbara Walters, media superstar, TV journalist

It's what my scientific husband would call "a highly selective sample." I picked these particular women because (a) they are all well known and move in the celebrity circle; (b) I knew a number of them and felt these women would be honest with me and hence with you. They have been.

PAT CARBINE

This leading editor-feminist, who has red hair and the skin that goes with it, comes from Villanova, Pennsylvania, and is a graduate of Rosemont College. Both parents were first-generation Americans of Irish descent. Her father was a self-educated man who became general manager of the Pennsylvania Railroad. Pat has had a distinguished career at *Look* magazine where she was executive editor, at *McCall's*, where she was editor and later vice-president ("I left because Gloria Steinem told me, '*McCall's* will survive and thrive if you leave; *Ms.* won't start if you don't.'") In just three years she has helped to turn *Ms.* from a new magazine with an uncertain future to a profit-making publication with many subsidiary operations. My reaction on the two occasions when we met has been, "She is just so nice. How can anybody so successful be so nice?" She really is.

Pat says, "My teen years had a strong influence on me. My dad died when I was sixteen. It was during the war. All my brothers were away, and it seemed natural for me to fill in the vacuum left by their departure, so I stoked the furnace, put up the storm doors and did the grass cutting. I saw the need, and started to fill it. I've been doing this ever since. Because my mother was one of thirteen kids, she'd had no real shot at education, so she was very fixed on her children's having an education. There were so many siblings—six of us—

that it mitigated any pressures she might have put on me to marry. But I am an aunt thirty times!

"Still, the sexual stereotypes have had their effect on me. I realize now that when I was beginning to compete in the professional world, I felt I shouldn't show my brains. Whenever I had an idea, I introduced it by saying, 'This is a wild idea' or 'This is probably the worst idea you ever heard but I'm going to say it anyway.' I find myself still lapsing. I don't hold back from winning but I do hold back from talking about it in the company of men. It's that stereotype again."

ON SAYING NO: "It's a root problem for me. I'm too much of an optimist. I have the notion that I'll get it all done. I have the crazy idea that with a little more effort I can participate in one more thing. Recently I said yes to something I had no business saying yes to because I have no time—I said I'd join the board of the International Design Conference in Aspen though I probably should not have, but I knew it would be a great learning experience. I find it so hard to say no.

"With friends it's even harder. I try not to commit myself. I say, 'I'll try.' Then at the last minute I call and say, 'I can't make it.' I get so mad at myself. I say yes to a speech request that I don't want to make and haven't got time to make, but a friend asked me. So there I am getting up at 5 A.M. to get to another city by noon to speak to a friend's auxiliary group. I get perturbed at myself and the sentence I hear in my head is, 'This was not worth it,' but I go right on doing it."

I asked, "Are you shy?" She answered, "Believe it or not—yes. I feel shy with someone I've just met socially. I don't like to reveal where I work until some kind of rapport has had a chance to take place. When I say what I do, I get a fascinating series of reactions. It puts folks on guard, adds an ingredient of tension. It takes longer for them to relate to me as a person as opposed to a 'type.' I feel shy at gatherings of men where I am the only woman. At first they are all in huddles talking to one another. I have no shyness about getting myself a drink, so I make my way to the bar. But there's that awful moment before I turn to someone and say, 'Hello, there.' I find myself using small talk. I ask, 'What did you think of so and so's comments?' Or I talk about sports. As a kid I was a touch football player, and I'm still a big sports fan."

ON BAD HABITS: "I have a terrible failing. I'm always late. I always think I'll get places faster than I do. And I procrastinate: about preparing a speech, losing weight, getting my apartment painted—it was supposed to be painted three years ago when we were launching *Ms.* and now I've gone through a whole lease; we have a magazine but I still have no paint job. Writing a will is another thing—all I've got is a piece of paper which will test the human flexibility of a court. Then there's getting clothes to and from the cleaner and entertaining.

"I'm a terrible correspondent. God never meant me to have to deal with all the pieces of paper involved in my life. I'm indirect but I hope I'm not manipulative. I use indirection to make a project seem more interesting than it is. I deliver a preamble that sets the scene for the 'wonderful' thing we're about to do. Everyone sits there waiting for the shoe to drop. Maybe I'm just keeping myself psyched.

"I find it terribly hard to make requests. I put off asking people to do things until the last minute. Next Monday I'm running a conference panel. It's Wednesday, and just today I've gotten to actually asking the panelists I want to participate. With me it's always last minute. I always procrastinate. I go through periods of thinking, 'There must be a better way!' "

WITH MEN: "I add an extra explanation for not being able to do something or be someplace. I want to explain so men won't view what I'm doing as being less important than their activities. Being successful and earning a high salary used to bother me. The perfect solution is to go out with someone in a different business. Now most of the men I spend time with are my peers. With them I don't often say, 'I want to do such and such,' but I don't feel it's because I'm holding back. If I've made nineteen hundred and two decisions in the course of the day, it's often a relief to have someone else make a few."

ON TAKING COMPLIMENTS: "I used to have a terrible time accepting compliments. I was helped a lot by a scene I once observed. I was out with a journalist. We encountered a colleague and my date stopped her and complimented her on a piece she had written.

"She said, 'Oh, it was nothing. It was O.K.' As she spoke, she looked off in the distance instead of looking at him. It was classic—just the way I had always reacted in the past.

"He said, 'You're going to have to learn to accept compliments. Did it ever occur to you to say simply 'Thank you'?

"It made a great impression on me. Now I say thank you."

ON DEALING WITH PEOPLE AT WORK: "In my career I always found it appalling when people behaved differently to different levels of people, nicer to someone higher up than lower down. At *Ms.* we all try to make decisions together. The newest assistant has as much right to present an idea as I do.

"*Ms.* has influenced my assertiveness. When I'm doing business with outside folks, I feel as if I'm taking a position not just for me but for the corporation and staff. If the position involves being faithful to the magazine's charter, I'm endlessly assertive. I'll go to the mat with anyone if the magazine's prerogatives are being abused. But in my personal life I still back off."

ON ANGER: "A lot of it stays inside. If something has gone very wrong at work, I can deal with it. I do it quickly but I get terribly cool and precise. But it's harder with close friends and my brothers and sisters. For example, one of my brothers made negative comments about *Ms.* I listened. I did manage to get out the sentence, 'Obviously, I don't agree with you.' But to this day he doesn't know how angry I was at him. If he weren't my brother, we'd still be sitting there and thrashing it out. I know I should have said, 'Your reaction not only offends me but is completely uninformed,' and then proceeded to tell him why. But I couldn't do it."

ON FRIENDS: "In a lot of ways I trust them to understand why I don't see more of them. I can't tell them about the pressures I have to live with. I say nothing or I minimize it. If I tell them why I'm an absentee friend, I'm afraid it will sound like boasting or I will sound crazy. I don't want everyone to love me. I do want them to understand me. My great concern is that my friends will run out of patience with me. I don't work hard enough at being their friend. That troubles me. I promise myself that I can change and will change."

LENORE HERSHEY

She is bubbly, lively, the kind of woman one describes as "extremely feminine." A graduate of Hunter College and a member of its Hall of Fame, she is married to Dr. Solomon G. Hershey, a distinguished anesthesiologist, and has one daughter. After fifteen years with *McCall's* magazine, she joined *Ladies' Home Journal* in 1968 and served as managing editor and executive editor before becoming editor-in-chief in 1973. She says:

"I was an only child. My father was director of a boys' camp and my mother helped out in the office. I was secure but lonely. I always knew I was a girl because there were so many boys around. I knew I wanted to be a writer, and my parents encouraged me to write and have a career. But by being special, I lived with loneliness and many anxieties. And I always had the feeling of trying to please.

"To this day, I am self-conscious about my looks. I always thought that if I had been a classic beauty, I could have owned the world, and the appearance hang-up still bothers me. I envy those tall, slim, beautiful girls I see. In my life, I've been called many pleasant things: cute-looking, smart, chic, now even handsome. But it's not enough. I always wanted to be beautiful, just that. Perhaps for itself, perhaps as a way of power over men. Silly, but that's my cultural baggage."

ON MARRIAGE: "I got married when I was twenty-one, and our life-style was the shared one that's routine today. I worked so he could finish his residency (and because I wanted to work). All my life, I worked full-time, and I've never wanted to stay at home. In our marriage, my husband is the dominant one. He's the organized, lean-on type; sometimes his preciseness and neatness drive me crazy. But I thank God I am married to a strong, dependable man. My success? He welcomes it and is proud of it as long as it doesn't make special problems . . . interrupted vacations, a clash of plans. Fortunately, he has always made more money than

I do. Men, no matter how unprejudiced, still have a thing about this, I'm convinced.

"The coy guiles and wiles don't work on Sol. In business, I can use flattery: 'I just know you can do this for me; you're so great,' and that sort of thing. But I know it won't work with Sol. We have a long-term gut relationship. We can't say anything to each other that isn't true and honest. Oh, yes, I've evaded sometimes. Even though we have a joint financial pot, I'm sure I haven't told the truth when I paid an outrageous price for something extravagant."

ON ASSERTIVE PROBLEMS: "Professional decisions have always come easy to me; I don't worry about my own judgments. But when I'm hurt or angry, I can never answer back. Two things bother me greatly: being lied to and being left out. I think I gave my novelist friend Joe Heller that line in his book *Something Happened*: 'Every time I pass a closed door, I think they're inside talking about me.' I've alway been thrown by tough criticism. I find it difficult to take put-downs that attack me as a person. This current job has developed strong new patterns for me: trusting my own decisions and backing them with action affecting other people, feeling like the boss, believing in myself as the boss, reducing my own vulnerability. Assertion can't be surface. Your insides have to feel sure. Now, after two years, when someone contests a choice of cover or headline and asks, 'Why do you think this will work?', I can say, 'Because I'm editor and I want it that way.' It took me two years to be able to say that coolly and mean it."

AT WORK: "It's still difficult for a woman to move up to the top jobs. Years ago, there was a change in management at *McCall's*. I went to Herb Mayes and asked for the top editor's job. He said, 'Don't be silly. No woman will edit this magazine. Be a good little girl and stay in your spot.' I was upset. I just sat there, feeling powerless. I said, defensively, 'Maybe I should look for another job,' and he said, 'Oh, no.' Something happened. A week later, I moved myself over to the *Journal*.

"Becoming editor-in-chief at the *Journal* was an accident of fate, and my big problem at first was role adjustment with the men I worked for and with. Earlier, I had been the office wife for several male bosses. They took credit for many of the things I did. I'd write their speeches and sit back and beam with pride while they read my words. I didn't mind; they had the headaches of responsibility, and, like many women, I enjoyed being the secret weapon, the power behind the throne, especially if the men appreciated my contribution.

"When I finally got the top spot myself, I stepped into the shoes of an adored big-Daddy image. He left, and I felt like one of the deserted children. A male associate said to me, 'My sister has suddenly become my mother,' so I guess we all felt that way. Later, I realized that my management pattern had to be different and my own. I believe I serve more as a mother figure who can be tough, stern, molding, but open; you don't have to take out the strap. Women bosses should develop their feminine assets into strengths, have a guiding firmness rather than the fear quality of the father.

"When men work for you, you find they release a lot of their general emotions about women on you. I think I have a good relationship with my male associates. I try to give them their own authority and dignity. Sometimes, they still like to surround themselves with adoring young women, but somehow I don't have to surround myself with adoring young males. I find women easy to work with, too. It's all professional now; no more vying for Daddy's love. We can talk without maneuvering."

ON ANXIETIES: "I've had to conquer a lot of anxieties. As a child, I was frightened of automatic elevators, driving a car [she still doesn't], flying [she criss-crosses the globe by air], public speaking [she makes several talks a month], and always, loneliness. Now I know a special kind of loneliness, in the executive suite. There are many decisions and many situations you simply must sweat out by yourself.

"My chief anxieties today are existentialist: dark thoughts in the night, time's winged chariot drawing near. Here I am in my fifties, and I look in the mirror and don't see a thirty-year-old with decades to spare and experiment with. I'd still like to write a novel, have more children, produce a movie, raise horses, learn how to ride a motorcycle, be an ambassador (preferably to Ireland), be President of the United States. Or at least, president of a company. Time's short, but maybe my energies will still get me some of these."

ON WOMEN: "I'm more impatient with women than men

in the working situation. A lot of women don't realize how hard they have to work to get ahead; they haven't been bred in the same work compulsion. And too many people—male and female—confuse aggression and assertion. You can push, but you don't have to shove."

DR. HELEN S. KAPLAN

She is small, quick, seems like the kind of woman who can handle anything—and does. Born in Vienna, she came here at ten, studied art at Syracuse University, then married at twenty-one, got both her M.D. and Ph.D., had three children, and is now divorced. Her pioneering work in sex therapy and her book *The New Sex Therapy* have brought her worldwide recognition from both professionals and the public. She says:

"I've achieved academic and professional success, enjoy my work, am sought after as a speaker, have wonderful friends, great kids, a nice apartment, am at ease with anyone in the world. My mother—and she represents millions who think just like her—thinks all that is 'nice' but that I'm a failure. If I were married to a man who made the success, that would be much better. Doing it myself isn't. I'll be O.K. in Mother's eyes if I catch myself a husband. Then I'll be successful. I'm an analyst, but it's only lately that I came to realize how many of my mother's values I had inadvertently adopted.

"I never realized I was bright. When I was younger, I wanted to be a psychiatrist, but I didn't think I was smart enough to go to medical school. During college I dated psychiatrists and I married one. Then, I realized, 'I want to be a psychiatrist, not just be married to one.' And I took proper action. My eleven-year-old daughter doesn't have these problems. She says, 'I want to be a lawyer.' But I was brought up to marry a successful man—not be successful myself.

"When I was married I didn't speak up for fifteen years. My husband never washed a dish or changed a diaper or took a sporty ski vacation—the kind I would have liked. I was totally submissive, just the way my mother brought me up to be. I'm afraid I might be that way again if I were afraid of losing the man. But I hope not."

ON SETTING PRIORITIES: "This is one thing I was always able to do. During the four years I was in medical school, just two things mattered—taking care of the one child I had at the time and my studies. One time my brother came to town from California. He was engaged. He invited us to have dinner with him and meet his fiancée. And I said, 'I'm sorry. I have an anatomy exam.' I was able to do this because I was secure with my husband. We had agreed on priorities. He encouraged me in my career. My priority fit into his needs. And that's all-important. You can't set priorities without considering other people.

"Time is the important thing. I have a budget system. I make a list and I set limits. I've learned not to go to pieces when I can't get a minor item on the list done. I know the people I love come first—that I must call the dentist for Peter and the school re Jennie, respond to Phillip's call from college, telephone a friend to accept a dinner invitation. Then there's my work. I must see patients, teach my students, arrange lectures. You've got to get over the guilt about what you can't do. There has to be a balance between your needs and others."

ON WORK: "Now, I don't have difficulties. I've thought through my own likes. I know I don't want to be head of a department of the medical college. I'm not power-hungry. I enjoy humanistic and creative activities more than administration, and I'll be damned if I'll get involved in a fight for power. I want only enough power so I can do my own thing.

"I've always been helped by men at work, never hurt. But I have used creative nepotism to get ahead. My husband was training director at the hospital and that opened doors to me. I made myself indispensable to the chief and helped him with important work. I know now that this was unnecessary. I would have made it on my own. However, during all the years of my marriage, in any professional papers and books where I did the work, I'd always put some man's name first as senior author. My mother again!"

ON FEARS: "I'm still afraid of rejection—though not as much as I used to be. In a social group—let's say a big cocktail party—I feel secure and usually have a very good time. But recently a friend gave a dinner party for six single people. I felt terribly shy. I still have my old hang-up of feeling insecure when I go to a dinner party unescorted.

"I have assertive problems in two situations. One is when I play tennis with a woman. I can hit one killer shot but I can't follow through if she returns it. I'm afraid to hurt my opponent. I used to have anxiety attacks on the tennis court. Now I can play doubles where the responsibility for aggressiveness rests on my partner, but I play a poor singles game. With women it's a fear of hurting a vulnerable person. I know it's irrational and unconscious but it's there.

"The other situation where I still experience anxiety is with a man whom I really love and fear will reject me. I can't talk straight. I'm overly nice. I become a totally different and unattractive person. In every conversation and action I'm completely deferential. I put his needs before mine every time. I don't express my own feelings.

"I used to do this with everyone. For instance, with my housekeeper. I'd worked a twelve-hour day, but my daughter had to be picked up from a friend's house. I'd ask the housekeeper, 'Would you please pick up Jennie?' If she made a face, I'd immediately say, 'I'll do it.' I was always afraid she'd leave.

"Now I know I can handle people, but I'm aware that I still have this pattern of going back to my old ways when it comes to an important emotional involvement. This is something I'm trying to work through."

ON THE FUTURE: "I have come a long way since my early years, when I was taught that material values and pleasing a man are the most important things in life. I see how destructive some of my patterns have been—particularly the ones caused by my insecurities. Now I know that people's feelings, love, and the expression of honest emotion are what matter. I still have a long way to go, but someday I'll get there. At last I am beginning to live by my own values—not those I learned as a child."

ANN BUCHWALD

She is a bright, blonde, vital woman. The adjectives hearty and sunny fit her. Married to columnist-author Art Buchwald, she moves at the top of the celebrity circuit (when she says "Ethel," she means Ethel Kennedy. Author of three books for children, she recently started a career as a literary agent, handles clients like Abigail McCarthy. Reared in Warren, Pennsylvania, a town of 15,000 people, daughter of a housewife mother and barber father, she is one of eleven children—nine of them girls. She says:

"After high school I had to get a job. Later I learned I had gotten a scholarship to college, but my mother didn't have the heart to tell me. We couldn't afford even the minimal expenses of college. I would have gone to Allegheny College and ended up teaching Latin and Greek. I started in the lingerie department at the local department store. Then I made a suggestion to a manufacturer about changing the color of a lingerie envelope from black to pink. The boss heard about it and said, 'Maybe you'd like to study advertising.' I did. Then the boss handed me a clipping from *Women's Wear Daily* about a job in Memphis. I borrowed $75 from my sister and a spring coat from a friend—it was cold and I had to sew a sweater in it—and went to New York for the interview. I got that job. Then I had a series of fashion jobs in Pittsburgh, New York, and then at Neiman-Marcus in Dallas.

"But when I thought of myself as a fashion director, something was amiss. What crumbled me was to be the director. Mother had always been the organizer of our family, telling us what had to be done (feed the baby, help with the ironing, etc.), but because she had to juggle so many people and problems, she ran the big show (she had to, to make the most of what resources we had). As a result I couldn't deal with big decisions or underlings. I'd try to do it all myself. I thought I didn't know enough to tell anyone else what to do. I also thought I'd go starkers if I stayed in the merchandising business. I didn't want to wear a good black dress and five strands of pearls. I decided to go to Paris. Up to then, all my life I had worked hard but been completely unassertive. I kept trying to please my mother and other people, to find out what it was she or they wanted, and give it to her or them."

Ann went to Paris in 1948, worked as a publicity girl for Pierre Balmain (1949–1951), met Art in 1949, started a public relations business in 1951 with two other American women, married Art in 1952, and stopped working. They have three adopted children—ages twenty-three, twenty-one, and twenty.

She admits, "We've been married twenty-four years and I still look to Art for decisions. At the airport, I ask, 'Where's the gate?' When I'm alone, I can find it easily. I love to have other people make my decisions. It was Art's idea I have a career as a literary agent. I thought, 'I'm a great housekeeper. Why learn something new?' But he told me to do it, so I did it. Without giving myself a chance to think it through, I launched into a career about which I knew nothing. The first year I felt so stupid I thought I must be losing my mind. I thought, 'I don't have the answers to anything—I don't even know the editors to match with writers or the writers for the editors.' I'd come up to New York once a month and tremble all the time. At home I'd cry and project what awful things would happen. But Art wanted me to do something 'interesting.'

"He also got me involved with my first book. He was having lunch with David Brinkley and a woman who ran a school teaching manners to children. The woman said, 'I need a writer to carry out a book project.' And Art said, 'Why don't you see my wife. She can't write either.' I signed my first book contract *without even reading it.*"

ON INDIRECTNESS: "I'm very indirect. I have a checking account for household expenses. Art used to say, 'How's your bank balance?' I'd say, 'I don't know'—I knew it was overdrawn but not how much. He'd get mad. When he asked me last month, I told him '$72.' He didn't say anything, but he gave me more money than he usually does and I knew he liked my straight answer."

ON SPEAKING UP: "Art thinks of me as dependent. But when I go away I come back to find that everything is broken and no one has fed the cat. It seems to me that everyone depends on me—for marketing, getting the roof fixed, paying the bills, taking care of three kids and their problems. I wonder, 'Why am I classed as dependent?' But I can't speak up.

"Recently we had a discussion. I was so tired of only heavy talk about politics, death, war. I said to Art, 'Look, I always tell you about the kids and the house. I leave notes on your bed so you'll be au courant—and what I get in return is that you keep on reading or nod at me. I want trivia.' So he started coming home at night and announcing, 'Trivia One.... Trivia Two....' It was hard for him. He's tired. And then he'd say, 'That's all the trivia for today.' But I heard him bragging to friends, 'I don't tell her the big things. She reads those. I tell her the trivia.' He was pleased because I finally spoke up about something."

ON ANGER: "My assertive failing is a tremendous temper. I guess I get so angry because everything in my childhood was black or white, good or bad. One word can trigger a reaction. I'm in the tub and Art will say, 'So and so is in from California with his wife and kids and I've asked them to dinner tomorrow night.' So I yell. Our maid leaves at four o'clock. It's my pride. I want to do it. I want to be a woman and make my family comfortable and entertain a lot. But he doesn't understand my workweek.

"Or he'll say in May, 'Let's see, I'll be in Pittsburgh on June 13. You could meet me there and see your mother.' He's so organized, but I panic and then I get angry and scream out, 'I don't memorize my date book the way you do.'

"I came home from Paris and he and my son Joe met me. He told me there was a problem with our daughter. Everyone looked relieved when I took it calmly. Their main fear had been that I'd have one of my anger outbursts.

"I'm still overcoming my own childhood. It's engraved on me. Of all of us—and nine of us are still alive—my mother understands me but possibly doesn't totally approve of me. She knows I'm working now, but if I'd told her I was planning to do it, I would have gotten negative vibes. Art still tells me, 'You undersell yourself.' But it's not easy to do what women are trying to do now. I don't want to prune the roses."

The interview had been held at my house. As Ann turned to leave, she asked me, "Where's the best place to get a cab to go to the Waldorf?"

I looked out of the window. It was pouring. I said, "Better

go to the northeast corner of Third Avenue. If you can't get a cab, you can get a bus there."

She looked hesitant. There was an awkward silence. Finally, she said, "I never know how much it is" [she lives in Washington].

"Ann, it's fifty cents now," I said.

She looked relieved. "I'm always afraid to ask." Pause. *"Why am I always so indirect!"*

ELIZABETH ASHLEY

She is lithe, wiry, intense and has the personal magnetism of the great actress. Child of divorce, she grew up in Baton Rouge, Louisiana, where she "didn't belong at all," came to New York some sixteen years go, plunged into the Greenwich Village scene, studied at the Neighborhood Playhouse. From her job as understudy to Barbara Bel Geddes in *Mary, Mary,* she went into *Take Her, She's Mine* with Art Carney, which led to a Tony before she was old enough to vote. Then followed *Barefoot in the Park*, films like *The Carpetbaggers* (with George Peppard, whom she married and with whom she had a son, Christopher, now nine). Following this marriage she took six years off, then divorced Peppard and made a "comeback." She has played Broadway most recently in *Cat on a Hot Tin Roof, Skin of Our Teeth,* and *Legend.*

ON SEX ROLES: "It was odd with me. My mother divorced my dad when I was an infant. She supported herself, me, my grandparents. She never remarried. She believed in independence. She told me it would be a tragedy if I got married: 'Any little snip can get married—don't get married and have some sorry man to support.' But I grew up in a small southern town with gender roles and culture myths. I wanted to be like my peers. Nobody's comfortable being on the outside when you're young. The double processing—the conflict between my mother's ideas and those of my peers—didn't give me alternatives but a horrible set of short circuits."

She shrugs off her first marriage to Jimmy Farentino. "I didn't want to get married. It was lust. Jimmy said, 'You have to marry me. You can't just have my body.' So we married. We were early hippies. It didn't last."

Marriage number two was to George Peppard (though in the course of the two-hour interview she never mentioned his name). "I never grew up around a father figure. I was always going to find me a daddy who was going to protect me from the world. I always felt all alone. So I was a hippie kid in Greenwich Village and I met an actor who was fourteen years older and who said, 'You are a real woman. Be my wife, the mother of my kids. You'll be happy.' He said he loved me. I thought what I ought to do was to live life as a woman, to have a real life. So I got married and quit working. I moved to Beverly Hills and my career became shopping, traveling, and lunch. But I wasn't able to fulfill the conventional female role. It didn't make me happy. It didn't make him happy.

"After six years I moved out. Those were six crucial years for an actress. When I called my agent and said I wanted to work again, he said he couldn't get me a guest spot on *Bonanza*. But I'm glad I did it. I am not capable of living with a provider. I don't need one. I'm not capable of being dependent. If I'm dependent on anyone, I tend to defend myself against being dependent. My mother always said dependency is imprisonment."

ON AGGRESSION: "When I was a child, I could never defend myself when attacked—whether it was physically, emotionally, or verbally. In the fifth grade, when I was ten, there was a girl who was bigger, richer and the class bully. Every day I lived in fear of her. If she didn't talk to me, no one else would. One day Cecilia walked up to me by the tree at recess and beat me up. I couldn't hit back. I froze. Very young I began to make sure that would never happen to me again. All I remember wanting was to be able to stand up for myself, to be a person nobody messed with.

"I'm overassertive. I never trust anyone to figure out I'm smart and strong, so I tend to come in a room announcing it. It's so unnecessary and defensive and born out of the fear that I'll be stupid and weak. When we start rehearsals for a play, I walk in and let it be known that I'm rough, tough, and mean and that's the way we'll get along. I tend to state anything I say without any sense of doubt—I've got a .38 in one hand and a club in the other. It's insulting and demeaning to the other people.

"With men I've always been the leaver. When any relationship began to murder my self-worth, dignity, and pride, the only way I knew how to handle it was to walk out. I've never been one of those women who didn't leave.

"I have rage, deep rage, and I express it constantly. I have a scarred ego that creates a performer. I became facile at using this overassertive manner very young."

ON THE ADVANTAGE OF BEING A STAR: "I lead a privileged life. I can express myself freely and not get fired. For example, recently I got to the Kennedy Center in Washington on a Monday. I was exhausted from touring. Then I learned we would 'tech' the show on Tuesday—that's twenty-four hours when you live on coffee, nerves, and uppers—then play two performances on Wednesday, Thursday, Friday nights, two on both Saturday and Sunday and have the press preview Monday. It was too much. I told myself, 'If you don't take a stand, no one else will.' So I told the people involved, 'Do whatever you want to do, but I won't do that schedule. I want Sunday off.' I won. It was a matter of what was just. I had the muscle.

"At work I don't care if they like me. Love there is based on my professionalism at the bottom line and artistry at the top. I'm an insurrectionist but they respect me because I'm good. My work is my lifeline. It's the only true, mature thing about me."

ON ASSERTIVE HANG-UPS: She freely confesses, "It's not so simple in my personal life. There are so many things I'm not good at. I'm shy. I'm awkward socially. I'm totally incompetent in situations where there's a formal social ritual—like small talk at cocktail parties. I can't do it. I don't read or answer mail. I don't send thank-you notes. I'm not good at juggling all sorts of things at one time—I get manic. I'm not concise. I'm articulate, but not with clarity. I use twenty words where one will do and I have the mouth of a truck driver. I'm not good at the maintenance of my career. I don't even have a press agent. I've done all right because I'm a great laborer. I work four times harder than other people. I'm Avis."

ON EXPRESSING TENDER FEELINGS: "Expressing anger is

easy for me, but expressing tender feelings is hard. It took me a long time. I'd walk into a room and think, 'What do the people want me to be?—I'll be it.' But somewhere buried down there was a self. I had values I didn't live up to because I needed total approval, total acceptance, total love. I'd say anything people wanted me to say to get approval.

"I've spent years of my life trying to work things out. I've been an emotional junkie—always shooting substance into myself that would hurt me; that's my addiction. I've never been able to live with a man, and I've lived with a lot. I gave up finding one. Now I'm blessed. I've found the mate I've been looking for all my life [third husband, James Michael McCarthy, whom she married in May, 1975]. He's free of the gender myth. I can fight with him. When I did that with other men, it was always carnage. I would always risk losing them."

ON SUCCESS: "Success is supposed to be a cure-all. It's worse then. The wounds still bleed. Nobody loves you. People lay down their lives to attain success and still have no life. I did that. But I was lucky. It happened to me young and I got the chance to get full-circle. Success and achievement aren't synonymous. Being a success—if that's all you are—is pretty horrible."

JILL WINE VOLNER

A willowy blonde, green-eyed, cool, intense young woman, Jill achieved national fame for her brilliant work as assistant special prosecutor at the Watergate hearings. She was part of the Justice Department's legal team which got conspiracy convictions in the trial of the seven Watergate defendants, and received particular recognition for her cross-examination of Rose Mary Woods, former President Nixon's secretary. Born in Chicago, she attended the University of Illinois, where she earned a journalism degree. She went to Columbia Law School, married attorney Ian David Volner, and then to the Justice Department. Thirty-two-year-old Jill is now with the Washington firm of Fried, Frank, Harris, Shriver and

Kampelman—with offices in the Watergate complex. She says:

"I come from a traditional home. My mother's aim was to be a mother. I rejected what she did for myself—though I think being a housewife is fine if that's what you want to be and it fulfills you. Sometimes I feel guilty, but I refuse to be bound by the stereotypes like women shouldn't be trial lawyers and wives should have babies and stay home and take care of them. Women should have the same options men have, and, at the same time, men should have the option to stay home. What I do, I do because I've thought about it and want to do it.

"My husband and I split the chores. Each of us does what each least minds doing. He does the bills. I order the groceries and plan the meals. We share the cooking. He was the one who paid for me to finish school, who encouraged me when I wasn't sure I wanted a career.

"I'm hardly a traditional wife. I think he gets cheated. When I'm tired, I'd like to have a traditional wife at home who'd take care of me. But Ian doesn't want a traditional wife. He wants a wife who brings something of her own into the situation. We have not had children. We're not sure we want them. But I can't stay home, and I'd feel guilty if I didn't. Children would change our life-style."

ON ASSERTIVE DIFFICULTIES: "In business I have no assertive difficulties. I know my job and how to do it. I can insist the client follow my advice. I can handle combat in a courtroom. That's what I was trained to do. But my trouble comes in social situations. I was a shy child and I played a role of not being shy. I wanted to be vivacious. I've played the role a long time, but it's not me. I feel shy at a gathering with more than a few couples, and, at a party, I always wait for another person to make the first move. When people call us, I can't say no, so my husband and I find ourselves seeing people whom we don't really want to see. Since Watergate, it's harder than ever; if I refuse, I'm afraid they'll think I'm being a snob.

"The Watergate publicity has helped. Now if I walk over to someone and say, 'Hello, I'm Jill Volner,' they know who I am. I used to even avoid telling people I was a lawyer. I'm less reluctant now. I tell myself, 'You're missing the opportunity of meeting people.' "

ON PUT-DOWNS OF FEMALE LAWYERS: "It bothers me to be called a 'lady lawyer.' When people say it, I always correct them with something like 'Lawyer is a neuter term. There is no such thing as a lady lawyer unless you mean someone of either sex who represents women.' When I started seven years ago, people assumed women practicing law were different from male lawyers and from other women. They were a third category of people.

"It's different now, but there are still put-downs. I've been referred to as 'the young lady' by the opposition instead of the correct 'learned opposition.' I react in one of several ways. When it helps me, I ignore it—jurors protect attacked women. But I can put a stop to it. I may call the opposition by his first name, actually shout back, or have a conversation outside the courtroom where I say, 'Please stop it.'

"In a similar sexist context, a lawyer took me by the arm as we approached the bench. He did it deliberately to make me look helpless. I jabbed him and said, 'Get your hands off me and never touch me again.' The judge watched this and so did the jury.

"Once I was terribly abused with male put-downs in a courtroom. I asked for a five-minute recess and went into an adjoining office and burst into tears.

"In terms of how I behave in court I'm not like a man. I try to be a person. I try to take advantage of the good qualities of women—sensitivity and warmth—and not the bad—shyness, being irrational. After all, as a lawyer I've been trained to be rational."

ON FEARS: "I want to be the best I can be. I get tense. I ask myself, 'Have I done everything I can to prepare?' But I refuse to let fear interfere. Training as a lawyer is training to be assertive. Right now I'm teaching at Columbia Law School. I'd never had any training to teach, but I told myself, 'If you can think in a courtroom where the judges really know, you can talk to third-year law students.' It works the same way at home. My husband yells at me and that intimidates me, but I yell back."

THE EFFECT OF WATERGATE: "The publicity gave me credibility, which gave me confidence. I'm the same person I was before. I have the same friends I had five years ago. But I feel more comfortable socially. I feel I've accomplished something. I don't have to push or always promote myself."

BARBARA WALTERS

Recently newspapers throughout the nation headlined the fact that Barbara Walters was leaving her spot as co-host on NBC's early-morning *Today* program to become co-anchor with Harry Reasoner on ABC's *Evening News*. In doing this, Barbara scored a series of firsts. She became the first woman ever to fill a regular network anchor slot (the most prestigious job in television journalism) and history's highest paid journalist ($1 million a year over the next five years). In addition to taking a new professional step for herself, Barbara did something else: her changeover marked the furthest advance of the women's movement in television. When I read about it on the front page of *The New York Times,* I thought, "Professionally, she has shown women can do it. She's one of us. She has done it for all of us."

Daughter of showman Lou Walters, Barbara grew up in Brookline, Massachusetts, and Miami, Florida, graduated from Sarah Lawrence College where she remembers primarily "being on the outside." Mother of eight-year-old Jacqueline, whom she openly adores, she is divorced from Lee Guber, her husband for thirteen years. Always eager and hard working, she started with the *Today* show as a writer in 1961, became an on-camera interviewer within three years, and co-host with Jim Hartz in 1974. She has interviewed such notables as the Shah of Iran, President Anwar Sadat, and Henry Kissinger—to name just a few. Today she reigns undisputably as queen of television.

I interviewed Barbara for this book while she was still with *Today.* On the day of our talk I came out of her small office thinking, "Success has changed her for the better. She's honest, real, and completely without affectation." I also realized that, despite her extraordinary accomplishments, Barbara is a product of the same societal conditioning that affects most women.

On fear of being thought aggressive: In Barbara's case there's an office with a bathroom on the seventh floor of NBC that symbolized a lot of things. She says, "First Hugh Downs had the office with the bathroom. When Hugh left *Today*, it went to Frank McGee. Then Frank died. I had seniority. The office should have been mine. I kept thinking, 'You have such a small office—why shouldn't you have the office with the bathroom?' But I was afraid the new host, Jim Hartz, would resent it if I got it. It might have become an additional problem, so I didn't ask.

"If I were a man, it never would have occurred to me to hold back. I would have said, 'Look, I've been here nine years....' But I'm not sorry I held back. I did have bathroom privileges. By the way, once I got to know Jim, I realized he wouldn't have minded if I got the bathroom.

"When Hugh Downs left, it never occurred to me to be co-host. Sally Quinn—who had no experience in TV before going on CBS—was a co-host before I was. I didn't ask because it would have caused more trouble than good. Just like the bathroom.

"My professional life used to be full of opportunities I didn't get because I didn't ask for them. I had never hosted a news special of my own. I have always co-hosted. But I've always been afraid I'd be thought too aggressive if I spoke up. Now not only do I have confidence, but I realize the atmosphere all around me has changed and such things are possible."

On stereotypes: "I grew up in a house where if my mother got the soft piece of steak and my father got the hard, she'd give hers to him. Like most men then, he didn't do chores. He'd never stop on his way home to buy a quart of milk. It's different with the younger generation now, but I'm dealing with me brought up as I was. To this day, with a man I often listen to his account of his day before I talk about mine. I encourage him to talk about his work. I have the feeling that I should. I still feel a little funny if a man makes me dinner at his home."

On criticism: "I can take it if it's really constructive. But I try to avoid reading about myself. I'm always hurt if someone says, 'She's aggressive.' My mother has sometimes been overly critical: 'That picture of you was bad' ... 'Why did you wear that dress?' I guess most of us haven't learned to overcome parental criticism. That's why I always try to tell my little girl how well she does."

ON SHYNESS: "I have a slight inferiority complex still. I go into a room and have to talk myself into going up to people. I used to feel they wouldn't want me to join them. Now it's easier—at least, if I walk into a room, everyone knows me. My little girl is so great in that area. She goes right up to people."

ON ASSERTIVE HANG-UPS: "On remotes, when we travel, if there's no cast or crew member to eat with, I eat in my room alone. I can't take a vacation alone, eat in a restaurant alone, have cocktails alone.

"Once, some time ago, I did have cocktails alone. I went to Monaco to interview Princess Grace. After the interview I went back to my little hotel on the French Riviera. It was the cocktail hour. Everyone was sipping apéritifs and having a good time, but no one talked to me. I left the terrace and went up to my room and had dinner alone.

"Last year there was a series of parties to show Rockefeller's newly decorated vice-presidential residence in Washington. I probably would have known everyone there, but I couldn't go alone. I asked a network executive to accompany me.

"If I were younger and had to go to singles bars to get a date, I'd never go out.

"If I'm dancing and my partner holds me, I'm marvelous. But I can't do any of those dances where the men and women separate and you dance alone. I just can't do it. It's not just shyness. I'm afraid I'm going to make a fool of myself.

"If I'm going to a strange city and someone gives me a phone number of a friend to call, I can't. Again, just too shy."

ON SAYING NO: "I sometimes tell white lies. It's hard to say no and always tell the truth. I don't like to hurt people's feelings. I make up excuses."

ON PLUSES AND CHANGES FROM HER JOB: "Socially I'm not afraid of expressing my opinion. I don't have to punch the way some women do. Most women are still afraid to be taken seriously. They fear speaking up. I don't have to hold back there. Also, many women speak up in little-girl voices because they think it makes them seem feminine. I don't have to do that.

"I've changed. Now I spray myself with perfume every day. I didn't three years ago. I don't knock those so-called feminine ways and I don't feel guilty about the perfume or the femininity. People say I look better, dress better, seem softer. I've stopped worrying that it's all going to end tomorrow. I feel easier about life, easier about people, easier about myself.

"My mother says, 'What about a rainy day? You should have someone to take care of you.' Now I'm able to answer her, 'But, Mother, how about all the sunny days right now?'

"After a while what you do as part of the job becomes part of you. But I still sometimes walk around saying, 'Is that me?' If *I'm* the epitome of a woman who is always confident and in control, *don't ever believe it of anyone.*"

I hesitated about including this chapter in this book. It offers no Assertiveness Training counsel, techniques, or exercises. All that will follow.

But, from the stories of these women, I do think certain conclusions can be drawn.

Despite their achievements, they all have personal hang-ups which take various forms.

Regardless of these hang-ups, they share one quality in common: They are willing to work hard.

This work has brought about success. As Barbara Walters pointed out, "What you do as part of the job becomes part of you." The role stops being a role and become reality.

You don't have to become a TV star or editor of a major magazine to become an assertive woman. If you practice even the simplest of assertive behaviors, they will become "part of you." The assertive role will become reality.

Chapter 3

Spotting Your Own
Assertive Blocks

"People take advantage of me."

"When people pick on me, I can't say a word."

"I always ask my husband, 'How was your day?' He tells me, and I listen, but I resent it that he never asks about my day."

"I can express anger to another woman—never to a man."

"I'm going nowhere."

Do any of these statements sound familiar? If you suffer from lack of assertiveness, they may. They are the sentiments of many victims—women of different dimensions, classes, beliefs, interests and incomes—united by common resentments, inertia, defensiveness, and the feeling of having no control over their own behavior or lives.

I collected these remarks during hundreds of hours of personal interviews with unassertive women as well as at some fifty women's Assertiveness Training group sessions. From these interviews and groups and from the wealth of data on the subject of assertiveness, certain fundamentals emerge:

Most women have trouble with assertion because (1) they grew up avoiding the assertive situation (One twenty-six-year-old social worker told me, "My mother brought me up to 'Think it but don't say it'—and that's what I've always done"); (2) as a result they have never learned to be assertive.

Thus, because of fears, rationalization, or training, lack of assertion has become a habit. You spend your time satisfying the needs, directives, and even whims of bosses, friends, family without ever taking a few minutes to figure out "Why am I always so afraid to speak up?" ... "What do I really want to do or say?" ... "How can I feel better about myself without hurting someone else?"

The quality of assertiveness possesses as many ingredients as a Brunswick stew. But essentially women with assertive difficulties can be grouped into seven problem types.

SEVEN ASSERTIVE PROBLEM TYPES

1. *The shrinking violet.* Because you haven't learned to stand up for yourself, you can't express opinions, wishes, or refuse to take on the most unreasonable request. You encourage people to walk all over you and rarely receive a thank you for your efforts. Unsure of who you are and what you want for yourself, you go submissively through life, continually feeling like the "poor relative" in a Victorian novel.

2. *The fear victim.* You're frightened of the fearful and anxious thoughts you get at the very idea of being assertive, whether making a demand of a friend or asking for a promotion on the job. You constantly tell yourself, "I'd like to say this ... do that, but I can't. I'm afraid to try. If it doesn't work, I'll feel even more insecure." Of course, when you take certain risks, you get anxious and encounter difficult situations, but the fear victim is so ruled by anxiety and the fear this arouses in her that she avoids the situation and thus avoids assertiveness.

3. *The sham assertive.* You seem very open, warm, even extroverted, but this seeming assertiveness often covers a lack of honesty. You utter lines like, "How wonderful to hear from you; I was just thinking about you" (completely untrue; you haven't thought about this particular person in months) or, "Darling, that dress is so becoming" (to yourself thinking,

"It adds ten years to her age"). Pseudo-assertiveness may work in the political arena, but in personal life, because of its lack of honesty, it leads to distance and misunderstanding. Often women in this category have problems in any but the most superficial relationship.

4. *The woman who wants the world to love her.* Your goal is to have everyone—husband, lover, children, boss, friends, shopkeepers, and even the man who comes to the door selling magazine subscriptions—think you're the greatest. Because of this you placate, aim to please, say yes to every request, do too much for others and very little for yourself. Rarely do you think, "Do I really want to do that?" Instead you think, "If I do it, will he/she like me more?" In seeking constant praise, you completely forget the all-important goal of self-respect.

5. *The split assertive.* I've used this phrase frequently in writing about assertive difficulties. You're a tigress on the job and a mouse in intimate relationships (One woman told me, "On the job I feel I'm competent. I know what has to be done and I do it. But in a close relationship, I feel I may be rejected if I say what I really think"). Perhaps you can express anger to superiors but not to peers—or the reverse. "Splits" have gradations. You can hold down a demanding job, have an excellent relationship with your husband, but be unable to fire your cleaning woman. In this category comes the woman who can stand up to everyone and everything but her own children.

Also within this category fall an army of women who are *brainwashed females.* You can be assertive with women, never with men. Whether from parental model or school conditioning, it's now second nature for you to take care of a man's needs before your own. Seeing yourself as the object, never the subject, you think the focus of life is doing things for and with a man. And Mama's admonition still runs through your mind: "Don't be a hot shot; that's the man's role."

6. *The manipulator.* You stoop to conquer with such womanly wiles as the iron-hand-in-the-velvet-glove technique. Instead of openly communicating your needs, you become involved in indirect maneuvering ("Darling, that idea you had about a vacation in Maine is terrific"—when he has never even

mentioned the subject, or you woo him in bed so that later you can reveal the horrifying size of your bill from Saks). This kind of cunning, intrigue, and desire to get the better of someone is not assertive. It is an assertive problem because these manipulative devices limit the closeness you can achieve with other people. Generally women who use these methods have low self-esteem.

Until Assertiveness Training I always thought that a certain kind of artful deceit was part of the man-woman game. One incident not only taught me how wrong I was but that I couldn't even enjoy the prize I had wangled so hard to get.

One day I spotted a jade bracelet in the window of a New York jewelry store where my husband had once purchased a tiny locket for me. I went in, asked the price of the bracelet, and then mused aloud, "Christmas is coming. I wonder how I could get my husband in here."

The store owner picked up my crafty thoughts. He suggested, "Why don't we call him, tell him that we were checking our files, noticed that he bought you the locket years ago and might be interested in this lovely bracelet."

"Go ahead," I said, "but don't let him know I was in here." At Christmas there was a bracelet in a tiny box under the tree. I exclaimed, "Oh, Herb, how beautiful. How did you ever find it?"

Herb looked at me with a hurt expression in his eyes and said, "I bought it because obviously you'd been to the store and the bracelet was what you wanted. I'm sorry I did it. It took the fun out of Christmas shopping for me, and it was a mistake."

I realized he was right. Christmas was almost ruined. I've worn the bracelet only once. Even looking at it makes me feel bad.

According to psychologist Andrew Salter, "There are some women whose life is one of chronic indirectness. Indirectness is based on fear. Sometimes you have to be indirect when dealing with someone in a power position, but it's an empty situation when your survival is always based on indirectness."

7. *The pusher.* You substitute aggression for assertion. With overemphasis on your own ideas, too loud a voice, inap-may be good, but you disagree with others so much and so propriate outbursts, you constantly create turmoil. Your ideas

violently, express your thoughts in such an unpleasant, hostile way that you turn everyone off. Usually you lose sight of your goal (whatever that goal may be) and turn everything into a fight and then wonder why people don't like you.

THE RIGHTS OF WOMEN

As her children neared their teens, Jane decided she wanted to take courses toward her M.A. in business administration with the future goal of returning to work. Looking through the catalog at the selection of available evening adult education courses, she thought, "No, that night is inconvenient for my husband," and then, "That night is bad for the kids." Sorrowfully, she reflected, "There's not much left for me to choose from. In this house I don't seem to have any rights."

Many women feel they have no rights. Or, if they have rights, these seem to exist only in abstract form (such as "the right to be happy") and never seem to apply to any specific situation. Some women feel they do have rights, but when a specific situation comes up, they don't feel they have the right to stand up for them. Or, if they do possess this last right, they believe exercising it may prove dangerous or disruptive (of course, it sometimes is, and you have to weigh alternatives, like loss of self-esteem). Some women suffer from the *get permission syndrome;* in order to take any action about their rights, they must first get permission from their man.

Yet, knowing your rights and standing up for them is a central aspect of assertion. According to Dr. Arnold A. Lazarus, professor of psychology at Rutgers University, some people are so concerned with an arbitrary range of "rights" and "wrongs" and allow themselves so little freedom of movement that they spend their lives in an emotional prison or confined capsule. To gain the desired "emotional freedom," they must first know their rights, do something about them, and attempt to do this within the framework of striving for emotional freedom.

Both Thomas Paine and Edmund Burke wrote about "The Rights of Man." What are the rights of women? To what should they be entitled? In determining this, it helps to think through (1) the basic general rights and (2) the specific rights.

The Seven Basic Inalienable Rights of Women

1. *The right to have rights and stand up for them.* This is a core right.

2. *The right to dignity and self-respect.* You have the right to expect others to treat you with dignity and to treat yourself the same way.

3. *The right to consider your own needs.* This does not mean you ignore the needs of others who are important to you. It does mean that you put your own needs in proper perspective and not always in last place.

4. *The right to self-fulfillment.* You have the right to be competent (even in this supposedly liberated age some women think that if they reveal they have lots of gray cells, men will reject them as "too brainy"), to practice and improve your abilities, and recognize that you have the right to do things that lead in this direction.

5. *The right to accept challenges.* This basic right includes the right to take risks, make mistakes, learn and grow from life situations.

6. *The right to determine your own life-style.* Society doesn't have the right to dictate where and with whom you live. This is your right. You don't have to apologize for being "only a housewife" if that's what you want to be. Do not go by others' values and standards; form your own on the basis of what's important to you.

In one instance, Ellen, a childless wife, had a very unhappy marriage. Following an operation for ulcers, she went to Arizona to recuperate. She went alone and began to flourish, making new friends and even starting a business. However, her family and friends deluged her with letters and phone calls, all saying the same thing: "Return to your husband." Ellen, a passive person, gave in to their pressure, and, in her words, "gave up the fight completely." Now she's severely depressed.

In carrying out this right, ask yourself, "If I live in this style, will it be destructive to myself or others?"

7. *The right to change—yourself, your behavior, values, life situations.* This includes the right to seek professional help when necessary.

From these basic rights stem the specific rights. Here are the specific rights the women I interviewed for this book were most concerned about:

a. *The right to reply to rudeness* (derived from right number 2: "the right to dignity and self-respect"). For instance, one recent Saturday afternoon I went to a department store to look for a new scarf. The salesperson kept ignoring me and giving her attention to others who had arrived after I did. Finally, I asked, "Don't you have any of the extra long wool knitted ones?" She snapped, "They're at the end of the counter. Go get them!" The order, the tone of it, and her behavior infuriated me. Very calmly, I said, "No. That's your job. It's my turn. Please wait on me in a civil manner or I will have to report you to your department head." Her whole attitude changed. Furthermore, she gave me a lesson in scarf-tying.

b. *The right to spend money you didn't earn* (derived from right number 3: "the right to consider your own needs"). Says one housewife, "I make no monetary contribution to the household, so I don't feel I have the right to buy without asking." Others can make a pins-and-needles purchase without permission but abdicate over major items like a refrigerator. In acting upon this right, evaluate your contribution to the household in terms of time and energy. This may help you to see your right more clearly.

c. *The right to be successful* (derived from right number 4: "the right to self-fulfillment"). You have the right to grow professionally, look for another job in which you can earn more money even though you adore your boss and your exiting for better things may leave him in a temporary hole, and make more money than your husband.

d. *The right to select and reject dates* (derived from right number 6: "the right to determine your own life-style"). See Chapter 7 for a discussion of "new courtship patterns for singles."

e. *The right to split the household chores* (derived from

right number 3: "the right to consider your own needs"). A well-known female psychiatrist says, "I contribute half the income, but I always have the feeling I should take complete care of the house. I feel guilty about saying, 'This isn't fair. I contribute half. Why should I do it all?'"

f. *The right to be left alone* (derived from right number 2: "the right to dignity and self-respect"). To take a bath without the children trouping in, to make a personal phone call without interruption, to read your mail in peace without the query "Who's that from?"

g. *The right to ask for information* (derived either from right number 2: "the right to dignity and self-respect"; or right number 4: "the right to self-fulfillment"): from a boss ("I've been here a year; just what are my chances for promotion?"); from a doctor ("You say you want me to go into the hospital for a complete checkup. Is anything really wrong? Please give me the facts and also what your charge will be"); from a husband ("Just what is our exact financial situation?").

h. *The right to reject impossible situations* (again derived from right number 2). In my own case I stuck with a famous gynecologist for years, even though he constantly broke appointments and sometimes failed to show up for them. He also would scream at me. I resented it but didn't think I had the right to pass judgment on someone so well known. I kept rationalizing, "He's supposed to be so good. I'd better put up with it." I didn't leave him as a patient until I was forced to it. One morning I read about his death from drug withdrawal—together with that of his twin brother—on the front page of *The New York Times*.

i. *The right to date a younger man* (derived from right number 6: "the right to determine your own life-style"). There's a report about a traditionally oriented analytic group in which a woman member happily reported that she was thinking of marrying a "very congenial" man. The group members, male and female, got all excited for her until she revealed that she was nine years the man's senior. Then their whole attitude changed, and they said things like, "You think it's a romance, but it's really a disguised mother-son relationship" and "He wants to be dominated." No one, including the therapist, pointed out that if the woman had been nine years younger, the relationship would have seemed completely appropriate. Instead they just reacted to the cultural tradition that a man should be older than his wife, and in so doing seriously influenced the woman. She no longer felt that she had the right to the relationship.

Decisions about rights must always be based upon your own individual feelings, the strength of these feelings, and the possible consequences of action.

You may deliberately choose not to exercise a right to which you feel entitled in order not to inflict hurt on another person. For example, Mary was very involved with Larry for two years. Then the affair ended and each married someone else. Seven years later they met on a bus. While feeling complete loyalty to their respective mates, they wanted to see each other occasionally for a drink on a friendly basis. Mary felt she had every right to this platonic relationship. When she discussed this with her husband, he objected. The situation became a source of tension in their marriage. Eventually Mary made the decision to give up the right to see her old beau for the sake of her marital relationship. She did this out of choice.

Like many women, you may mistakenly feel that it is someone else who is placing the obstacle in the way of your standing up for your rights. Many times it is. Often it is not.

In my own case, while writing this book, I had spent a nine-hour day in solitary confinement with my typewriter. Stir crazy, at 5:30 P.M. I took myself off to a party, honoring the late newsman Bob Considine, at the Overseas Press Club. At the party I had a wonderful time but at 7:30 P.M. I began working myself into a fit. I wanted to stay on, socialize with all those old-time, white-haired newspapermen who reminded me of my adored newsman father. I wanted to call up Herb and say, "Go out to dinner. We'll have the fish tomorrow." I couldn't do it. I told myself, "You don't have the right to enjoy yourself and let him come home to no wife and no dinner."

Over the horrible fish filets I told Herb just how I felt.

"You were wrong," he answered. "I never get the chance to be alone. I would have loved the opportunity to go to Harvey's and have sea food. You won't ever go there because they clang the plates."

"You wouldn't have gone," I retorted. "You would have fixed the fish yourself and then I'd be the bad wife."

"I might have fixed the fish or I might have gone to Harvey's," he said. "That would have been my decision. But after your day you had every right to some fun. *Don't try to make me feel guilty because you didn't do what you had a right to do.*"

By ignoring your rights you demean yourself. By believing in them and taking action you work toward your goal of becoming an assertive woman. As Emerson wrote, "Take the place and attitude to which you see your unquestionable right and all men acquiesce."

POWER

In *Assertive Training for Women* by Susan M. Osborn and Dr. Gloria G. Harris, the authors write that "While men accept the fact that they have the ability to affect, to influence, and to change persons and social situations, many women are very reluctant to acknowledge having any power whatsoever. Like the term aggression, they reject the notion of power and any suggestion of their ability to effect change."

In determining your own use or lack of power, it may help to ask yourself some questions:

1. What does power mean? It can mean serving as president of the United States, holding an elected office where you have the authority to control jobs and contracts, or having a plum job where you make scads of money, and the money and position give you power. But, in its most basic definition, power means "the possession of sway or controlling influence over others." Are you capable of this or do you always abdicate?

2. When you use power, what kind of power do you use? Do you use strong power bases like *legitimate* power ("I'm your supervisor and this is the way I want it done") or *expert* power ("I know this is the way to do it because I've handled this sort of thing so many times")? Or do you rely on weaker bases like *indirect informational* power (you leave travel brochures lying around but—because you don't want the other

person to know he/she is being influenced—you don't say, "I want to go to the Grand Canyon this summer") or the *helpless* technique in which you try to get others to do the things you can't or won't do for yourself?

In a series of studies relating to power use, Dr. Paula Johnson of the University of California at Santa Cruz found out that women who felt less competitive or powerful often chose helpless power. They didn't like themselves for using it but found it effective in interpersonal relationships for the short run—but less effective than expert power.

3. What is your basic attitude toward power? Are you happier being dominant or submissive? To determine this, you might try the "Slave Market" game used by Dr. George R. Bach at the Institute of Group Psychotherapy, Beverly Hills, California.

SLAVE MARKET GAME

STEP ONE: Get a partner who agrees to play "Slave Market" with you. Set a time limit. For your first experience this can be from ten minutes to a half hour. You will be reversing the roles of "master" and "slave." Jointly decide who plays which role first.

STEP TWO: The "master" orders her/his "slave" to perform various tasks (from errand to back rub). The "slave" is expected to perform these tasks as well as possible and in a spirit of good will.

STEP THREE: Reverse roles. The "master" performs as the "slave" for the same length of time.

STEP FOUR: After the completion of the game, analyze your feelings. Were you more comfortable as the "master" or the "slave"? During the exercise were there any moments when you resented your partner? What were they and how did you handle your feelings at the time?

4. What specific behaviors detract from your having power?

• *Do you constantly apologize?* My husband told me of a very unassertive woman patient who gave the key to her apartment to her boyfriend when she went on vacation. Upon her return she saw (from bobby pins and other left-behind articles) that he had entertained other women in her home. She hesitatingly accused him. He didn't deny it but answered, "You said I could use your apartment. How dare you talk to me like that!" She immediately backed off with "I'm sorry." Women perpetuate their lack of power by their compulsion for apology. The next time you find yourself apologizing, ask yourself what you are apologizing for.

• *Do you always work for the approval of others?* If you do, you limit your own growth because you always concede the power to someone else. If you base your security on what other people feel—anger, liking, admiration—you deal with things that go beyond you. You move into the area of least power. Someone may not like you for reasons that have nothing to do with you. He/she has a headache, had a fight with a close friend, or is in trouble on the job. If your security is based on the reactions of others, you have only minimal command. Conversely, if you base your security on meeting your own standards of what makes you respect you, you are then acting in terms of maximum control.

Throughout this book I will be showing how assertiveness will enable you to determine the course of your own life, stop accepting unjust blame, make your own decisions. Right now your tasks are:

1. To think through the kinds of power available to you
2. To analyze the effectiveness of different kinds of power in different kinds of situations. Your word may be law with a five-year-old, but what happens when he's fifteen?
3. To recognize the kind of power you most respect yourself for using
4. To stop saying "I'm sorry" when someone steps on your foot

SPOTTING YOUR OWN ASSERTIVE PROBLEMS

Before you can take any action about your own assertive difficulties, you must know what they are.

The following two quizzes may help you to determine your own individual problems in assertion.

FEMALE ASSERTIVENESS INVENTORY

STEP ONE: In your Female Assertiveness Notebook make up a chart with three columns. The left heading should read "Degree of Discomfort," the middle one "Situation," and the third "Response Probability."

STEP TWO: In FAN copy the following list of typical assertive problems. Some are mine. The form and many of the questions have been adapted from the excellent Assertion Inventory devised by Dr. Eileen D. Gambrill of the University of California, Berkeley, and Dr. Cheryl A. Richey, University of Washington, Seattle.

STEP THREE: Go over the questions and mark your "Degree of Discomfort" (that means how much of any kind of uncomfortable feeling you get in that situation) in asserting yourself in each of the situations. Use the following scale to indicate degree.

1—none   4—much
2—a little   5—very much
3—a fair amount

STEP FOUR: Go over the list a second time and indicate, after each item, your "Response Probability"—the likelihood of your displaying the behavior if actually confronted with the situation. Be sure to cover your "Degree of Discomfort" rating as you do this. If you don't, one rating may affect the way you answer the other. Use the following scale to indicate your "Response Probability":

1—always do it   4—rarely do it
2—usually do it   5—never do it
3—do it about half the time

For instance, in an intimate relationship if you rarely tell the man when he does or says something that upsets you, you would mark a "4" after that item.

STEP FIVE: Indicate situations you would like to handle more assertively by placing a circle around the number.

Degree of Discomfort	Situation	Response Probability
_____	1. Turn down a request to borrow money	_____
_____	2. Compliment a friend or co-worker	_____
_____	3. Receive compliments	_____
_____	4. Ask a favor of someone that will mean time/work/effort for him/her	_____
_____	5. Resist sales pressure from clerks who try to sell you merchandise you don't want	_____
_____	6. Apologize when you know you've done something wrong	_____
_____	7. Return merchandise	_____
_____	8. In the close relationship tell the man when he does/says something that upsets you	_____
_____	9. Start a conversation with a stranger or new acquaintance	_____
_____	10. Admit "I don't know" when you're ignorant about something	_____
_____	11. Ask personal questions	_____
_____	12. Answer personal questions	_____
_____	13. Apply for a job	_____
_____	14. Ask for a raise	_____
_____	15. Delegate authority to a woman	_____
_____	16. Delegate authority to a man	_____
_____	17. Quit a job you don't like	_____
_____	18. Say no when someone makes a completely unfair demand of you	_____
_____	19. Tell someone "I like what you did"	_____
_____	20. Tell someone "I don't like what you did"	_____
_____	21. Get off the telephone with a long-winded friend	_____
_____	22. Make social overtures (dates, dinner) to a female, a couple, a new man	_____
_____	23. Answer a hostile, unjustified put-down	_____
_____	24. Discuss a justified criticism of your behavior with the other person	_____
_____	25. Refuse a date when you don't like the man	_____
_____	26. End a relationship with a man which has become unsatisfactory	_____

Degree of Discomfort	*Situation*	*Response Probability*
_____	27. Resist sexual advances when you have no interest	_____
_____	28. Ask for a better table in a restaurant when the *maître d'* puts you and a friend next to the kitchen	_____
_____	29. Send back food in a restaurant when it arrives and isn't what you've ordered—for instance, you want well-done calf's liver and it comes blood red	_____
_____	30. Stand up for yourself when your mother-in-law attacks you	_____
_____	31. Request the return of borrowed items	_____
_____	32. Say something when another person takes credit for your work	_____
_____	33. Tell another person when he/she has done something that has offended you	_____
_____	34. Tell good news about yourself to: friends, family, husband/lover	_____
_____	35. If single, be able to go out with a couple and no man for you	_____
_____	36. Go alone to a party	_____
_____	37. Tell a man—whether boss, lover, husband, friend—when he has done something wrong in a professional sense	_____
_____	38. Speak up at a meeting	_____
_____	39. Feel you have the right to choose your own life-style even though others may disagree with it	_____
_____	40. Say "I love you" aloud and mean it	_____
_____	41. Express a sexual want to your partner	_____

The ultimate goal of Assertiveness Training is to help you achieve a sense of control over your own life, a feeling of self-mastery. Alternative ways of handling situations exist; you want to learn to analyze these alternatives and then *choose* your own behavioral approach to the situation, not have it chosen for you by mate, child, co-worker, boss, friend, or even salesperson. The key is always, "Which action will make me respect myself the most?"

Always remember assertive behavior tends to produce more assertive behavior. It increases self-confidence. As you act out of assertiveness, you feel good for acting that way, confident, and want to try it more.

Admittedly, it is difficult to change a lifetime pattern of unassertiveness. Before you can take any action, you must have the desire to change and the ability to assess your own problems in this area. The following "Spot Your Own Assertive Block" quiz covers a variety of typical situations involving female lack of assertion. In answering try to identify the unassertive behavior and the action you might take to change it and become a more assertive person. The comments at the end reveal the implications of each answer.

SPOT YOUR ASSERTIVE BLOCK QUIZ

1. You're single and applying for a job with a major company. The male interviewer asks you various questions about your background and then thrusts, "Are you going to stay or are you just using this to fill in the time before you get married and pregnant?" Do you:

   a. Turn on your heels and exit with the line, "My personal life is none of your business"

   b. Answer, "I can't project my life so far ahead"

   c. Answer, "If I didn't feel committed to work and the chance for this particular job, I wouldn't be applying for it. Why did you ask that question?"

2. You've always been bad at figures. Now you're dating an accountant who seems interested in you. Tax time is nearing. You'd like him to help you fill out your form. Do you:

   a. Say, "Joe, could you give me some help in filling out my tax? It would help a lot, but I'll understand if you're too busy to take time for this"

   b. Say nothing, fill out the form yourself and feel you did a bad job

   c. Say nothing and feel increasingly annoyed that he didn't volunteer to help you. This resentment grows until one night you lose your temper at him for something trivial

3. You do a presentation of a proposed new project at an office seminar. When you finish, the boss comments, "What a good job." Do you:

   a. Smile shyly and hang your head

   b. Say, "Thank you. I worked very hard on that point about such and such. What part did you like best?"

   c. Say, "Oh, thanks. I don't feel completely satisfied with it"

4. For the past three years you've organized the annual fund-raising luncheon for a local charity group. Now the president telephones and asks you to handle the chore again. You don't want to do it. Do you say:

   a. "I'd rather not. It's just too much work"

   b. "Well ... (long silence) ... O.K. But this is the last time"

   c. "No. I don't have the time. Let someone else have a chance"

5. You're the mother of three children, ranging in age from six to twelve, who continually fight at the dinner table. On this particular night you cannot stand the squabbling any longer. Do you:

   a. Start yelling at them and saying things like, "Why can't you be like Mrs. Jones's kids? They're decent children"

   b. Burst into tears, scream, "I can't stand it" and leave the table

   c. Quietly state, "I think I have the right to a decent dinner. If you must fight, take your plates to the dinette and do it there, or wait until after dinner and continue your fight out of my hearing"

6. Obviously in a bad mood, your husband comes home late from the office and greets you with "What a terrible day I've had." Do you:

   a. Immediately counter with an account of your terrible day

   b. Start diagnosing his difficulties by telling him all the things he does wrong on his job

   c. Say, "I'm sorry you had a bad day. You mix drinks and we'll talk about it over dinner"

7. You'd like to ask an internist male friend out to the summer house you share with a mixed group for the weekend. Do you:

   a. Say, "Would you like to come out to my summer house for the weekend? There'll be a nice crowd"

   b. Stifle the impulse because Mother taught you "Nice girls don't call men"

c. Ask a series of questions like, "Do you have a busy week?" . . . "Will you be on call this weekend?" . . . and keep on until you have all sorts of information about his social life. When you have this, you'll decide whether or not to extend the invitation

8. You've sat in the same job for six years, doing very good work but receiving only limited raises and no promotions. Now there has been an office reorganization and you see a vacant spot where you could make a major contribution. Do you:

a. Wait for one of the executives to have the same thought

b. Gripe about the situation to your peers and tell them all what you could do if you had "that job"

c. Go directly to the executive in charge of that job and ask for it. Be prepared to say what you can do and also have this outlined in a written memo which you leave with him

9. You attend a big cocktail party where you know nobody. Do you:

a. Get a drink, hold it clenched in your hand, and die a thousand deaths inside, worrying that "nobody will talk to me"

b. Stay a half hour and go home, feeling like a wallflower

c. Go up to someone and start talking

10. You don't feel completely happy with your sex life. Your man's performance in bed leaves you frustrated and dissatisfied. Do you:

a. Play Dr. Freud with him. You initiate a discussion where you analyze his sexual problems, even pointing out his strong attachment to his mother (who has been dead since he was seventeen)

b. Continue to say nothing, resenting the situation but remembering your mother's words, "Not all women enjoy sex"

c. Have an open discussion with him in which you talk over the situation and take up what both he and you can do differently about sex

ANALYSIS OF ANSWERS

1. Assertive block: *inability to answer put-downs.* Right answer: (c) You respond in a way that clearly indicates your interest in the position and are simultaneously nicely assertive. By querying the interviewer, "Why did you ask that question?" you bring his chauvinism out into the open and also maintain your own self-respect. Answer (a) is aggressive and (b) is a cop-out.

2. Assertive block: *inability to make a request of someone else.* Right answer: (a) In this you state your request directly, show what it would mean for you, and also recognize he has the right to refuse. In answer (c) you commit two mistakes: You expect him to be a mind reader, and because he isn't, later you explode over something that really has nothing to do with what you're angry about. You're angry at yourself for not asking the favor. In answer (b) your lack of assertiveness leads to feelings of dissatisfaction with yourself.

3. Assertive block: *inability to respond to compliments.* Right answer: (b) Here you show you appreciate the boss's praise, affirm the fact of your hard work, and invite further discussion of your project. Answer (a) is passive. In answer (c) you demean both yourself and your work. Even if you're not completely satisfied, this is not the time to bring it up.

4. Assertive block: *the ability to say no.* Right answer: either (a) or (c). Answer (a) is advanced—for people who have little trouble refusing a request. In answer (c) you also state your position firmly and clearly and you follow the rule that works well for people with difficulty in saying no; the very first word of your answer is no. Answer (b) is completely unassertive.

5. Assertive block: *standing up for your rights.* Right answer: (c) Do you feel you have a right to eat the dinner you've cooked for all those long hours at the hot stove in peace? If you do, as an assertive woman you must at least try to stand up for this right. If the children don't listen and continue to fight, you continue the "take your plates to the dinette" routine. In answer (a) you're aggressive and do nothing to help the situation. In answer (b) you're unasser-

tive. You also forget that you have the obligation to serve as an assertive model for your children so that they can have the learning experience of seeing how an assertive person behaves.

6. Assertive block: *inappropriate communication.* Right answer: (c) Here you show you care and open the way for appropriate and close communication. Many people with assertive difficulties continually say things that they think are open and honest but in reality are inappropriate. This form of behavior can lead to numerous interpersonal difficulties, creating distance rather than closeness, dissension rather than helping the situation. In answer (b) you may be right—your husband may be mishandling the office situation—but obviously this is the wrong time to say what you think is the right thing. In answer (a) you show complete insensitivity to his own needs. You think you're being assertive; in reality, you're inconsiderate.

7. Assertive block: *indirect communication.* Right answer: (a) By making the direct request, you'll get a direct answer. If he refuses, it means he's refusing the weekend, not attacking you as a person. In answer (b) you're still letting Mother run your life. In answer (c) you're maneuvering and being manipulative. The internist won't know what you're really getting at and may be turned off by your indirect questioning.

8. Assertive block: *setting goals.* Right answer: (c) In this you go after the position in a prepared, organized, direct fashion. You've set a goal and you make the attempt to reach it; up to now you've been passively waiting for something to fall in your lap. Of course, the person to whom you go for the position depends on your specific situation. In real life pick the person according to the realities of your particular firm. It might be wise to go to a friend at the top. Answer (a) is unassertive, and (b) is passive in another way. You're not putting yourself forward to the right people. Complaints to peers won't lead to a job change.

9. Assertive block: *lack of skills.* Right answer: (c) The art of initiating a conversation is a learnable skill. The assertive thing is to force yourself to go up to someone and start a conversation. There may be two problems involved: (i) You don't know how to do it. If so, try making a starter statement

like, "I know very few people here—do you know a lot?" (ii) Who's in command—you or your anxiety? There are many women who go to cocktail parties all the time and also feel anxious. Don't let the anxiety take over. Go over. Start that conversation. As you do, the anxiety will go down. Answers (a) and (b) are complete unassertive cop-outs. You haven't even tried to reach out to anyone else—female, male, or couple. If you do, you may find he/she/they feel(s) as insecure as you do.

10. Assertive block: *lack of assertiveness about your own sexual needs*. Right answer: (c) By speaking up frankly and taking some responsibility for the sexual actions between you and your mate, you will go a long way toward a more satisfying sex life. Maybe you'll learn he has been feeling equally dissatisfied and would like you to take more responsibility. In answer (a) you're being aggressive and hostile and taking no step toward improving the situation. In answer (b) you're being unassertive and living in your brainwashed past.

STARTING ASSERTIVENESS TRAINING

1. Be certain you understand the concept and goal of Assertiveness Training. The idea is not to teach you how to manipulate others but to enable you to stand up for yourself by learning certain tested skills. As you practice these skills, you'll find that you'll like yourself better and that others will respond to you in new, different, and more satisfying ways.

2. Learning the skills is important—but not enough. You must *deliberately* use them. This involves keeping lists, giving yourself assignments, and, as I do, asking yourself every morning, "What assertive problem do I attack today?" I can't stress enough the importance of keeping a record of every success or failure in your Female Assertiveness Notebook. Don't make the mistake of thinking it too mechanical or simplistic to jot down what you do, don't do, and your thoughts at the time you did it or didn't do it. According to Dr. Arnold Lazarus, "Those who make the most impressive psychological gains usually turn out to be the ones who take the trouble to chart their responses and to compute their daily or

weekly averages." Keeping a record will help you to monitor your changes in assertiveness.

3. Realize that two factors may be major holdbacks in terms of your learning to be an assertive woman:

• *Your beliefs about the relationships between men and women.* Analyze your mistaken beliefs by asking yourself some key questions:

Was I brought up to believe that men are and should be the more assertive sex?

Do I fear a danger in becoming "overassertive" and having the world perceive me as "unfeminine"?

Do I feel I must protect the fragile male ego?

Have I learned to get what I want by not asking directly—by using the so-called feminine behavior patterns? Writes Dr. Estelle Ramey, "In order to get what she wants, a woman learns to wheedle, to pout, to manipulate, to be essentially an outsized child. And it works very well unless what she wants to do is grow up."

Have I avoided certain professions that interest me because they "belong to men"? Do I hold back from expressing anger to a man because he's stronger and may become violent?

Have I been taught not to compete—and if I compete, I shouldn't win?

• *Your rationalizations.* Many women keep themselves from living assertively with such thoughts as, "If I don't take on that extra assignment, my boss will fire me" ... "If I tell my husband he's got to do some chores around the house, we'll have a terrible fight" ... "If I go alone on a trip, no one will talk to me." Are these reasons valid? Would the outcome be so terrible? Or are they just excuses to maintain your fears and general lack of assertiveness?

4. Identify your target behaviors. Think through the general areas where you are unassertive: at work or home, with strangers, acquaintances, or in a close relationship. Then break down the behaviors in each category that you can perform differently. These are your target behaviors. These are what you are trying to learn. For instance, you have assertive problems at social gatherings. Think through what you could do differently and the skills you must acquire to do it. Do you cling to the sidelines and make no attempt to talk to

anyone because you don't know how to start a conversation? Could you change things if you developed a couple of good conversational openers and made the deliberate attempt to talk to three different people at every social event *even though you feel anxious?*

5. Systematically work on changing your target behaviors and learning new assertive skills. As your first behavior, start with something you can reasonably expect yourself to accomplish fairly quickly (perhaps speaking up to a rude salesperson where there's no close interpersonal relationship). Then go on to something that's harder. Learning to be an assertive woman when you've been a patsy or pusher all your life will require a lot of thought and effort. However, the benefits that will accrue to you from this work have the potential of influencing your entire life.

Chapter 4

Exercise Class

Learning to be assertive is like going to an exercise class.

In the typical diverse group of women there are a few who excel at everything, whether cartwheels or headstands, and can even do forty instead of the required twenty leg lifts. But, if you're like most of us, at first you feel clumsy. You can manage the basic breathing and simple muscle exercises, but little else. Slowly you learn to make your body do what you want it to do. Gradually you master the various thrusts and bends until you feel the security of being competent. You feel in control of your muscles, no longer embarrassed over your inadequacy, but you still default on the leg lifts. However, because you see progress, you realize that someday, with effort on your part, you'll be able to conquer these too.

The assertive assimilation process works in the same way. At first you learn what to do. You start small—from where you are now. If, in the most impersonal situation, you can't speak up to a rude salesclerk, you learn how to do that first. Then you apply that same assertive technique to speaking up to a close friend or husband, where the relationship matters. With each new success you go on to changing other behaviors until eventually you work on the one that is hardest for you.

It may help to think of it as a learning curve that has dips and plateaus. At times you may not seem to get anywhere in your learning-to-be-assertive campaign. This may be followed by a sharp upward curve.

In my own case, I first worked on the setting of goals which, although I had never realized it, had emerged as one of my major assertive problems. That proved comparatively simple to master. I then attacked something harder—making requests of others. I worked at this until now it has become an almost automatic process. But I'm still working on saying no. Like the leg lifts, I can't say no without enormous contortions, anguish, and self-flagellation. But now I manage to get that two-letter word out about half the time—and that's progress.

SETTING AND ACHIEVING GOALS

In his *Autobiography* Benjamin Franklin candidly tells of his attempt to achieve certain personality goals, namely, the "habitude" of the thirteen virtues of temperance, silence, order, resolution, frugality, industry, sincerity, justice, moderation, cleanliness, tranquility, chastity, and humility.

To do this, he devised a "little book." He allotted a page for each of the virtues, ruled each page with red ink so as to have seven columns, one for each day of the week, and marked each column with a letter for the day. And he gave a week's strict attention to each of the virtues successively. By concentrating for that week on one particular virtue and leaving the others to "their ordinary chance," he supposed that if he "could keep that line in his book free of fault marks, the habit of that virtue would be so much strengthened and its opposite weakened" that he might "venture extending my attention to include the next, and for the following week keep both lines clear of spots."

Franklin's technique was to do a thirteen-week stint—one for each virtue (order gave him the most trouble)—and then begin again. For the week he concentrated on temperance, his fault-mark chart looked like this:

Form of the pages.

	S.	M.	T.	W.	T.	F.	S.
TEMPERANCE.							
EAT NOT TO DULLNESS. DRINK NOT TO ELEVATION.							
T.							
S.	*	*		*		*	
O.	* *	*	*		*	*	*
R.			*			*	
F.		*			*		
I.			*				
S.							
J.							
M.							
C.							
T.							
C.							
H.							

Franklin confessed that after several years of this routine, "I was surprised to find myself so much fuller of faults than I had imagined, but I had the satisfaction of seeing them diminish.... I never arrived at the perfection I had been so ambitious of obtaining but fell far short of it, yet I was, by the endeavor, a better and happier man than I otherwise should have been if I had not attempted it."

This happened during the eighteenth century. Even then Benjamin Franklin was following many of the rules that behavior therapists today advocate for people who want to change themselves and their lives: He thought through his goals, did the easiest thing (for him) first, and kept a record.

To achieve your goals, you must possess certain skills, namely, the skill of working toward a goal. A variety of unsatisfying behaviors enables the "no goal" syndrome to control you and your life.

You lack the ability to get work done in a productive fashion. As a result of childhood experiences and environment (overprotective parents, an indulgent teacher), *you were trained not to work and you've never outgrown the habit.*

You may have acquired the habit of working only when you feel like it. When you don't, any little task seems overwhelming. You've never learned the concept that you perform work because it has to be done, not because you're in the mood. Or, in the course of living, you've *never managed to develop good work habits.* Not knowing how to organize your tasks or your time, you move from crisis to crisis, continually procrastinating, and eventually do a poor job.

You let work control you, keeping other needs from surfacing. You may keep compulsively busy so that you don't have time to experience emotions. You may be a workaholic who never takes time to relax.

You let other people control you. You may overcommit yourself because you can't say no. Or you spend your days as a martyr, always doing things for other people.

You don't have realistic expectations—either you expect too much of yourself or too little. Rationally you know a certain task will take three hours. However, you make the unconscious demand of yourself to complete it in one hour. When you can't, you become discouraged, lose interest, or stop. But you don't connect this behavior with your unconscious fantasy goal. On the other hand, you may think, "I'd like to do such and such" and then you add the thought, "I can't do it—I'm bound to fail." This brainwashing can lead to a depressed state where even the most trivial task becomes a burden.

Says Dr. Herbert Fensterheim, "By setting goals and attempting to achieve them, you become aware of the specific behaviors you have to change—regardless of how these behaviors originally developed. Having goals helps you to separate the important from the trivial so that you can make decisions about where to expend time and energy. Long-term goals give you a feeling of movement through life. Sub-goals provide a sense of accomplishment."

How do you set up a goal program that gets you where you want to get? The following pointers may help:

1. *Define your goals.* In doing this, ask yourself some of the same questions that industrial psychologists use to develop achievement motivation in industry. What are your goals? How can you accomplish them? How do you deal with the obstacles? For example, you want to move up on the job, but the next logical position open to you would require some knowledge of marketing which you now lack. Can you learn this on your present job? Should you take a course? How can you get help?

2. *Concentrate on sub-goals.* According to Dr. Norman R. F. Maier, professor emeritus of psychology at the University of Michigan, "To set up goals, think about them. Ask yourself what you want out of life. Then divide your life into sub-goals. That means, What do I want to accomplish today?" For instance, your long-range goal is to "become an assertive person." But this involves many sub-goals. You may want to emulate Franklin's list (but if you do, improve on his technique—mark your chart *when you perform an assertive act well, not when you don't*), and keep a graph in which you record such assertive sub-goals as "ask a favor," "say no," "express anger." Remember, sub-goals provide encouragement. Without them, you can get discouraged.

3. *Make it easier for yourself to get started.* Once you have formulated your goals, write them down. Without a specific statement of intention, it becomes easy to fool yourself that you've carried out your objective. Make your list concrete and specific. Don't use vague generalities like, "I will stop procrastinating" . . . "not be late any more" . . . "be more orderly" . . . "dress better." Instead, if your goal is to be on time at work, be very exact: "I will be at my desk at the office no later than 9 A.M." Warning: Do not think you're wonderful because you've written down your intention. Move on to the next step of action or you just become a master at writing intentions.

● Seek out models. Talk with your friends who have managed to achieve goals you want and see how they have handled the problems you anticipate so much that you don't even attempt the goal. For instance, you want to go back to work (main goal) but can't figure out how to cope with the cooking (obstacle). By talking with a friend, mother of three teen-agers who has successfully managed to hold down job and kitchen detail, you may find out that she spent a month learning how to use the freezer efficiently and that, in addition, each child cooks dinner once a week.

• Break goals down into specific acts. For example, your goal may be to have a spotless apartment. Your sub-goal may be to do spring cleaning. Break this down into specific acts: "do linen closet today" . . . "hall closet tomorrow" . . . "send draperies out Thursday."

You can apply this "specific acts" technique to almost any goal. In one case, a woman had graduated from college with a major in drama, married almost immediately, and spent the next twelve years as wife and mother. She wanted to go to work but claimed, "I have no skills." She set up a series of "specific acts": Read the want ads, prepare a résumé based on volunteer jobs ("No one had to know I didn't get paid"), spend time thinking about her talents. By doing the latter, she realized she possessed considerable knowledge about art. She told every friend she had about her desire to work, and eventually one friend came through with a two-day-a-week volunteer job at an internationally known museum. She took it, and six months later was hired on a full-time basis.

4. *Don't let others set your goals for you.* There are many people who love to tell you how to run your life—when to leave a party, what school to choose for your children, what to serve when you entertain, why you should go back to work, whom to marry and whom not. They do this, even though when it comes to handling their own lives they aren't such paragons. When what they preach isn't nonsense, you should listen. But the actual decision about your goal has to be yours.

5. *Set priorities.* Pace yourself—at such and such an hour, you'll do certain things. When you have to do something really important, try to defer everything else until the next day. Do the deadline chore first. Establish your own value system with a selection-rejection process. You can't be the Renaissance Woman and do everything simultaneously.

6. *Use your fantasies.* You may have daydreamed about certain goals all your life and always put off doing them. Why? Some may be impossible to achieve (like my fantasy of winning the Nobel Prize for literature and walking across the stage in Stockholm in a Dior dress), but others may be within your grasp. I had always fantasized about running a literary salon, like the one Madame de Caillavet held twice a week for Anatole France. When I left my *Seventeen* job, I realized that I might not be able to swing this every Wednesday and Sunday as she did, but I could hold a dressed-up at-home once a month on Sunday. And I started doing it.

7. *Understand your limitations.* Talent and age obviously affect your goals. At forty you might learn to play the violin, but, obviously, you have started too late for a career as first violinist with the New York Philharmonic. If you lack coordination, you can't become Billie Jean King, but you can spend your vacation at a tennis camp with the goal of a better game. No matter what your years, you can start a career. One housewife of forty-five realized she spent most of her time advising friends about their professional and love lives. Doing this wasn't her idea of a lifetime goal. Thinking about it, she realized she had a strength—that something about her invited confidences from others. So she enrolled in a three-year psychological program with the goal of becoming a lay analyst.

You also have to accept the possibility of failing when you try to achieve your goal. One homemaker enrolled at the local university to get her long-dreamed-of college degree and found "It was too much to be a student-housewife-mother." Feeling very disappointed, she had to put off this goal until her younger daughter finished high school.

8. *Realize that good goals have time limits.* The danger arises when you lack any sort of goals and hence have no sense of purpose in life, and when you keep on living according to a goal ("raise my children") that is no longer appropriate (the kids have flown the nest).

If you have trouble setting goals, the following two exercises may help.

a. *Play the ring toss game.* This is the game many of us played as children, but which you can utilize to determine your actual achievement motivation. Put a spike at one end of the room. Take a handful of rope rings to pitch onto the spike. Do it. At the end take notice of where you stood to make your pitch.

When industrial psychologists at the Boston-based firm of McBer and Company conduct this experiment with business people, they find that some people stand very close to the spike, thus easily ringing it—and quickly lose interest. Others stand relatively far away, fail to make any ringers, and become discouraged. But a few stand just far enough away to make the toss challenging, yet not so far away as to make success impossible. Highly motivated people always set goals high enough so that they present challenges, but within reach so that at least some of them can be realized quickly. Thus you get "accomplishment feedback," the success experience of realizing your goals.

Evaluate your level in the ring toss game and take action to change. If your goals aren't hard enough, make them harder. If they're too hard, switch them to something you can do.

b. *Ask yourself, "What kind of woman would I like to be?"* Dr. Dorothy J. Susskind, associate professor of educational psychology at Hunter College of the City University of New York, uses the Idealized Self-Image technique for confidence training in which the goals are the creation of a "more positive identity and an enhanced self-esteem."

EXERCISE IN IDEALIZED SELF-IMAGE (ISI)

1. Close your eyes and see yourself as your ISI with all the qualities you'd like to possess. The women I interviewed for this book often chose the following: "very feeling," "able to accept compliments," "able to express anger," "very unflappable," "an easy sense of give and take," "emotionally stable," "professional competence," "to be comfortable with myself."

If you have trouble thinking of traits, you might get some ideas by conjuring up characteristics of certain women you admire: Jackie Bouvier Onassis for her charm, Shana Alexander for intellect, Katherine Hepburn for courage and cool.

2. Go to your desk and put what you've just imagined in writing. Be very specific. Include the way you'd like to look, subjects about which you'd like to be knowledgeable as well as the personality type you'd like to be ("serene" would be my choice because I'm not). You should have about twenty items on the list.

3. Redo your checklist, listing the items in order of their importance to you. Do you have any of the qualities now? Are you "very unflappable" but not "very feeling"? What can you do to develop the qualities you already have? What can you do to minimize the discrepancy between the traits you have and the way you'd like to be? Pare your list down to some ten items. Eliminate any characteristics that are absolutely beyond you. For instance, I'd love to be "mechanically adept," but since I've nearly killed myself three times by sticking a fork in the toaster and broken two blenders in two years—to name just a few mishaps—that goal is obviously impossible for me.

Work on your ISI. Make a commitment to yourself to achieve those goals just as Benjamin Franklin did. You won't attain your ISI by daydreaming about it or wishful thinking. Start working on one of the qualities right now. If it's "to be better-looking," go for a make-up lesson. If it's "to be more curious," read the editorial page of the daily newspaper or take two new biographies out of the library.

When in doubt about what to do in a situation, ask yourself, "What would my ISI do?" "What would my ISI do if another person took credit for my work?" "What would Katherine Hepburn do in my spot?"

9. *Strengthen your goal resolves with rewards.* This is the principle Dr. Arnold Lazarus taught to Jane Graham, an unhappy divorcée who came to see him because she felt so depressed by her messy apartment—a shambles of dirty dishes, uncompleted tax forms, unread magazines and newspapers. "It would take me a lifetime to straighten it up," she said, "and I can't even bear to think about it."

Says Dr. Lazarus, "We set up a system of sub-goals. Each week she had to do one task—for instance, the first assignment was to wash and put away all the dishes. But we added a contingency contract. Jane collected art books, and they were the one clean thing in the whole apartment. If the dishes weren't put away clean, she would have to destroy one of her cherished books. But if she did do the dishes, she could buy herself a new art book. The next week Jane walked in triumphantly with a brand-new copy of *Picasso's Theater*. Tidying up took six months. She had relapses and had to tear up several art books. But she kept her bargain and at the end had a lovely new library of art books."

Giving myself rewards has enabled me to write five books. Now, if I get up at 6 A.M. and do twelve pages, I present myself with a Bloody Mary and steak tartare for lunch. When I finish the first draft of a book, I buy myself some sort of antique—patchwork quilt, piece of Meissen china, tole tray. When I deliver the manuscript, I do something indulgent and luxurious that I have planned beforehand—treat myself to a day in a sauna, spend four hours reading in the bathtub, cut hothouse grapes with my silver grape shears that I acquired as a from-me-to-me present.

Setting up your own system of reinforcements can be very helpful in achieving goals. You might:

• Give yourself every Friday afternoon off. One harried executive found herself feeling very annoyed by work pressures, so she decided on a new strategy. She says, "If I have given my all for four and a half days, I stay on the premises of my job but essentially I quit work. I get my hair done at lunchtime, write personal letters, and make personal phone calls in the afternoon, and sometimes just stare at the wall and think."

• Start the course you've always wanted to take.

• Buy yourself something you've always wanted.

• Go to a museum every Saturday.

You can make your rewards harder and harder to earn. First you must pay one bill, then three bills, then all bills to earn your present. Or you must amass a series of points. But always keep in mind the precept: If I don't meet the goal, I don't get the reward.

You can give these rewards to yourself or you can get them from others. Encourage your husband, lover, children, friends to praise you as you move toward your goal. They should not comment on any lack of progress. The idea is to reinforce your progress. In addition to the reinforcing qualities of praise, the knowledge that others believe in us and are counting on us acts as a self-fulfilling prophecy and helps us to achieve goals that they think we can achieve. Leontyne Price, the great soprano, got her first job, as a maid, with a family that predicted she had the makings of a star—and made it a self-fulfilling prophecy by convincing Miss Price herself.

It's a twist on Parkinson's law: If you enlarge the opportunity, you will expand to fill it.

ASSERTIVE ASSIGNMENTS

Have you ever ordered a rare steak *au poivre* in a fancy French restaurant and had it delivered well done—and short on pepper? Have you ever been taken a roundabout way to your destination by an opportunistic taxi driver who, after you tip him despite his hi-jinks, complains, "Lady, I ain't never gonna get rich off people like you!" While traveling abroad, have you ever decided to treat yourself to a weekend at some posh resort and been put in a tiny cubicle across from the cleaning room quarters?

What did you do in those or similar situations? If you're like many women who lack assertion, you suffered and did nothing.

To treat people who have these specific problems in assertion, Assertiveness Training offers a method called behavior assignments. The therapist gives out certain tasks—some involving impersonal situations in stores, restaurants, theaters, supermarkets, and others that concern social interaction with friends, co-workers, husbands, relatives. The premise behind these assignments: knowing what you should do is not enough. You must carry out assertive acts in the life situation. The purpose of these assignments: to get you to start behaving assertively in an organized way.

Here are some assertive assignments that may help you to get started on the assertive life. In your FAN workbook list them in order of difficulty for you. By doing the easiest first, you know you can perform an assertive act and thus you have the knowledge that you can go on to others. Use the following assignments as a guide and then tailor-make your own to your individual needs.

BEHAVIOR ASSIGNMENTS

Ask for something in an impersonal situation:
- In a store where the price list isn't posted, ask to see it.
- If you're driving and aren't sure of the turn-off to your destination, stop at least two people and ask for directions.
- In the course of the week go into stores and ask for change of one dollar. Don't buy anything. The second week ask for change of $5 and the third for change of $10. Again, don't buy anything. The point here is not to amass a collection of change but to have the courage to ask. (Note: this assignment is a favorite of behavior therapists who specialize in Assertiveness Training.)
- Take the classified section of the newspaper and find jobs for which to call. Practice saying, "I read about your job in the *Times*. Can you tell me a little about the job and just what it would entail?"
- If you have difficulty coping in a business situation that is primarily male-oriented (for example, dealing with people like auto mechanics), go to a garage and get an estimate of what it would cost to do a repair job on your car, even though you don't plan to have it fixed.

Put you first:
- Take an hour every day to do something for *yourself* in your own home. It can be something as simple as reading a new best-seller. Repeat this over and over until you are able to do it without feeling guilty.
- During the week take at least four hours for *yourself* for "fun time" outside of the house.
- Make the deliberate effort to go to a store and purchase something for *yourself*—not for a friend, colleague, spouse, children, or mother-in-law.
- Enroll in a course—typing, karate, finance, or credit toward your M.A.
- At work tell your boss you need an extra two hours to

do a personal errand (naturally, this assignment presumes you do not have the habit of goofing off). This task is particularly good for women who feel a male authority figure will view them as a "female stereotype—flighty and gabby" if they take time for a coffee break or an extra long lunch hour.

Break a pattern:
- Do one thing you've procrastinated about for a long time: make an appointment for a checkup, fix up your personal phone book, write your aunt to whom you've owed a letter for six months.
- Open your own checking account.
- Sign up for volunteer work requiring responsibility. Or ask for more responsibility on your job.

Make a social contact:
- Get in touch with someone you haven't seen for a long time and make a date.
- You pick whom you and your husband socialize with for the next three Saturday nights.
- Talk to a stranger. One Westchester housewife tried this and found both a work project and a close friend. Enrolled in the School of Continuing Education at Sarah Lawrence College, Joan was drinking carrot juice one day at the health food bar and made herself speak to the woman on the next stool "who just happened to be another grown-up." Says Joan, "It turned out that she was like me—a middle-aged housewife trying to move out of the house and reenter the working world. We liked each other. I thought she'd be perfect to star in the film I was making as part of my course. I said to myself, 'How am I going to ask this lady if she'll be in my movie?' Finally I said, 'Would you like to be in my movie?' and explained I was doing this as my major project. She answered, 'I'd like to do it. If you get sick of me or I get sick of you, we'll just quit.' So we made the movie. We also became good friends and now we get together as couples."
- Make two social overtures in the next week—for instance, invite a couple whom you have never seen socially over for dinner; suggest to a fellow worker that you lunch together; invite a woman in your exercise class who seems worth knowing to join you for coffee.

• Ask a man out. If he refuses, don't go to pieces.

• Initiate a contact at a singles bar. (Note: This is a favorite behavior assignment of therapists, but I must confess it's too advanced for me. I couldn't do it.)

• Try making a personal friend of someone you'd like to know better—and who frightens you. In the course of writing my book *The Second Wife*, I interviewed Julia Perles, the internationally known lawyer whom *New York* magazine has described as a "low-key dynamo." Miss Perles not only gave me a two-hour interview but even volunteered to go over the two chapters pertaining to legalities involved in remarriage. I was terribly impressed—by her knowledge and warmth. For months I thought, "I'd like to be friends with her." Then I'd negate the wish with, "She wouldn't be interested in me."

One day I summoned my courage and called her. To the secretary I said, "My name is Jean Baer. I interviewed Miss Perles for my book, but probably she won't remember me."

But Miss Perles did. "Jean, how nice to hear from you. How is the book coming?"

I plunged. "The book will be out in June, but that's not why I called. I enjoyed meeting you so much. You were nice to me. I wonder if I could take you to lunch."

Dead silence.

I died. "Of course, I realize how busy you are, so I'll understand perfectly . . ." I trailed off.

Miss Perles interrupted with, "The shock of being asked to lunch shut me up. You know, in the past year I must have given forty interviews and not one reporter has even written me a thank-you note much less asked me for lunch. I'd love it. How about next Wednesday?"

We had a lovely lunch at the Clos Normand. As we sipped coffee, Julia (I had progressed to her first name) invited me and my husband to a cocktail party she was giving that Sunday. I hesitated, saying, "Herb is giving a professional talk somewhere and we wouldn't be able to get to your house until seven o'clock."

She said, "Let him come when he can. You come at five."

Again, I demurred, "But do you want a woman alone?"

She laughed, saying, "We'll take care of you." She and her husband did. I had a marvelous time meeting the legal lights of New York. The next day three of the party guests telephoned with invitations (they all used the same sentence: "How wonderful to meet someone who isn't a lawyer"). Julia and I became fast friends—the kind that call each other on Saturday afternoon and say, "Doing anything tonight? If not, I'll cook." Recently she told me, "I can't believe we've known each other only three years. I feel I've known you forever."

It is such a satisfying and rewarding friendship, and all because I forced myself to call her when my basic insecurity kept saying, "What would she see in you?"

As well as the above assignments, you should also *watch for situations in which you can practice being the assertive woman.* For instance:

1. When a waiter puts you at an undesirable table—by the kitchen, street door, or next to a group of ten women hostessing a bridal shower—ask for another.

2. The next time that food you've ordered in a restaurant arrives and is unsatisfactory, send it back. That applies to the steak you've ordered rare and shows up carbonized, the veal that's so tough that you practically break your knife trying to cut it, or the casserole of creamed chicken that comes lukewarm instead of hot. Offer no apologies. Just state firmly what is wrong.

3. Seek out opportunities to respond to male-chauvinist-pig put-downs. For example, if you are shopping with your husband and the salesperson directs all his attention to him and ignores you, speak up. Use a line like, "Please talk to both of us about the mechanics of this. I'll be the one actually using the washing machine."

Or if you are about to make an expensive purchase (auto, stocks, etc.) on your own, and the salesperson or broker asks, "What does your husband do?" refuse to answer. Say, "I'm making this purchase with my money, not his, and you have no right to ask that question." If the person insists, take your money elsewhere.

4. Look for the chance to ask people to do minor favors for you. For example, a switchboard operator at a large company felt very uncomfortable about asking another employee to cover for her while she went to the bathroom. At the time

she was being treated by Drs. Barry Lubetkin and Steven Fishman at the Institute for Behavior Therapy, New York. They gave her graded assignments. First: To ask a fellow worker, "Can you just cover for thirty seconds while I look out the window?" Second: "Can you cover for a minute while I get some stationery?" Third: "Can you cover for two minutes while I get coffee?" Gradually she worked up to the ladies' room.

5. When salesclerks, co-workers, even friends take advantage of you, view it as an opportunity to practice assertiveness. To the salesclerk who puts pressure on you, you might say, "This isn't quite what I want. I'll come back another time." To the manager who gives you a tiny cubicle at a hotel, you might say, "This room is really stifling. What else can you show me?" To the co-worker whose loud voice hampers your concentration, try, "Would you mind speaking a little softer? I can't do my work."

6. The next time your parents or husband make critical comments regarding how you spend your time or bring up your children, express disagreement instead of sitting there mute.

As you do these assertive assignments, you may think to yourself, "They're hard. Why do them? Maybe I should just stay the way I am."

This is the time to remember these words of philosopher William James from his *Principles of Psychology*: "Keep the faculty of effort alive in you by a little gratuitous exercise every day. That is, be systematically ascetic or heroic in little unnecessary points, do every day or two something for no other reason that you would rather not do it, so that when the hour of dire need draws nigh, it may find you not unnerved and untrained to stand the test."

SAYING NO

One day playwright Moss Hart was talking to Garson Kanin, who was about to direct a new Broadway play. Hart asked Kanin how he really felt about the actress he was considering for the lead, and Kanin admitted he really didn't care for her, but said the author of the play liked her. "Don't have her," Hart told Kanin firmly. "Don't say yes. Listen to what I'm saying to you. All the mistakes I ever made in my life were when I wanted to say no and said yes."

The ability to say no is an important part of being assertive. People—whether bosses or mates, strangers, co-workers or your college roommate—will almost always make demands of you. If you can't say no when you want to say no and feel it appropriate to do so, you are letting others run your life.

Yet, when it comes to uttering this one-syllable, two-letter word, women particularly feel anxious. Among the definitions given for the word "feminine" in *Webster's Third New International Dictionary* are "receiving or enduring action" ... "passive." Many women automatically assume that to be "feminine" means being submissive and indecisive. Some feel it's a "woman's place" to nurture, to always take care of other people's needs before they do anything about their own. For them it's easier to say yes rather than deal with the guilt they may feel by refusing a request, no matter how unreasonable. Because of a lifetime of being conditioned to be a second-class citizen, others lack confidence in their own decision-making ability. They reason, "How can I disagree? He/she knows more than I do. My wishes don't matter." Others don't say no because they feel it will lead to conflict, reprisals, or "the other person won't like me." Some diehards even think that for a woman to be taken advantage of is status quo.

If you don't say no, the consequences can run the gamut from minor distress and annoyance to a psyche at the zero level.

You end up feeling complete lack of self-respect. For example, when Anne Gerard had been married for about six years and had a five-year-old daughter, an acquaintance called with a request. "Look, Anne, you can really help us out. My husband and I want to go to Europe for three months. Will you take care of Cynthia?"

Anne said yes when she wanted to say no. She knew she was making a mistake. Then came the consequences. For the next twelve weeks she dealt with a sixteen-year-old. Not only did she have to cook and clean for her but found herself dealing with late curfews, dates she didn't approve of but felt she lacked the authority to forbid, and the pressure from the divorced father, who felt now was his chance to win love from his child. Anne says, "I had to deal with all this adolescent rebellion. It produced such a strain in the household that it nearly ruined my marriage, which up to then had been so happy. The kid was so sloppy, and she started to compete with my little daughter for my affections. There was nothing in the situation that benefited me. I didn't even make the arrangement with the mother to have Cynthia act as a mother's helper. It was all because I couldn't say no. In the end the acquaintance returned, the daughter went back, and we hardly ever saw each other again."

According to Dr. Herbert Fensterheim, "The inability to say no is the greatest single cause of unwanted promiscuity among young single women. I see it over and over again in my clinical practice. These patients don't see it as such. They rationalize it by saying, 'You have to go to bed these days to be popular' or, 'If I don't, he won't ask me out again,' so they do—and then they hate themselves."

In your eagerness to have the whole world love you, you find yourself with no time to do the things you want to do and have to do. For example, not too long ago I was up against a deadline for a major magazine piece. In the mail I received a letter from a French friend—not a close one, but the kind you exchange Christmas cards with and meet for lunch if she comes here or you go to Paris. "I have a chance to take a charter flight to the United States," she wrote. "Can you put me up?"

It was extremely inconvenient for me. I had many work assignments plus the magazine piece. In addition, there's no extra bedroom, but there is a convertible sofa in my office–dining room–library.

I couldn't say no, so I rationalized it. "Poor thing," I reasoned to myself, "she has the chance to come and no money." And I promptly wrote back explaining the circumstances, pointing out that she might not be too comfortable, but that she would certainly be welcome *for a little while*.

Nicole arrived with five suitcases. From then on my life

became a nightmare. The telephone rang constantly *for her*. I couldn't get into my kitchen because she was always asleep in the next room. Her underwear hung over the backs of chairs. And she entertained constantly—with my liquor.

Three weeks later, when I felt ready to lose my sanity, I asked, "Nicole, how long is your charter ticket for?"

She answered, "Forty-five days!"

I knew I must do something or lose my mind. So, for two days, I rehearsed and finally said, "Nicole, *we* have a problem. Do you have any other friends with more room with whom you could stay?"

She gave a Gallic shrug. "Of course. Why didn't you tell me right away? Lots of my friends have extra bedrooms." Two days later she moved into the Cosmopolitan Club, a very fancy, private Manhattan club for women. During the rest of her time in New York she never called nor did she write a thank-you letter upon her return home. My next month's phone bill was for $182.43—about five times the normal amount.

Instead of making her love me more, my inability to say no had lost me a friend, and cost me that extra $150 for her phone calls because I didn't have the guts to ask her to reimburse me. But even worse, I fizzled completely with the magazine article. For the first time in my life I not only turned in something late but had it rejected.

You don't come to terms with your passivity. Instead of facing this quality in yourself, you say yes because it's easier than saying no. For example, I always used to take my stepmother's dog when she went off on vacation. Did I say, "No. Lee can do it. She doesn't work"? Of course not. Instead, I rationalized, "If I say no, I'll hurt Helen's feelings. She wants me to take care of Brownie." It was quite a shock when, after Assertiveness Training, I finally refused to take Brownie for a two-week stint and heard my stepmother say, "Oh, it really doesn't matter. She'll be better off in a kennel."

Because you don't speak up honestly, you and the other person end up doing something neither of you wants to do. For instance, your husband says, "Let's go to the movies," and you say yes. In actuality, you want to read the new Book-of-the-Month-Club novel. But you think *he* wants to go to the movies. In actuality, he doesn't. He'd like to watch the Jets game on TV. By suggesting a movie, he thinks he's pleasing you. This kind of dishonesty blocks communication.

You virtually ask other people to take advantage of you. If you're always Jeannie-on-the-spot, volunteering to do chores no one else wants to do, naturally people will say, "Let Jeannie do it."

Sometimes people count on you to say no and feel disappointed when you don't. This is especially true in relation to your children. Or your spouse may expect you to set limits. For example, your husband indulges in compulsive socializing. He may want you to say, "No, I'm too tired to go," and thus set bounds on his hyperactive social life.

You let the resentments build up and spend most of your life feeling antagonistic to others. In reality, you're mad at yourself.

You don't have to wend your way through life as the patsy who always says yes. Research at the University of Wisconsin has proven that saying no is a learnable skill.

1. *Start your answer with the word no.* If you don't, you'll end up saying "maybe" or "yes."

2. *Speak in a firm voice.* If you say a whispered, hesitant no, your words say one thing and your voice another. The other person will seize the chance to pounce.

3. *Keep your answer short and clear.* If you start in with long explanations, you become apologetic or defensive and start giving in. Aim for clarity and honesty.

EXAMPLE ONE: Your mother wants you to come home for a visit this summer. But on your limited vacation you want to do something else.

Wrong way: "Oh, Mother, I'm not sure of my plans yet. I'll try though."

Right way: "No, I just can't afford it. I'm going to stay here and go to my beach house on the weekends."

EXAMPLE TWO: At work collections for gifts have gotten out of hand. Several times a week someone asks for a small contribution for a co-worker who is leaving for another job, getting married, retiring, or having a baby. You don't even know most of these people and feel enough is enough. Now you are asked to contribute again for a stranger and don't want to chip in your dollar. How do you say no?

Wrong way: You don't and fork over your dollar.

Right way: "No, I don't even know her." Or, "No, this is the third collection this week. I'll skip this one."

4. *Don't let your anxiety keep you from saying no.* For example, you and a date have agreed not to see each other any more. You have no interest in him. He telephones and asks you out. The proper dialogue might go like this.

HE: Joan, I'd like to see you.

JOAN: No, I don't think it's a good idea for us to see each other.

HE: I've changed.

JOAN: No, I really don't want to see you or continue this conversation.

If you're not firm, you send the message, "I'm not sure. I can be convinced." The example dialogue is honest, and honesty usually works.

5. *Don't send double messages.* For example, Helen had a sixteen-year-old son who was graduating from high school. He wanted to give a party for the entire senior class of thirty students. Their pre-AT dialogue went like this.

HE: I'd like to have a party for the senior class.

SHE: What kind of party?

HE: A nighttime one.

SHE: What about having it in the country?

HE: Can they stay overnight?

SHE: Is it a coed party?

HE: Of course.

SHE: You can have it in New York in the daytime.

HE: That won't do.

SHE: I don't see why not. Anyway, you can't have the party at all.

HE: You don't have to be there.

SHE: It's my house.

HE: I don't see why I can't have the party where I want it.

SHE: Because I don't want to be responsible.

In this dialogue Helen made two mistakes: She didn't say a firm no and she tried to convince her son that he shouldn't have the party. She failed to follow the rule, "If it's no, it's no."

After an Assertiveness Training session, she was able to have the following dialogue.

HE: What about the party. Can I have it?

SHE: No, you can't.

HE: Why not?

SHE: Because I say no. It's completely unreasonable. You're only graduating from high school and I can't be responsible.

HE: All the kids are expecting it.

SHE: The answer is no. Let someone else have the party.

6. *You have the right to say no.* You have the right to tell your mother-in-law you can't run an errand for her, a cousin you can't afford to lend money, a door-to-door salesman who gives you the "help send me through college plea" that you have enough magazine subscriptions.

You also have the right to stick to your own time schedule—even though it differs from other people's. In my case I rarely make luncheon dates. I work from early morning until about 3 P.M. So I'm constantly having conversations like the following:

FRIEND: Let's meet for lunch.

ME: No, I just can't.

FRIEND: Why not?

ME: That's when I write.

FRIEND: Oh, you can write at any time. It doesn't matter when.

ME: It matters to me. No, I can't.

You can even say no to unreasonable requests on the job. One of my fellow Assertiveness Training groupers told the story of how she, a social worker, had sent a doctor all the material about a disturbed child three days previously. The doctor was scheduled to make the presentation on the case at noon to a group of residents. He called her and said, "Look, kid, I haven't had the chance to read the material. So just brief me quickly on the problems."

She answered, "No, I can't do it. I'm seeing a patient myself. I sent you the material. You're just going to have to read it." She adds, "Before Assertiveness Training, I would have dropped everything and gone to help him out."

7. *Practice.* Think of five unreasonable requests that have been made of you lately. Now think of how you could have said no in a better way—more firmly, directly or honestly. Write down the answers you would like to have given. It also helps if you use a tape machine. Put the "unreasonable request" on tape, answer it in a way that pleases you, and then listen to your response. Repeat this until you are satisfied.

8. *Be prepared.* It helps if you have various model ways to say no at your fingertips. Some that work for me: "No, I'm just too committed. Much as I would like to I can't accept" . . . "No, I've already done more than my share. Give someone else a chance" . . . "No, I'm just not in the mood to do that today. I'd rather do such and such" . . . "No, I just can't. I've already taken on something else that conflicts."

Remember, you don't have to say no immediately. If you don't know what your answer can or should be, you can ask for time to think. Because it's so hard for me to say no, I frequently use this technique. Then I rehearse my saying no answer until I feel confident of my ability to say it.

9. *Don't say no when there's a valid reason to say yes.* The art of saying no is not meant to spur selfishness. You have to take everything into consideration, including the feelings of the other person and your feelings for the person. It is a deliberate decision.

For example, recently I asked my stepmother, whom I adore, to come into New York to celebrate Mother's Day with lunch and an afternoon at the ballet. She accepted and then added, "Let's not go out to lunch. Why don't you make your wonderful cheese soufflé and then we can eat at your house. I can see your new wing chair cover." I was scheduled to give a dinner party for ten the night before. Making the cheese soufflé not only meant all that egg beating and the worry over will-it-rise-or-not but cleaning up the house immediately after the party. I didn't want to cook lunch. I wanted to take Helen to a restaurant where someone would wait on me. But her needs mattered more than mine. I willingly said yes, even though I wanted to say no. I did it out of choice.

10. *Don't say no when you want to say yes.* This is carrying things to the other extreme. A close friend, who is a successful newspaperwoman, told me that some years ago she was offered the job of Sunday feature editor at a Washington newspaper. She and her husband then lived in Chicago, and she recalls, "I didn't even tell Jim about the offer. I just refused. It wasn't him. It was me. It was crazy. I felt like a fool when, a year later, he told me he had always dreamed of living in Washington."

If you have problems with saying no, start saying it right now. For the next month make it a point: when in doubt, say no. Say it to unreasonable requests from your kids, your mate, your sister-in-law, your best friend from college. You'll find it gets easier and easier.

And remember, you aren't alone in having trouble in this area. When thirty-six-year-old Empress Farah Dibah, wife of the Shah of Iran, was in the United States recently, she gave an interview in which she commented about her frantic pace in which she frequently campaigns for as many as four causes on the same day—ecology, women's rights, the arts and education. She said, "It's just not normal to jump around so much. It's tiring. When I get tired I don't eat and I get depressed . . . *I must learn to say no.*"

Even Empresses have problems saying no.

I-TALK

Recently, Alice Nelson, a young reporter, came to interview me. I told her the story of how some years ago I had become sick with a severe ear infection. Since I was running a high fever, was single, lived alone in a business neighborhood so isolated that stores would not deliver, and was too sick to cook for myself, food—the little that I wanted—became a real problem. I had spent years running to sick friends with containers of chicken soup and tasty casseroles, but these same friends didn't come with food for me when I needed it. I have never gotten over the hurt and fury I felt at their neglect. Years later when I complained to my husband about this, he asked, "Why didn't you ask them to bring you some food?" It had never occurred to me to make the request of someone else.

About a month after the interview, Alice telephoned me. "It's unbelievable!" she exclaimed. "I'm in bed with flu and I thought of your chicken soup story, so I telephoned a few friends and asked for help. To each I said the same thing: 'I'm sick. I'm alone. I need help.' That night one friend brought a chicken, one a pot roast, another left three mystery books outside my door, and still another sent the most beautiful tulips. Being assertive really works."

How is anybody going to know what you want or don't want if you don't tell them? Like me, many women have difficulty using the pronoun "I." They've been taught that to use I is egotistical, that if they come right out and say what they want, others won't listen, approve, like them. But they have also been taught by society that it's perfectly acceptable to be "cute and coy," "use womanly wiles," "stoop to conquer." The result: They try to get what they want by indirect means.

They play games like:

Flattery: You say, "That was a wonderful idea you had for a vacation in Greece." (You're trying to make your husband think it was his idea when it was yours.)

Suffering: Instead of asking your husband to take the dishes out of the dishwasher, you sigh, look put upon, and try to signal, "After all I do for you, why can't you for once do something for me?"

Play-acting: You ask, "What restaurant shall we go to tonight?" You know very well that you long for Italian food and have every intention of going to Angelo's.

Manipulation: You ask a close friend, "Will you be near Fifth Avenue today?" (You're pressed and want her to buy stockings for you.)

Sabotage: You work at a retail store, and your boss asks you to start coming in on Saturdays. You object very much to this, but instead of saying anything to him you get even by making no attempt to sell and have a very low total sales figure on Saturdays. You want him to get the idea that it's better for you to work a Monday-through-Friday week.

These games may have temporary benefits, but usually the results of indirectness can be costly.

You dilute your message. You say to a man, "I hear there's a great show at the Strand next week." He may answer, "Thanks for telling me. I'll try to go." You end up with no date. If you had said directly, "I hear there's a great show at the Strand next week. I'd like to go with you if you're free," you may or may not get the date, but you've stated a preference and you'll get an answer.

You make the mistake of expecting the other person to be a mind reader and second-guess you. For example, you say, "Do you have plans for the weekend?" instead of, "I'd like you to come out to my beach house for the weekend." With this kind of indirectness you leave it to others to pick up your hints and clues. And so you run the risk of being misinterpreted.

You submerge your own identity. You say what you think other people want to hear. I made this mistake with my third book, *The Second Wife*. I hate my husband's ex-wife (whom I've never met formally, only seen at graduations and in court). I hate her because I work so hard and she gets lifetime alimony. I have experienced much hurt from his three children. But did I say a word of these feelings in the book? No, I was so afraid that other people would think me "bitchy," "against first wives," "the wicked stepmother" that I wrote all 275 pages in nice-Nelly style, crediting anecdotes that had actually happened to me to "Jane A." and "Mary B." I couldn't contain myself completely, and at the very end I wrote just four pages which expressed my resentments. A noted critic commented, "If only Miss Baer had written the entire book in the very feeling style of the last chapter, she would have had an even better book." By holding back my feelings and not using the pronoun "I," I had written a second-best book.

You may have the false impression that you do show inner feelings when you explode with rage. But explosion of rage usually stems from holding back of feelings. If you had been able to express your honest feelings before they built up to the high voltage point, you would rarely have had the occasion to have an anger explosion.

Assertiveness Training encourages women to recognize the value of being direct, honest, and nonmanipulative. In this way you control your own communication. You pursue what you want directly and don't have to wait to see if others fall for your manipulative ploys. One AT technique to aid you in the expression of honest and appropriate emotion is I-Talk. This is my term. I borrowed it from psychologist Andrew Salter's more technical term "feeling talk," which is the "deliberate utterance of spontaneously felt emotions." It is a technique that is specifically designed to aid people with deficiences in the expression and experience of feeling.

The Use of I-Talk

1. *Say what you want to say when you want to say it.* Writes Andrew Salter, "There is no harm in honoring social amenities and ethical conventions when they do not oppose our feelings. But we must forgo premeditated utterances and say what we feel when we feel it. When a cat is happy, it purrs. When a dog has his paw stepped on, he howls. Let the inhibitory go and do likewise."

2. *Say what you feel.* At many times it is important to say what you think, but think-talk is not expression of feeling. Statements about what you think reveal nothing of you. Make a distinction between verbs of feeling and thinking.

Feeling	*Thinking*
cherish	suppose
adore	guess
approve	imagine
enjoy	understand
get pleasure from	believe
covet	conclude
long for	presume
care for	deduce
hate	assume
dislike	think
detest	let's go
despise	verbalize
want	let's discuss
love	let's put our minds to the problem

3. *Deliberately use the pronoun "I" as much as possible.* Follow this with a feeling verb.

"I want to pay the bill this time."

"I like this beef stew."

"I detest Senator————and everything he stands for."

"I cried over what you said to me last night."

"I've been dying to meet you."

"I feel terrible about the way I spoke to you yesterday."

"I'm afraid of you when you show so much hostility."

"I resent the way your mother treats me in my own home."

"I don't care for the way you always show up late."

"I admire the job you did on that report."

"I love you more than I've ever loved anyone."

4. *If you have trouble using the pronoun "I," two AT exercises may help.*

  a. Count the number of times you use "I" in the course of a day. You might want to invest in a golf counter and click it each time you get the word out. Keep score in your Female Assertiveness Notebook.

  b. Make a deliberate attempt to use the following three pairs of phrases as often as possible:

● "I agree with what you've said" . . . "I disagree with what you've said."

● "I want you to do this" . . . "I don't want you to do that."

● "I want to do this" . . . "I don't want to do that."

In using them, start with the easiest for you (many women find the "I agree" . . . "I disagree" simpler than the "I want you to do this" . . . "I don't want you to do that"), keep a daily count in FAN and total weekly. After a few weeks analyze your progress.

Using I-Talk will not make you seem self-centered. It will make you sound direct, natural, and enable you to take that mask off your face.

CASE

For two years Kitty, a twenty-eight-year-old divorcée, had been involved in a relationship with a man who was unable "to give, unable to say, 'I love you.'" She says, "He was aware of his problem. He'd tell me, 'If I say it, I sound like a sissy.' I kept asking myself, 'Kitty, why are you with this guy? He gives you nothing.' But when I was with him, I'd stay silent. I couldn't get out the words 'I want. . . .' My AT group made me see my feelings mattered. Finally after rehearsing— by myself and with friends—I got out the words 'I want more from you.'"

When Kitty finally spoke up about her own needs, her man answered bluntly, "I can't give it. You'll have to get it from someone else." Kitty felt pain at this but also a new sense of self-confidence and dignity. She says, "For once I had expressed what I wanted. The affair ended badly, but I felt good about myself."

CASE

Madge was dating a man she liked very much. Then a recently separated platonic friend called and said, "I'm in the city. I need a place to stay." Madge broke her date and let the friend use her living room convertible couch. Her date was disappointed and angry. He couldn't understand why she couldn't work out a compromise. Madge realized it wasn't just a case of saying no. She had told neither man the truth. To the date, she hadn't said, "Look, this man is an old friend. He needs me right now. This is something I want to do." To the old friend she hadn't said, "Look, I'm getting involved with a man I'm starting to care for. If I let you stay, it means I can't see him. I'd like to make it another night."

But Madge learned. When the platonic friend called the next time, he called her at her summer beach house and wanted to come for the weekend. This time she responded, "No, I have a guest. But I'll be back in the city on Sunday and I do want to see you next week. What night is best for you?"

CASE

A fifty-year-old woman had spent her life as the perfect wife. She had put her spouse through his Ph.D., raised five kids, never developed any skills of her own, concentrated solely on domesticity. Finally, aware of her own dullness and subservience, she decided to take up nursing. The husband objected, saying, "You won't be free to take trips with me." Finally, after thirty years, she spoke up, saying "I want something for me." But it was too late. Shortly afterwards, he fell in love with a woman in his own profession and dumped his wife. She had waited too long to say, "I want."

5. *Don't simulate agreeability when you're seething inside*. Use sentences like, "I feel hurt" . . . "I don't like what you've said" . . . "I feel you have no right to talk to me like that."

Often people don't realize they've made you angry. In my Payne Whitney AT group, one young physician had great problems expressing rage. Once, when she got into an argument with her husband, she was completely unable to express her feelings. Her solution was to put a pillow over her head. The next week she reported to the group, "I'm not going to put a pillow over my head any more. I'm going to say what I feel." She did, and her husband said, "What a relief to know what's wrong."

In another instance, one cousin continually criticized my writing. I particularly resented it coming from her since she barely knows an adverb from an adjective. But I never said a word. Following a TV appearance one day, she called me. "I saw you on TV," she said cheerfully.

I waited for the barb.

It came. "Your voice didn't sound the way it usually does," she said. *"Did you have your teeth out yesterday?"*

Fortified by AT, I let my feelings show. "Listen, Linette," I said. "I feel hurt because you constantly criticize me. You don't know a thing about books or TV, but that doesn't stop you. You don't realize the effect you have on me. *I want you to stop*. Unless you're going to say something nice, please don't say anything."

She hasn't said a hostile word since.

6. *In expressing your feelings, make sure you express them appropriately.* Expressing your feelings directly doesn't mean a complete loss of control.

7. *In expressing your feelings, make sure you understand the difference between a request and a demand.* It has nothing to do with the way you phrase a question. It has to do with whether, in your expectancy, you are giving the other person the right to say no. If you say, "I would like Chinese food tonight. How do you feel about it?," this can be either a request or demand. If he/she says no and you feel disappointed or unhappy, it was a request. Even though you don't like the answer, you recognized the person's right to refuse. If your reaction is anger, depression, a feeling of humiliation, then it was a demand. You are thinking, "He/she should have said yes." You don't recognize his right to say no. When this happens, ask yourself, "Am I recognizing the other person's right of refusal?"

8. *Suit your actions to your words.* I-Talk also involves body and facial talk.

a. Eye contact. Look straight at the person to whom you are talking. Don't try to give those coy little glances that some women mistake for femininity. You don't have to stare, but keep your eyes on his/her face, not on the floor or at the door waiting for a "better prospect" to walk in.

b. Match your facial expression to your feelings; don't smirk when you express anger. Don't look away when you say, "I care." Don't look sullen or moody when you express love.

c. Stand proud. The way you stand influences the way you feel about yourself. If you hunch over in a fetal position, you show irresolution and passivity. If your head is up, feet solidly on the ground and eyes level with the other person, your body evinces assertiveness.

d. Make gestures. Show emotions with your hands and arms as the French do. You can pound a table for emphasis. You can put your arms around the other person to show warmth. Try to shake hands with people when you enter a room. You create a passive image if you keep your hands and arms against your body.

e. Make your voice strong and sure. Some people think

a little, soft whisper means femininity, and Jackie Bouvier Onassis certainly gets away with this. But baby-voiced women—when it's an obviously assumed tone—often annoy rather than attract people. Also avoid the hysterical high-pitched squeal, the monotone, and the strident voice. Read a short story or a poem into a tape recorder and then listen to it to hear how you sound. If you don't like your voice, do something about it. You can talk clearly and firmly and still sound like a woman.

f. Your clothes are another way of saying "I"—"This is what I am." Certain outfits make assertive statements. When I feel in a blue mood, I try to wear a favorite red Parisian pants suit. It gives me confidence, and wearing it makes it easier for me to say, "I want" . . . "I won't."

By practicing I-Talk you learn the skill of expression of feelings. Eventually you won't need to practice. The skill will be automatic, and you will have developed your own style of saying, "I want you to" . . . "I don't want you to."

Says one AT graduate, "I always used to feel guilty when I was direct with a man. But recently I spoke up to a man I was dating fairly steadily. We were planning a vacation together, but he wouldn't make any definite plans as to when and where. I told him, 'Look, I want you to tell me one way or the other. I have to know.' "

"You're being aggressive," he said.

"No," responded Sally. "I'm being assertive."

He made the plans.

ROLE REHEARSAL

When I got fired from *Seventeen* magazine, I managed to get $4,661.60 in additional severance pay. This happened because (a) I asked for it, and (b) before I asked, I spent three hours role-playing the way in which I would ask for it with my husband.

As I pointed out in the Introduction, during my last year at the teen publication I was sure that the new powers-that-be would eliminate my job. More and more, I was excluded from meetings, forced to the humiliation of "justifying" any expense-account items, prevented from going ahead with any new projects, however worthwhile they might be. I made the deliberate decision to sit it out bcause, after so many years, I wanted that severance pay. Because I wanted to be prepared when D-day came, I researched what all the others from the old regime who had been fired had gotten. I knew to a penny their various percentages, which in most cases came to two weeks' salary for each year worked.

When I returned to my office after a vacation in Colombia with my husband, I found myself with literally nothing to do. In the three weeks we had been away, two other staff members had departed: the top boss and the top executive secretary who had served three successive regimes.

The situation was intolerable to me. I called Herb and said, "I can't stand it. Maybe I should quit."

He counseled, "Obviously, your days are numbered. Stick it out until Friday. If nothing happens by then, go in at 3 P.M. and quit."

Two days later I received a summons from the general manager. "Sit down, Jean," he said. I knew what was coming.

"We've decided to disband your department," he said.

I let none of my jubilation show, saying simply, "This isn't unexpected, Steve. I'm just surprised that after all my years of service I didn't merit the courtesy of being dismissed by Phillip Wright" (the new boss whom I'd met once by introducing myself in front of the entrance to the men's room).

Steve was embarrassed. Obviously he hadn't wanted to do the dirty job. "We tried to find a new spot for you, but there was nothing," he said.

I ignored this statement, and said, "You've obviously worked everything out. May I ask the amount of severance pay?"

He named a figure. The amount came to little more than one week for each year worked.

Because I felt very sure of my facts, I was able to be quite assertive. "That's too little. Everyone else got two weeks for each year."

Steven seemed sympathetic, saying, "You certainly can take it up with Phil."

"I will," I replied and exited.

That night I told Herb about my getting fired. He

promptly got out a bottle of champagne from the refrigerator. I couldn't drink it. I told him, "I can't respect myself if I don't at least fight for the money to which I'm entitled. I'm not scared, because I've got nothing to lose. But I don't know how to do it."

Herb suggested role-playing it. The following is an almost verbatim reconstruction of our role-playing session.

HERB: How would you start?

JEAN: Mr. Wright, I'd like to talk to you.

(*Pause. I was stuck.*)

HERB: Go ahead. How do you get into this? What do you want? Is your problem that you don't know what you want?

JEAN (*Not role-playing*): That's no problem. I want that extra money and also to let him know that I'm angry that he didn't have the guts to fire me himself and let an underling do it.

HERB: O.K. You want to spell out those two things. How could you say it?

JEAN (*Not role-playing*): I think I can manage.

JEAN (*Role-playing*): Mr. Wright, my dismissal yesterday came as no surprise to me. I estimate in the past three years some thirty people have been let go. But I am a major department head and have been one for twenty-one years. I was surprised you didn't do the firing yourself instead of leaving it to a subordinate.

HERB (*Role-playing*): This is the way company organizations do things.

JEAN (*Role-playing*): In the past this organization didn't. However, I was even more surprised at the amount given me for severance pay after my twenty-one years of service.

HERB (*Role-playing*): I don't understand. We all felt it was very good severance pay.

JEAN (*Role-playing*): No, it's not. Jane Jones got two weeks for each year worked, and so did Trudy Randall and George Marks and many others.

HERB (*Coaching*): No, that's no good. Tell him what you're going to tell him. You're being indirect.

JEAN (*Role-playing*): Mr. Wright. The general policy has been to give an employee two weeks' salary for each year worked. I can cite you case after case of this. As a department head for so many years, I followed this rule myself when I let someone go. You have given me a figure which works out to slightly more than one week for each year worked. I consider this very unfair and would like to have two weeks for each year—the figure which has been the policy with others.

HERB (*Role-playing*): We have no policy. Each case is different, and, again, I consider this excellent severance.

JEAN (*Role-playing*): I do not. Furthermore, I've had an outstanding record. I built the editor of *Seventeen* as a public personality, I am known by virtually every women's page editor and women's commentator in the country, and have won many awards for the public relations job I have done for *Seventeen*.

HERB (*Role-playing*): All this has nothing to do with the situation. The economy is in a bad state and, like other organizations, we have to cut down on operations we consider superfluous. We are not firing you. We are disbanding your department. And we have been very generous.

JEAN (*Out of role*): I don't know where to go from there.

HERB (*Coaching*): Jean, you're getting off on the wrong track. What is the line of your argument?

JEAN (*Out of role*): After twenty-one years of loyalty and hard work I'm being let go. Twenty-one years earned me the right to the same money others have gotten. Besides I did my job so well. I'm not asking for anything special—just what's fair.

HERB (*Coaching*): Do you think that's a good line of argument? Put the emphasis on fairness to you. Now let's try it again.

JEAN (*Role-playing*): You're penalizing me. I know the magazine is cutting back, but I certainly gave *Seventeen* the best years of my life.

HERB (*Coaching*): No. Try something like, "I'm not asking for special treatment—only for fair treatment that I've earned." Put him on the spot. Now do it again.

JEAN (*Role-playing*): I'm not asking for special treatment. Only the fair treatment that I've earned with twenty-one years of service. (*Out of role*) What do I do if he says a flat no?

HERB (*Coaching*): You're bringing up another problem before you've solved one. Now let's start from the beginning again and take the problems one at a time. Remember that in this kind of role-playing there are certain common problems: (1) Even after we got the line of argument, you went off on a different track. (2) You seem to have a feeling of being overwhelmed. As soon as you see the light on one thing, you take off onto others. (3) I can't give you the answers. You know your professional world better than I do. I can only help you to find the answers for yourself and frame them in a way that communicates.

I thought the last point an extremely good one. Therapists, no matter how experienced, don't exist in the day-to-day rough world of business. Thinking the whole thing through again, I realized that maybe Mr. Wright probably expected me to ask for more and perhaps the offered amount was testing me, that Mr. Wright didn't have the final word on the subject (he took his orders from the company headquarters in Pennsylvania, and the men there barely knew my name), and that I had absolutely nothing to lose by asking and everything to gain, including my own self-esteem.

Realizing that, like me, Mr. Wright always got to work early, I purposely stuck my head in his office before nine the next day so I wouldn't have to deal with his secretary. Because I felt so well prepared, I was able to come on strong, confident, and assertive, not passive or aggressive. The dialogue, which turned out to be slightly different from what I had prepared, went something like this.

MR. WRIGHT: Come in, Jean.

JEAN: Thank you. I'll get right to the point. As you know, yesterday Steve fired me. I was surprised you didn't do it yourself.

MR. WRIGHT: But I don't even know you.

JEAN: You knew me well enough to make the decision. But that's water over the dam. I've been here twenty-one years, and, if you'll check, you'll find I've done an outstanding job. The severance pay I've been offered is $———. That comes to just a little over one week for each of my years of service. I want the two weeks that others have gotten.

I'm not asking for any special treatment—just fair treatment.

MR. WRIGHT: We felt we were being very fair and that we were giving you very good severance pay. After all, we're not firing you. We're simply disbanding your department. We can't keep you if there's nothing for you to do.

JEAN: I see your position perfectly, and I'm not questioning your reasoning on letting me go. However, Mr. Wright, the general policy has been to give an employee—and certainly a senior employee—two weeks' severance for each year worked. And this is what I feel would be fair in my case.

MR. WRIGHT: We have no policy. Each case is different, and we feel we've given you excellent severance.

JEAN: I can cite you case after case where *Seventeen* has given two weeks for each year worked. You did it with Margie Smith just last week ... and George Marks and Trudy Randall. And I can name at least twenty-two others. Furthermore, Mary Smith and Nancy Jones got a full year's pay. I'm not asking for that. I want two weeks for each year worked.

MR. WRIGHT: I didn't know anyone ever got a full year.

JEAN (*Inspired and taking Herb's advice to "Put him on the spot"*): The point is that while I have given much to *Seventeen, Seventeen* has given much to me. In these twenty-one years it has enabled me to gain a national reputation as well as the chance to set up events which have even made *Seventeen* page-one news—something that may happen at *Time* and *Newsweek* but not often at other women's magazines. I feel tremendous loyalty to *Seventeen.* I always will. That's why I wouldn't want to do anything to spoil things—like crying here now, or telling any of my newspaper friends of the severance trouble, or even taking legal action as one former employee did. I just want fair treatment. I want that two weeks for each year worked. If I don't get it, I'll feel terribly unhappy.

MR. WRIGHT: We wouldn't want you to feel unhappy. I'll see what I can do.

With that he stood up. We shook hands and I returned to my office, drafted a brief, three-paragraph memo reiterating what I had said, and waited. Fifteen minutes later there was a call from Steve. He said, "You'll get the two weeks for each year worked. The check will be here on the twenty-seventh."

I felt victorious, but not only over the money. If I hadn't role-played with Herb, I might have gone in and picked a fight. Or I might have gone in and been so weepy and tense that Mr. Wright might have thought the only way to pacify me was to restore my job—something he could not do. In which case, I would have gained nothing. Or, and most likely, I might not have gone in at all. With a few hours of role-playing I achieved an extra $4,661.60 for myself.

Role-playing, also known as behavior rehearsal, is a central technique in the process of Assertiveness Training. According to Dr. Herbert Fensterheim, "It serves as a training process in which individuals who have problems in their social or interpersonal behaviors receive direct training in more effective alternate behaviors. To do this, we use response rehearsal, modeling, and coaching. With unassertive and inhibited people we work in three steps: (1) We teach the individual what the assertive response is. (2) We have him practice it. (3) He applies it to the life situation. Naturally the purpose of the first two steps is to achieve the third."

How to role-rehearse on your own. If you are in therapeutic treatment, whether individual or group, you have the benefit of the therapist's coaching to improve your role-playing techniques. But you can also do it on your own with the assistance of a friend, co-worker, husband. Role rehearsal has many advantages; primarily, you can experiment in a non-risk situation so that you build up the confidence to try to get what you want in the risk situation.

EXERCISE IN ROLE REHEARSAL

1. **Be specific.** Figure out the exact situation you want to role-play and then stick with it. When role-playing, many people make the mistake of trying to handle four or five situations instead of one. Then they feel helpless. Defer other problems for another time, even if they're related. Stick to one specific behavior at the practice situation. For example, you're twenty-two and your mother still makes almost all your decisions for you. She tells you what to wear, how to style your hair, and makes your dental appointments for you.

You feel you have the right to govern your own life. When you role-play, decide on one situation for your initial practice session—for instance, telling your mother to stop making your appointments with the dentist.

You may want to utilize the scriptwriting technique DESC that Sharon Bower uses in her Assertiveness Training classes at Stanford University's Institute for Behavioral Counseling. The initials stand for:

Describe the problem to the other person.

Express the points you want to make.

Specify the behavior change you want the other person to make.

Consequences—Stipulate what you'll do if the other person continues to behave in the same way and if she/he doesn't.

Writing out an assertive DESC script in which you cover the four above points may clarify the issues for you.

2. Find a partner. This can be a friend, co-worker, your spouse. Your choice of partner depends on the situation. If it's a work problem, the best technique would be to role-play the problem with a person in the same field who understands the business difficulties involved. You can effectively role-play personal or social problems with a good friend, male or female, or your mate. With friends you have options: to pick someone who has assertive problems similar to yours or someone who is strong, confident, secure—all the things you'd like to be. As a general rule, pick someone with whom you'll feel at ease and take it from there.

3. As you role-play, you might follow this format.

a. Outline the situation. The situation should be one that occurred recently (when you didn't make the request you wanted to make or let someone put you down) or one that is likely to occur in the near future (going for a job interview, telling your husband something he did that you didn't like).

b. First role-play. You play yourself and the other person plays the other party (whether boss, committee chairman, neighbor, mother-in-law). Start small. Don't take on anything too difficult. Give your partner specific instructions on the role you want him or her to play. Take from one to five minutes to play the scene. At the conclusion of the scene discuss what you liked and didn't like about your performance. Your partner should also offer comments.

- Play it again. Repeat the performance, making the desired changes.

- Reverse roles. You play the other person. Your partner models how you should behave. He/she can also model the things you do wrong—like saying, "Er ... er ... er" or keeping your eyes rooted to the floor instead of looking the other person in the eyes.

- Replay it. Discuss again. Did you face the real problem? Does your solution work? Did you communicate what you really wanted to say or get off on a series of tangents? Were you still compliant the way you've always been? Did you directly request a new way of behavior from the other person ("John, I want my own checking account" ... "John, I feel bad when you wake up in a nasty mood and start picking on me for no reason").

4. In role-playing, suit your strategy to your personality. Don't do anything that isn't you or you'll never be able to do it in real life. Try talking into a tape machine and see what technique suits you.

5. Watch for expression as well as the actual words. Did your voice, expression, and gestures communicate what you feel? Did you overexplain, become apologetic, or talk in a weak, little whisper?

6. Realize that as you rehearse, one of the consequences may be a reduction of anxiety. The "reciprocal inhibition principle" of Dr. Joseph Wolpe, professor of psychiatry and director of the Behavior Therapy Unit at Temple University School of Medicine, states: "If a response inhibitory of anxiety can be made to occur in the presence of anxiety-evoking stimuli, it will weaken the bond between these stimuli and the anxiety." Thus when you role-play a scene and express anger, affection, or any feeling other than anxiety, you make it less likely that you will experience anxiety in the life situation.

7. The actual troublesome situation may be too upsetting for you to role-play it on the first try. In that case use a step-by-step approach which psychologists call a hierarchy. For instance, you want to tell off your sister-in-law. You might first rehearse telling off a very good friend toward whom you feel no fear or hostility. Then you can enact a scene where you tell off a fellow worker. Gradually you work up to the difficult sister-in-law.

In one case, a woman wanted to leave her job as administrative secretary for a big corporation. She tried to role-play interviewing for a job with a friend, but that didn't work. She still felt too anxious to take action. So she tried the hierarchy approach.

First she read through the classified section of the Sunday paper and made a list of jobs she didn't want. She telephoned each of the numbers given and got information about these possible situations. During the week she made eight calls and did not feel anxious. She knew she didn't want any of the jobs.

Second, the next week she made calls to get information about jobs for which she might be qualified. She made no appointments. She felt even less anxious.

Third, she called and made appointments for jobs she didn't want and for which she was not qualified. At one of these interviews, she got terribly anxious because she was offered the job for $50 a week more than she was getting. This frightened her, but it also drove home the point that she was underselling herself.

Fourth, she began going out for interviews for jobs she really wanted. At this point she felt much more confident and was able to start a systematic search, working with employment agencies, calling on contacts, enlisting the aid of friends. She no longer felt anxious, and in three months had landed a new job.

Don't get discouraged if the role-playing doesn't work completely or doesn't provide you with the perfect solution to your immediate problems in real life. You may not get that raise or change the way your sister-in-law behaves to you. But you will feel good because you changed your own behavior.

You may find that role-playing not only solves the problem but that the other person is just as delighted with the new result as you are.

For example, Audrey, wife of a successful lawyer, felt miserable because her husband wouldn't let her get a part-time job. He insisted woman's place was in the home. Audrey wanted him to go for therapy with her, but he refused. So determined to get a job and become "an individual in my own right," she went alone. Three sessions of behavior rehearsal (a form of role-playing) solved this particular problem. Working with Dr. Arnold Lazarus of Rutgers University, Audrey pleaded and protested her case, and Dr. Lazarus, playing the husband, easily argued her down. They tape-recorded the dialogue and Audrey said, "That's typical of our arguments." Then Dr. Lazarus replayed the tape and suggested some judicious arguments she might have used. They kept rehearsing with Dr. Lazarus modeling. Occasionally they switched roles. After the third session, Dr. Lazarus, role-playing the husband, was unable to win the argument either "by rhetoric or verbal abuse" and told Audrey she was ready for a confrontation.

At the next session Audrey reported she had won her husband over and already acquired a part-time job. A few weeks later the couple went out to dinner and Audrey had the pleasure of hearing her husband boast, "My working wife—I'm so proud of her."

CONFRONTING AND CONTROLLING ANXIETY

Anxiety and assertive problems often feed on each other. Because you feel anxious, you can't make yourself do the assertive act. Because you don't perform the assertive act and/or because of the consequences of your lack of assertiveness, you become anxious.

This is complicated by the fact that many people become passive in the face of anxieties. When they become anxious, they let the anxieties build up and take over instead of taking command themselves or keeping the anxieties in perspective.

This passivity seems more true of women than of men.

Writing on "The Phobic Syndrome in Women: Implications for Treatment," Dr. Iris Goldstein Fodor, a New York psychologist, explains, "Many women have been trained for adulthood as child women. Under the realistic stresses of adult life and marriage, these 'stereotypic' emotional, passive, helpless women become anxious, wish to flee, dream of being more independent or of rescue or escape. For some the emotional stress is too great and phobia provides another solution.

Thus, they cling to their childish fears or return to them under the realistic stress of the adult role or conflict, sinking further into an exaggerated version of the stereotypic feminine role, becoming dependent on those around them, and avoiding autonomy, initiative, or assertiveness. This route is available for women since their socialization experience has not prepared them to be mature adults."

Anxiety and tension can stem from many causes.

You may be in the midst of an anxiety-provoking situation—for instance, your mother is dying of cancer. In situations like this, the appropriate response *is* anxiety. Too many people forget this and feel guilty and "sick" for showing this anxiety response.

In the process of becoming an assertive woman, you may be performing tasks that are new to you. Often when you do something unfamiliar, you experience anxiety. This is natural.

You may feel anxious because of conflicts, lack of knowledge, or because you have trained yourself to be an anxious person. The latter is my problem. I keep thinking that if I obsess enough and build up a high degree of tension, I can make the anxiety-provoking situation not happen.

Whatever the cause, there are two major approaches to controlling anxiety:

1. In the actual life situation when you try to perform an assertive act, you must train yourself to do it *despite your anxiety*. Initially, you must focus your attention on the action (like going to a party when you feel shy with strangers) and not on your feelings of anxiety. After you perform the act many times, your anxiety level will fall.

2. You must learn to control your tensions. Assertiveness Training tries to put *you* in command, not the anxiety. You can lower the amount of tension you feel by deliberately training yourself in the art of relaxation. Several methods are used for this purpose, but the most common ones are based on the work of Dr. Edmund Jacobson, a Chicago physician, who in the 1930s showed that just as you can learn to hit a golf ball, you can acquire the ability to relax yourself in minutes. See page 293 ff. in Appendix I for a typical relaxation exercise in which you deliberately tighten various parts of the body—and then relax them.

Research shows that methods based on the Jacobson system tend to have certain advantages over such other methods of relaxation as yoga exercises and relaxation induced by hypnosis. With all these different types of exercises, you tend to get similar subjective feelings of relaxation, and the muscles over which you have voluntary control become relaxed. But with the exercises based on Jacobson's method, you get a deeper relaxation of the involuntary muscles such as those concerned with respiration, circulation, and digestion.

However, there are some people who relax their bodies but still have tension because anxious thoughts continually race through their minds. The following exercise—to my knowledge presented here for the first time in print and used by my husband, Dr. Herbert Fensterheim, in his private practice—should help you gain *deliberate* control over your thought processes so that you control your anxiety. You will do this by evoking a series of images.

EXERCISE IN THOUGHT RELAXATION

STEP ONE: Put the exercise on tape so that you can use it when tension is building up and you want to relax. You might have a friend with a soothing voice record it for you. Another alternative: Have a friend read it to you. However, this latter technique is not as effective because he/she may not be around when you need the anxiety reduction.

STEP TWO: Allow five minutes for the exercise.

STEP THREE: Allow a seven- to ten-second gap of silence between each question.

STEP FOUR: As you do the exercise, lie down or sit back in a comfortable position. Find a quiet place where you will not be interrupted. Take the phone off the hook. Keep your eyes closed throughout.

STEP FIVE: Now begin. I am going to ask you some questions. They are phrased in such a way that they can be answered "yes" or "no." You answer inside yourself, not aloud. Your answer can be "yes," "no," "maybe," "sometimes," or even no answer at all. Actually, your response to the question is your answer.

Can you let your eyelids feel heavier and heavier?

Can you let your right arm feel more relaxed than your left arm?

Can you imagine looking at an object in the far distance?

Can you imagine watching a beautiful sunset over a body of water?

Can you imagine what a painting of a sunset might look like if it were done by a modern abstract painter?

Can you remember the smell of fresh strawberries?

Can you remember as a child the good taste of ice cream on a summer day?

Can you imagine a country lake in the summertime?

Can you imagine a country lake in the winter?

Or in the fall when the leaves are turning?

Have you ever smelled fresh bread or cake baking?

Can you count the colors in a rainbow?

Can you imagine looking at a campfire on a pleasant summer night?

Can you let yourself feel the warmth radiating from that campfire?

Can you let your legs and thighs feel pleasantly heavier?

Can you imagine looking at a beautiful flower right in front of you?

Can you imagine smelling that flower?

Can you listen to the sound of your own breathing?

Can you imagine a pleasant scene or think of the word "calm"?

Can you allow your whole body to feel calm and relaxed?

Calm and relaxed?

Calm and relaxed?

(Additional ten-second pause.)

Now you may open your eyes but stay relaxed. The exercise is over.

STEP SIX: Practice this exercise often enough so that you remember the questions and can go through the routine without a tape. You can even do it riding a bus on your way to a tension-making appointment.

Chapter 5

Handling Criticism, Compliments, and Anger

It took me seven years to respond to one particular put-down, and when I finally managed it, it wasn't in person but in bed. I have had one particular friend since grade-school days. We both left Mount Vernon, got into the communications industry, and specialized in public relations. Both of us dreamed of writing books. I did. She didn't. When my second book, *The Single Girl Goes to Town*, was published, Marge looked at me one day and said, "Anyone can write the books you do. You just sit down and do them, that's all!"

I was furious and speechless. Unable to think of anything to say, I changed the subject. For the next seven years I used to fantasize about what I could have said to Marge to put her in her place. One night, after Assertiveness Training, I woke up around 3 A.M., poked my husband and exclaimed, "I've got it!"

"Got what?" he mumbled.

"What I should have said to Marge: '*And you don't, do you?*' "

I was so excited over the brilliance of my postponed retort that the next morning I telephoned her, recalled the circumstances, and then told her what I should have said.

There was a long pause, and Marge said, "You're right. I only said it because I was so jealous. I'm glad you called me."

Finally I felt vindicated, but I had wasted seven years suffering from the "I should have said" syndrome.

The assertive woman can evaluate criticism. Her ego is not destroyed by it. The unassertive woman can't cope with it. When your self-esteem is low anyway, it's easy to interpret any critical comment as "he/she is rejecting me." You evaluate any criticism you receive from others as further proof of your worthlessness.

This attitude can produce severe consequences. You may fear criticism to such an extent that you anticipate it and thus avoid parties, challenges, closeness, new friendships, a better job, or any situation where you might encounter it. In this way you limit your life and reduce your ego even more. Or you can set up what psychologists term "the self-fulfilling prophecy." You're so sure you're going to be criticized by others—for your voice, dress, certain behaviors—that you begin to act in ways that will bring about the criticism. You make the decision, "They're right. I am that way." And you become that way.

What are some of the most common mistakes women—and men too—make about criticism?

You fail to realize that every criticism doesn't mean something is wrong with you. In actuality, in many cases criticism can stem from respect, a genuine wish to help you, and desire for emotional closeness. There are three kinds of criticism: justified; justified but said in a hostile, inappropriate way; and the put-down. If you don't understand these gradations, you will never learn to handle criticism.

When I completed my first book, *Follow Me!*, I nervously handed it in to my editor, a courtly British-born gentleman named Cecil Scott. Three weeks later he took me to lunch at The Four Seasons, where I anxiously awaited his verdict.

After I had made two trips to the ladies' room and had had two Bloody Marys, Mr. Scott said, "It's all wrong. You've written a series of fifteen magazine articles. It's not a book. What happened to all those anecdotes you told me about originally?"

I said, "They were about me. You don't want *me* in the book."

He responded, "That's just what I do want. Personalize it. Take your time with stories. Let one go on for five pages, another for three. And get rid of all that alliteration and those darling cute phrases."

Somehow I got through the lunch. Devastated, I felt like a complete failure. But that night I realized that this brilliant editor had paid me the compliment of criticism. So I rewrote the book.

You interpret every comment as a criticism. Your mother-in-law calls and tells you what a wonderful luncheon she went to and you think, "She means I'm not a good house-keeper." Your husband says, "Your friend Abby is certainly making good money on her job," and you think, "He wants me to go to work. He isn't satisfied with me as a housewife."

You set yourself up for criticism. You constantly ask questions like, "Did I do that well?" . . . "What do you really think of my work?" You set yourself up for a critical response and feel depressed when you get it. I am a second wife. When I first got married, I used to constantly inquire, "Am I a better cook than Doris?" . . . "Don't I work much harder than Doris?" . . . "Do I have more charm than Doris?" I was terribly interested in Doris, whom, at the time, I'd never seen, but my husband was not. Finally, he got so fed up with my constant interrogations that he started answering, "No, she's a better cook" . . . "She's got a lot of charm."

You've never learned to handle criticism and always become apologetic or defensive when you get it.

How can you learn to react assertively and constructively to criticism instead of with denial ("I did not do that!"), defense ("I've always done it that way"), attack ("What a bastard you are!"), standing on your dignity (the icy glare and the queenly posture), agreement ("Mea culpa!"), or door-slamming to be followed by seething, sulking, and drawing up plans for "I'll get back at her/him/them"?

THE ASSERTIVE WAY TO COPE WITH CRITICISM

1. *Ask yourself, "Have I really been criticized?"* For example, a boss may say, "You've done a fine job on this re-

port. It will be perfect when you polish it up a little." That's the simple truth—not a criticism.

2. *Consider the source* of the criticism and the motives of the critic. The question, "How's your social life?" coming from a very popular single friend may well be a veiled put-down. The same question coming from a happily married friend may be the prelude to introducing you to a new man. Spite, sour grapes, jealousy, envy lie behind many criticisms.

3. *Make sure you understand exactly what has been said, instead of automatically looking for a blow to your ego.* In one case, a cousin, with whom I'm very close, commented, "Why do you write such junk?" about a series I had done on "The Other Woman Today." Even though the words were harsh, I knew she didn't mean them quite that way, so I countered, "What do you mean by that?"

She answered, "I want you to write that serious book about French history—the one you've wanted to write so much all these years. I think you could do a great book." In actuality, her words—hostile as they might have seemed—stemmed from her pride in me.

4. *Try to make your critic be specific.* What can you do better? Why is it "no good"? Don't accept cracks like, "You have a father fixation!" Maybe you do, but so what? What is your husband really upset about? Find out.

5. *Don't take criticism in the close relationship at face value.* For example, you plan to take off on a European tour by yourself, and your child says, "You're a mean mother." What the child means is that she will miss you. Or you barely make it home before your husband, with the result that dinner is not ready. He walks in and yells, "I work. You don't. Can't you even have dinner ready on time?" His words may be the result of a bad day. Wait before you explode.

6. *Ask yourself, "Is this criticism familiar?"* Maybe you should accept repeated criticism (of your lateness, untidiness, etc.) as truth and do something about it.

7. *Learn the technique of handling put-downs or justified criticisms that are expressed in an inappropriate way.* Remember, the world is filled with people who criticize destructively and woundingly just for the feeling of superiority and power it gives them. They pick at others' faults to elevate their own virtues. You don't have to let them do it. You can assert

yourself. Your response has to fit your own style. Here are some suggestions to get you started.

A Put-Down Primer

If you feel put-down by the comment, you must answer. Forget the justification or truth of the comment. If you interpret the remark as a crack against you, you have to make a reply.

The reply should not have the aim of changing the other person. Your goal: to say something that will make you feel better about yourself.

Take your time before you reply. You don't have to take seven years as I did, but a brief pause often enables you to think of an effective answer.

Be prepared. Learn some stock phrases. Some women with difficulty in the put-down area can't think of an on-the-spot response. Learn some sentences that you can call upon almost automatically—for example, "What are you so angry about?" ... "Was that a put-down?" ... "How come you're in such a bad mood today?" If you have a date with a particular friend who always puts you down, it helps to plan in advance. Figure out what crack he/she might make this time and how you might answer it.

Do not use the words "I", "me," or "because" in the first sentence of your answer. Starting off with any of these makes you sound defensive immediately.

Break the above rule when it comes to the close relationship. Answering a put-down from a husband or child is different from responding to a salesperson or a co-worker whom you know only superficially. With people to whom you are close, your intent is to increase communication, not counterattack. Lines like, "I really feel hurt by what you said" or, "That remark really bothers me. Why did you say it?" work well.

Don't get involved in any lengthy reply. You want to put the critic on the defensive. Here are some examples of putdowns I have collected and suggested answers:

THE HURTFUL CRACK IN FRONT OF OTHERS

SITUATION ONE: You, your husband, son, and mother-in-law are guests at a Thanksgiving dinner. As everyone munches on turkey and sweet potatoes, your mother-in-law turns to you and comments, "You certainly chased after my son until you got him." What do you say?

Wrong response: Tears or the "You always do this to me" routine.

Right response: "And we've been so happy. We're both lucky. Aren't you glad we have such a great marriage?"

SITUATION TWO: You graduated as valedictorian of your college class, tried working in retailing, and eventually decided to work as a secretary in a public service organization. You meet a friend from college days who exclaims, "I never thought you'd end up just a secretary."

Wrong response: "I tried to get other jobs and couldn't."

Right response: "And a damn good one. Are you good at your job?"

THE MALE-CHAUVINIST-PIG CRACK

There is a small booklet entitled "Here Are the Answers to Those Male Chauvinist Put-downs," published by Feminist Invention Group, Box 8J, 333 East 49 Street, New York, New York 10017, and available for $1. It suggests such answers as:

Male Put-down	*Woman's Retort*
"How about a little smile?"	"How about a little respect?"
"I'm a male chauvinist pig and proud of it."	"I bet you're proud of being a racist too."
"I don't feel like helping you clean up tonight."	"Help? You're not helping. You're just doing your share."
"You're just the girl I wanted to see."	"Girl? I'll be back when you realize I'm an adult."
"If you're so liberated, when are you going to take me out?"	"When I take home your pay-check."

Women in certain professions seem particularly vulnerable to m.c.p. put-downs. A pediatrician in one of my Assertiveness Training groups told me, "I was doing my internship. In hospitals today you almost always circumcise a boy baby after birth. A male head resident said to me, 'It's your turn. You're used to castrating people.' I went into the other room and cried."

"What would you say now?" I asked.

Her first response was too defensive: "My business is to take care of children. I'm not in medicine for my grudges. I have no negative feelings toward men." After a little thought she did better: "*You* might be a little bit better with the knife."

From a Washington-based TV reporter, I heard the story of how she had scored a real beat during the Watergate hearings. She telecast her scoop on the 11 P.M. news; the next day *The Washington Post* carried her story with credit. As she walked into the newsroom that night, the male chief editor wisecracked, "And I suppose now you'll be impossible to live with." At the time she couldn't think of an answer. Alone at home, with no one to hear, she did: "Why aren't you happy for me instead of jealous?"

A lawyer told me, "Men always tell me, 'You don't look like a lawyer.' When this happens, I say, 'Neither do you!'"

THE WELL-MEANT CRACK

Parents and friends have a way of hitting with a remark that comes across as a jab, though it may be only a small jibe.

Comment	*Right Response*
"Why aren't you married? You aren't getting any younger." (from Mother or someone close)	"Mother, I understand your concern, but I'm self-sufficient and doing fine."
	"That's your need, not mine. I feel a pressure from you."
"Why aren't you married?" (from a friend)	"Sheer luck."

"Do you have a lot of boy-friends?" (from a married female friend)

"A lot. I'm very happy."
"A lot—and I can always use more."

"What are you doing working full time? You're not making a home for your husband. You're going to lose him." (Mother, again)

"Mom, I'm happy and handling my own life. What's happening with you?"

THE CRACK THAT'S PURE BITCH

SITUATION: At a party, an older woman says, "My dear, with your skin, you should never wear that shade of red."

Wrong response: "I thought it was becoming" (inviting the response, "It isn't").

Right response: "Don't you wish you were young enough to wear it?" (Sometimes a bitchy crack deserves a bitchy answer.)

THE COVERT PUT-DOWN
(achieved by implication rather than words)

SITUATION ONE: You are dean of admissions at a university. Your group consists of two peer deans and the head dean—all men. Even though advertising involves your department, you discovered that yesterday the three men had a meeting with a new agency. You find this out through office gossip. What do you do?

SITUATION TWO: You attend an office meeting. The participants: six male co-workers and a male boss. The boss asks you to serve the coffee. You resent this. What do you do?

SITUATION THREE: You've known a man at the office for quite a while. You start dating him. For a time you refuse his invitations to bed. One night you say yes. Ten minutes after you've slept with him, he goes to the door and says, "I don't think I'll be calling you again." What do you do?

Here are some suggested ways of handling these situations:

SITUATION ONE: the dean who is left out of the meeting. You ask for an appointment with the chief dean and then say, "You excluded me from the meeting with the advertising agency—and it will eventually be my responsibility to deal with them. I'd like to be included in the next go round." In this way you show you felt put down, speak up assertively—and from his answer you'll learn your job status.

SITUATION TWO: the coffee request. Some people may disagree with me but I think on-the-spot speaking up would make for office awkwardness. I'd pour the coffee, then go and see the boss and explain, "Really, coffee isn't always a woman's job. I'll be glad to take my proper turn." You may learn the boss thought he was making a nice gesture and didn't realize you would interpret it as a put-down.

SITUATION THREE: the man who makes a quick exit after sex with you. In actual life, the woman whose incident I used cried for a week. She says, "I was so crushed I couldn't be assertive. Now, after AT, I'd say, 'You are really a bastard. You were using me to screw all the women you hate. You're a sorry case. And I feel sorry for you!' And then I'd literally kick him out."

Even if you've spent a lifetime suffering from what the French call *l'esprit de l'escalier* (the wit of the staircase, meaning you think of what you should have said on the staircase en route to bed), you can learn to handle put-downs. The rules I've given are for novices. As you achieve greater creativity in riposte, you can break them. As an example, I offer the legendary quip of Sir Winston Churchill. After his capture in the Boer War, Churchill joined the South African Light Horse Division and grew a mustache. A friend of his mother's told him she cared neither for his politics nor his mustache. Responded Churchill, "Madame, I can see no earthly reason why you should come into contact with either."

RAISING YOUR COMPLIMENT QUOTIENT

Some women can accept criticism but not praise. From whence does this inhibition stem? For some it's the inability to know how to answer ("If my husband tells me, 'You look nice' or, 'Joan told me you're doing a great job at work,' it just doesn't register. I change the subject," says one woman). Others see the "you look nice" variety of compliment as a female put-down (A working wife comments, "I was so programed by my parents to look perfect, instead of being brought up with the idea of being a competent professional, that when I hear that 'you look nice' phrase, I just rebel"). Some feel the proper response to a sincere compliment is the show of embarrassment rather than pleasure. Others believe any compliment signifies false flattery, expressed because as a group women are "so vain" and require constant reassurance. Some awkward women feel they must return a compliment with a compliment.

Some pointers to help you accept compliments in a graceful fashion.

1. Be sure you respond nonverbally as well as verbally. Look the giver in the eye and don't turn your head or body away.

2. Answer. And not with just an "mm . . . mm" or a nod. A simple "Thank you" will do, but you can improve communication by adding a thought that expresses how you feel about the compliment. Try to use the pronoun "I." Here are some situations involving compliments that came up in an AT group.

SITUATION ONE: A date says, "You look nice tonight."

Wrong response: "This is an old dress—I've had it for years" (rejecting the compliment) or, "Nothing but the best for you" (too flip and even a little hostile).

Right response: "How nice of you to say that" or, "I just bought the dress. That really gives me a lift."

SITUATION TWO: A highly competent co-worker says, "You did a great job on that presentation."

Wrong response: "It was easy because there was so much material."

Right response: "Thank you. Praise from you means a lot. Did you like that part about the Lesham study? I really enjoyed working on that." Here you show something of yourself and invite the other person to reveal something of himself.

SITUATION THREE: You may receive a compliment from someone with whom you are angry. For example, your date was supposed to pick you up at 7:30 P.M. He arrives at 8:30 P.M. and says, "You look lovely."

Wrong response: "Why didn't you call" or, "Thanks but I looked even better an hour ago" or, "I know you're buttering me up." Any of these three can lead to a "You're in a bitchy mood tonight" crack from him.

Right response: "Thanks for the compliment, but I'm really upset about you being late."

Acknowledging compliments lets people know that what they've said matters to you. Since it usually does, why not respond appropriately?

THE EXPRESSION OF ANGER

Since childhood women have been trained to hold back and control their negative feelings. The admonitions come early on: "Forgive and forget" ... "Not to care" ... "Someone has to keep peace in the family" ... "Talk about it when you've cooled off" ... "Nice girls don't get into fights." This kind of conditioning results in two types of women:

Type A: For whatever reasons, she has never learned to express her anger. Instead she rationalizes, "Men are supposed to be aggressive—it's all right for men to express violent emotions." No matter what the provocation, she clenches her teeth and holds in her resentments. In some cases, she isn't even aware she is angry.

Type B: She too has not learned to appropriately express anger. Instead of ever showing displeasure over the minor, irritating day-by-day episodes that take place in everyone's life, she says nothing at the time. Then, an office mate, salesperson, or friend makes a chance remark that triggers a red flash of rage, and, on an unpremeditated basis, she lashes out in violent anger. This fury has unfortunate consequences: She feels terrible and she alienates people.

Both are extremes. Assertive anger means knowing your rights, appropriately expressing your feelings when someone tries to interfere with your rights, places an obstacle in your path, or violates your dignity. You must also realize that uncontrolled lashing out is not an assertive expression of anger. The hallmark of assertiveness is integrated behavior where, taking everything into consideration, *you* decide how best to express your anger.

According to Dr. Theodore Isaac Rubin, "We are taught—incorrectly—that anger is a dangerous, powerful emotion. We believe that if we really get angry, we will lose somebody's love, provoke anger at ourselves in return, or that people won't like us. In fact, we've got this pretty much backwards. It is the *repression* of anger, not its *expression,* that is dangerous. Besides, it doesn't matter a bit whether everyone likes you. That's an impossible goal, one that is guaranteed to frustrate you. People won't like you any more if you never get mad—in fact, they may like you less for it."

The consequences of suppression of anger or inappropriate expression of it can affect your whole emotional and physical being:

Depression: This can be anger that you turn against yourself because you feel so hopeless about a situation. The resulting depression can become so severe that you think of suicide, even carry out the thought.

Displacement: Unable to face what you're really angry about, you shift it to another cause. For example, something goes wrong at a cocktail party. You say nothing, but later blame your husband for something he didn't do.

Long fights: These often don't concern what you're really angry about. They occur because you've shifted your goal from sharing of feelings to one of hurting the other person. You forget where you want to go. Your anger takes over and you can't stop yourself.

Temper tantrums: This is inappropriate, uncontrolled expression of anger which can be set off by anything, whether some trivial current happening or something that took place long ago and which you've stewed about for years.

Psychosomatic illnesses: Your repression of anger can cause tension, insomnia, ulcers.

Anger is a very real part of everyone—not just men. The time has come for women to learn about anger, accept the fact that they have a right to it, and learn to express it.

A Learning Plan to Express Assertive— Not Aggressive—Anger

1. *Recognize your rationalizations for not expressing anger as rationalizations.* Don't pay attention to such thoughts as, "I'm afraid to say anything because I'll hurt the other person's feelings" ... "If I show anger, I'll sound aggressive and that's wrong for a woman." Statements like these are ways of explaining to yourself why you don't do what you've never learned to do. Instead of dwelling on the reasons why you don't express anger, concentrate on learning how to do it.

2. *Target your anger behaviors. Get the pattern of your anger.*

   a. *The way you express anger*

   Do you show too little?

   Do you come on too strong, too weak, or not at all?

   Do you express anger days, months, even years after the provoking incident?

   Is your nonverbal communication of anger appropriate?

   Do you mouth angry words but say them in a whisper that the other person can barely hear?

   Do you slouch or keep your eyes on the floor as you say them?

   Do you fall into the trap of attributing your anger to someone else ("You make me angry")?

   Remember, you own your own response. When you express anger you should try for an amalgam that combines your feeling with what the other person has done: "I'm angry because you always leave your underwear on the floor."

   b. *The different situations in which you have difficulty*

   Is it at work? If so, break it down. Does your anger have to do with co-workers, subordinates, superiors?

   In impersonal situations? Some people always get angry with taxi drivers, and others can never express annoyance with them.

   Friends and acquaintances? With some people the more distant the acquaintance is, the easier they find it to express anger. With others it's the reverse. The closer the friend, the easier it is to say, "I'm furious." There are some people who feel that the only time they're "being honest" is when they express anger.

Social situations? Can you get angry in a group conversation but not one-to-one? Do you feel safer in a group—or the reverse?

In a close relationship? Some women can express anger only to a husband or lover. When I asked one such woman "Why?" she answered, "He's the only one in the world who wouldn't leave me if I show anger." Because of his love, she gave him a constant hard time.

In trying to find the pattern of your anger, you should also look for other variables, like time of day (Do you get angry in the early morning before you've had your coffee or before dinner when your blood sugar runs low?), month, and even year (You never have inappropriate outbursts on vacation).

3. *Recognize that a woman has a right to feel anger and express it.* Men have always been told "fight for what you want." Women haven't. But they can learn. Anger doesn't have to lead to violence. If you have doubts about your right to be angry, perhaps you've done something you don't like, feel you'd like to yell at yourself, and instead want to take it out on another person.

4. *Avoid indirect expression of anger.* Perhaps you sit and sulk, seething inside, but refuse to say why you're angry. Or you communicate hurt instead of anger ("You shouldn't have done this to me"). Or you use sarcasm to express anger, making it difficult for the other person to cope with the situation. He/she knows something is wrong but the sarcasm pushes her away and she can't pin down just what bothers you. For example, two women meet at your house, become close friends. However, they don't tell you that they see each other and exclude you from their meetings. You find out and feel angry, feeling their secrecy is an affront to your dignity. But you don't express these reactions. Instead, you comment sarcastically to one of the women, "How nice that you and Norma have become such close friends. I'm so pleased I was able to introduce you."

5. *Express your anger when you feel it.* In this way you can frequently avoid unpleasant consequences. For example, not too long ago I had lunch with a friend from my *Seven-*

teen days. We were chatting amiably until she asked me, "Jean, do you know anyone who understands teen-agers and has entree to top psychologists who could do some psychological pieces for us?" Since I had just finished telling her about various psychological articles I had been writing for various magazines and about my book award from the American Psychological Association, I was absolutely dumbstruck at the impertinence of the question. It was just like a producer asking a documentary film writer, "Can you give me the name of a good documentary film writer?"

Did I say, "That's an insult for you to ask me that, and it really annoys me. Get your name from someone else"? Not at all. I meekly gave her a list of six names! I was so furious at myself for doing this that when, six months later, I met Lois at a press reception, I nodded icily and ignored her. We haven't spoken since. I'm not sure Lois even knows what she did. I do know that by my not expressing my anger on the spot, I finished a valued friendship.

6. *Don't make the mistake of not going far enough in your anger.* Some women make tentative stabs at expression of anger—and then abort it. For example, Andrea, a pretty, thirty-two-year-old divorcée, got involved with a man who came to her on the rebound. George told her he had completely broken off with the other woman. Then, one night a depressed George showed up at Andrea's apartment and revealed that the other woman had just thrown him out again and that he had been sleeping with her as well as Andrea for the past six months.

Andrea did manage to get out the words, "I'm angry. You've used me and hurt me," but she stopped there and began to mother the two-timing George while he told her how upset he was from this second rejection by the other woman. She kept thinking, "Go back to this other woman or in any case stay away from me. How dare you have lied to me in the way you have?" but couldn't get the words out. She missed her chance at satisfaction. George went back. She never saw him again.

7. *Realize you have the right to raise your voice.* Forget that ladylike routine. It's perfectly all right to pound the table, swear, shout, and do all the things Mother told you not to do. One woman says, "I always have trouble deciding

when and if to holler. I ask myself, 'Is it O.K. to raise my voice?' I usually don't. I go into my cold, distant routine." In deciding "when and if to holler," differentiate between the close personal situation and the work one. In the former, showing of angry feelings can clarify and facilitate communication. In the latter, doing this may be counterproductive. You may want to raise your voice—but just slightly.

Expression of anger doesn't involve merely a higher voice tone. It's the words you use, body position and movement, facial expression. One member of my AT group was role-playing a situation in which she wanted to express anger at her husband. Only her words showed anger. As she role-played, she sported a half-pleasant, half-contemptuous smile, sat back in a smug, untouchable way in her chair. Everyone in the group got the feeling that her manner really expressed, "I'm above all this. Nothing you do can get through to me. I'm impregnable."

The group members taught her to put an angry look on her face, lean forward, glance directly at her husband. Suddenly we all felt much more comfortable. Now she was really showing anger, the kind of anger with which her husband could deal.

8. *If you've never learned to express anger, some of the following Assertiveness Training techniques may help.*

a. Role-play. Start by playing angry scenes from plays. Then call upon a friend for aid and role-play with him/her the angry woman in imagined circumstances as well as past and present real-life situations. In this way your fear of anger will diminish and you'll learn how to carry over your new confidence to real-life circumstances.

b. Monitor yourself. Each time you do express your anger make a note of it in your Female Assertiveness Notebook. A word or two to recall the situation will be sufficient. Then, after some time has elapsed, take an hour or so to go over your notes, and for each situation rehearse in your mind better ways in which you could have expressed your anger.

c. If there is someone to whom you feel close, but with whom you have trouble venting anger, write down all the things from the past that have made you furious with this person. Ask him/her to do the same. Then make an appointment to get together and at this time each of you reads his respective list. Discuss the lists. Try to use the phrase, "I get angry with you because————." You may learn you've been wrong or that the relationship isn't worth continuing.

d. If your anger brings about tension and begins to interfere with other things, get it out of your system with physical exercise. This works when you're not in a position to express the anger—for instance, the other person is out of the country.

Buy a bataca (a cloth-covered bat). Enlist the aid of a friend and have a bataca battle. You each hit each other. One shouts "yes," the other "no." Rules: No one hits the other in the head and the fight is limited to three minutes. Use an egg timer.

In your bedroom, hit your pillow for two minutes. Curse aloud. Release that anger.

9. *Make the deliberate decision not to express anger.* During initial Assertiveness Training, the expression of any anger you feel is important. When you're more advanced, you can make choices. For example, I frequently see red with my stepmother because she uses a dated social worker technique with me; in any discussion she invariably takes the side of the other person (my sister or cousin, my husband's ex-wife). But my stepmother is getting older and frailer, and I don't want to have words with a woman who has meant so much to me. I often make the deliberate decision not to express anger, and I feel good because of this.

10. *Remember, your choice is not limited to expressing anger or not expressing it.* Sometimes you can use a supportive approach. I remember one occasion when my boss not only commanded me to do something I considered completely unprofessional but yelled at me as she did it. I counted to ten and then said, "Is something wrong, Mrs. Finch? I know there must be or you would never speak to me in that way."

Her eyes filled with tears as she answered, "I've just learned my favorite niece is dying of cancer. How good of you to understand, Jean." There was a pause, and she added, "I was completely wrong to speak to you in the way I did. Just forget the conversation ever took place."

Chapter 6

Asserting Yourself Socially

"I'm afraid to go to big parties. I don't know how to go up to people and start talking."

"I'm bored. I've had the same friends since college."

"I came to the big city and got a job, but I know no men. I won't go to a singles bar. I'd rather die."

Many women make statements like these. Often these same women can speak up to a rude salesclerk, hold down a demanding job, and build up a bank account, but they fail to carry over this assertiveness to an all-important life area: their social lives.

Sometimes a deficient social life is based on reality. You have never developed the skills that enable you to go up to a stranger at a party, leave a bore, entertain in your own home. You may have the skills but don't use them. Or you may have had the skills once but they've grown rusty from disuse; suddenly you move to a new town or become widowed or divorced and you need to relearn those social techniques.

You may have an unsatisfactory social life because you have misconceptions. You may think, "If I ask that terrific couple to my house, they're bound to refuse and then I'll feel terrible," or you feel you don't have the right to make social errors. If you fizzle at a party or give a dinner where the cheese soufflé falls, you will have committed a ghastly mistake. Fear of failure keeps you from even trying.

You may have a very active social life with very unsatisfactory relationships. You don't like your own behavior because you echo others and fail to express your own opinions (Says one twenty-eight-year-old woman, "When a man says, 'I love to ski but not in Europe,' I find myself saying, 'Yes, America is much better,' *when I'm from Switzerland!*"). You may keep relationships from developing because you can't reveal anything meaningful about yourself and thus all your friendships remain on a superficial basis. Conversely, you may reveal too much too soon and frighten people away because you have no emotional barriers. Because of your passivity, you may continue relationships that provide you with little or no happiness. You may lack a social life because you're married and live in relative isolation, expecting your husband to satisfy every social need.

It's only the rare woman who wants to live like a female Robinson Crusoe. Everyone needs a satisfying social life— one that has versatility (friends for work and friends for play, the close friend to whom you talk every night and the ex-roommate with whom you lunch once a year), suits your particular needs, constantly changes, offers you opportunities to grow and change, and serves as a base for social security, not emotional insecurity.

ACHIEVING AN ASSERTIVE SOCIAL LIFE

Think through the areas of your social life that bother you.

To trigger yourself, you might answer the following questions:

1. Are you a loner? Do you go virtually for weeks with no contacts except with salesclerks and co-workers?

2. Have you had virtually the same friends since childhood?

3. Do you feel able to make social overtures to women but rarely to men?

4. Conversely, do you feel able to make social overtures to men but rarely to women?

5. Do you sit back and wait to be asked or do you assume social responsibility and deliver invitations to others—whether to parties in your own home or outside events?

6. Is your social life composed completely of sporadic contacts with acquaintances and no close relationships?

7. Can you manage at a party if you go alone?

8. Do you opt to stay home and read a good book rather than take the risk of being unnoticed, left out, or rejected?

9. Do you speak up freely about your own desires and needs in a relationship with the opposite sex?

10. Do you do the things you have to do to meet new people: join organizations, make small talk in groups, prepare for encounters so that you come across interesting and different to others?

By evaluating your answers to these questions, you should be able to set some long-range goals:

- An expanded social network
- New friends that suit your adult interests
- The ability to make overtures to the same sex . . . to the opposite sex . . . to couples
- To make the shift from the superficial to the close relationship if that's what you want
- To go places alone without a fear of rejection
- To carry out an active program of self-improvement that will enable you to act and react more successfully in social encounters

Many social fears are irrational. In interviewing for this book, I heard the following statements again and again: "If I don't make a date for the night the guy suggests—even though it's terribly inconvenient for me—he'll never ask me out again" . . . "If I don't listen to my girlfriend's problems and have that nightly phone conversation with her, she won't like me and I'll feel awful" . . . "If I tell my guy off for something he has done, then he'll get so angry he'll end the relationship and then I'll never meet anyone else."

These irrational fears are often based on incorrect beliefs. You have learned (or been taught) to have erroneous ideas about life experiences. These wrong ideas influence the way you feel and the way you act. If you correct these ideas, both your feelings and your actions should change.

It was to change such "irrational beliefs" that in 1955, Dr. Albert Ellis, a New York psychologist, developed Rational-Emotive Therapy (RET). In the method, Dr. Ellis uses an A-B-C-D approach to changing personality.

A is the *activating* event that set off the disturbed consequence. It may take the form of someone criticizing you, going to a party, or taking on a new work project.

C is the *consequence* of that event. It can be feeling worthless, depressed, being upset, having stomach pains.

B is the *belief system* that comes between the activating event and the consequence. This is the part many people overlook. They tend to see A leading naturally and directly to C. In reality, an outside event cannot cause or create a feeling in you. It is the meaning the event has for you that sets off your reaction. There are two parts to the belief system: the rational beliefs (rB—for example, "It would be highly unfortunate if he rejected me; how frustrating that would be") and the irrational beliefs (iB—for example, "It would be awful if he rejected me. I couldn't stand it. What a worthless person his rejection would make me!").

D is to *dispute* these irrational beliefs in order to change them. First, you must identify your irrational belief that was active in the specific situation involved: "Why would it be awful if he rejected me? Why couldn't I stand it? Where is the evidence that his rejection would make me a worthless person to myself and the rest of the world?" Then, through logic and action you must learn that this belief is wrong and another belief is more correct. It is this new learning that changes the way you feel and act.

Dr. Ellis lists the following as very commonly held irrational beliefs:

- People must love or approve of me.
- Making mistakes is terrible.
- People should be condemned for their wrongdoings.
- It's terrible when things go wrong.
- My emotions can't be controlled.
- Threatening situations have to keep me terribly worried.
- Bad effects of my childhood have to control my life.

• I can't stand the way people act.
What are your irrational beliefs?

THE NO-COP-OUT SYSTEM: Exercise in Exorcising "The Worst Will Happen" Thinking.

STEP ONE: Take a page in your FAN workbook. At the left side list in descending order A, C, iB, rB, D. Be sure to leave space in between. You should take a recent irrational belief and show how disputing it might have led to different feelings and actions. Here is a sample form:

Example

A. Activating event you recently experienced about which you became upset or disturbed

"At a party Saturday night the attractive man I just met spoke to me only briefly and spent most of the evening talking to others. He took several phone numbers and didn't ask for mine."

C. Consequence

"I felt depressed when I left the party, and Sunday morning I felt terribly edgy."

iB: The irrational belief you had about the activating event

"If this attractive man rejected me, it means I'm dull, unattractive, and worthless. I'll go around being constantly rejected by men I like. It will always be like this."

rB: Rational belief you could have about the activating event

"I was attracted to him and was disturbed that he didn't pay attention to me."

D. Disputing, questioning, or challenging you can use to change your irrational belief. This can take the form of both logic and action

Logic: (1) Just because the man didn't pay attention to you doesn't mean you're worthless. Think of other incidents where men did pay attention to you. (2) Just because it happened once or even several times doesn't mean it will always happen.

> *Action*: (1) Make a list of times in the past where men you were initially attracted to at a party did pay attention to you. (2) Ask your friends to help you recall similar incidents. (3) Think back to parties where men were attracted to you and *you* discouraged them.

STEP TWO: Take other pages in FAN and use the same exercise to identify other irrational beliefs and their effects. If you really do a job on this, you should: (a) be able to understand how much you catastrophize, (b) reduce your anxiety, and (c) see that many of your fears are groundless.

When you recognize your irrational beliefs and try to replace them with rational ones, you can begin to act on the basis of these new beliefs. For instance, recently I decided to give a paella party for about twenty people. I invited eighteen people and then fell prey to my own irrational belief. I wanted to invite a male editor I had met twice and liked. He had a wife, but I didn't know her, so I would have to call him. I thought, "He'll think I'm trying to sell him a book idea and, if he refuses me, that will mean not only that he doesn't like me and that I'm pushy but that he thinks I'm a bad writer. I couldn't stand his rejection. It would upset me too much, and I'd feel like the nothing I really am."

After brooding about this for several days, I decided I was crazy. If he refused me, it would mean he was busy or maybe didn't want to come, but it wouldn't be the end of my professional career (rational belief). After all, eighteen people had accepted. I picked up the phone and called. He answered. I delivered the invitation. He said, "We'd love it. I've told my wife all about you and we've been wanting to call and make a date." I could have spared myself days of agonizing.

Make a deliberate effort to expand your social life.

Some assertive pointers:

1. *Go places to meet people.* If you continually wail about your "terrible" or "nonexistent" social life, you are probably enjoying (or not enjoying) the pleasure of your own com-

pany far too much. Remember, nothing comes to the woman who waits except a bus—and you'd better make sure you're waiting at a bus stop.

What activities do you find enjoyable? Take the following Social Life Action Inventory, adapted from one by Drs. Eileen D. Gambrill of the University of California at Berkeley and Cheryl A. Richey of the University of Washington as an aid to help you evaluate what you might do to improve your social life.

SOCIAL LIFE ACTION INVENTORY

Action	Did this in the past month	Would like to do more often
1. Attend adult education classes (such as foreign language, crafts, cooking, technical skills, history, etc.)	_____	_____
2. Go to a bar	_____	_____
3. Go to a coffee house	_____	_____
4. Attend cultural events (concert, opera, play, ballet, foreign film, lecture, etc.)	_____	_____
5. Attend church socials	_____	_____
6. Play games (bridge, chess, checkers, etc.)	_____	_____
7. Do group volunteer work (politics, fund-raising, community projects)	_____	_____
8. Participate in a hobby club (photography, gardening, book review)	_____	_____
9. Play a musical instrument in a group	_____	_____
10. Sing in a local choir	_____	_____
11. Go dancing (folk, square, discotheque)	_____	_____

	Did this in	Would like to
Action	*the past month*	*do more often*

12. Participate in a special "life situation" group (singles group, Parents Without Partners, Remarrieds Inc.) _____ _____

13. Participate in sports (golf, swimming, tennis, bowling, horseback riding) _____ _____

14. Go camping or hiking _____ _____

15. Participate in special-interest groups (Save Grand Central, P.T.A., environmental action, college alumnae) _____ _____

16. Go to parties _____ _____

17. Visit others _____ _____

18. Other activities that occur to you. Name them _____ _____

Taking this quiz should enable you to see a pattern. Do you have very limited social activities with others? Do you spend your time at cultural events because you think you *should*, when, in reality, you'd prefer to take up folk dancing but fear being thought "square"? Have you given up certain hobbies, like playing in the community orchestra, that once gave you great pleasure? Would you like to play bridge but don't know how? Use the quiz as a learning tool that can help you embark on new, different or long-forgotten social activities.

Incidentally, if you're concerned about what places to go to better your social life, it helps to check them out. Sit in a coffee house or bar for ten minutes and see for yourself what kind of crowd goes there. Try just one hiking trip. Take one bridge lesson. Attend a meeting of a volunteer organization and find out if you'd enjoy working on their agenda of activities or would hate it. Concerts serve as a wonderful way of meeting people. There's a twenty-minute intermission and you have freedom to move around, but none of that matters if you hate music. A singles bar will produce available men, but also anxiety. Try it once and see if you have the necessary stamina. Remember, going isn't enough; you have to talk to people.

2. *Start from where you are now.* If you are extremely shy, you do not begin a social improvement campaign by going to a resort which is expensive, competitive and a high-risk situation usually most productive for aggressive types. Go somewhere where you are comfortable, but at the beginning *don't take your enjoyment too much into consideration.* You do what must be done to increase your number of friends without worrying, "I don't like him/her too much." Later, when you have established some sort of social network, you can select and reject.

3. *Give yourself assertive assignments that relate to bettering your social life.* For example, a thirty-five-year-old secretary in an AT group wanted more contacts with men. She knew "no one eligible." In the group she was given four assignments, all of which she carried out successfully.

Week One: Have two conversations with two different men. The conversations must be longer than a greeting and must be with "availables." No eighty-year-olds or married men.

Week Two: Arrange a continuation of the encounter with one of the men. The meeting should be from fifteen minutes to a half hour. In this instance, the secretary was able to invite one of the men—a co-worker new on the job—to join her for coffee.

Week Three: Arrange a longer meeting. She said to the co-worker, "There's a great movie coming to the Rivoli. Would you like to go?" He was delighted.

Week Four: Invite a man for dinner.

4. *Select your target groups with care.* Go places where you have a special interest. If you're a lawyer, try a political organization that will welcome you because you possess expertise. If you care about ecology, join an organization like the Sierra Club. If you're a tennis buff, join a tennis club or spend your vacation at a tennis camp. The point: If you join a club, you must try to get involved. This can prove difficult when you're the newcomer and everyone else knows each other and has served on the same committee for years. One

technique: Write a letter outlining your qualifications to the head of the committee on which you would like to work. This is what I did after six wallflower months as a novice member of the Overseas Press Club of America. I was so intimidated by the noted newspersons and their equally famous by-lines that I would go to the events, always taking a woman friend with me for support. No one ever spoke to me. I spoke to no one and I knew no one since my sponsor had taken off to serve as a foreign correspondent in Afghanistan. Toting along a female prop and always paying for her cocktails, lunches or dinner got to be rather expensive, so finally I wrote a letter offering my services to the head of the hospitality committee (I figured serving on that particular committee would insure meeting fellow guests). Soon after a Mrs. X called me. She said, "We'll be glad to have you on the committee but you'll have to work hard." I did work hard, but participating was easy because here were definite projects to be involved in. And thus, I got to be an "in" member of the OPC.

5. *Renew your contacts.* Sometimes because of anxiety, inhibition, or just failing to take any action on your own, you have let certain social contacts lapse. This kind of passivity is characteristic of unassertive people. Whom could you call that you haven't seen for some time and make a luncheon or dinner date with? One young woman gave a "Patch Up Party" to which she invited four long-lost, still-single boyfriends. They came, but not one invited her out. However, all wasn't lost—one did introduce her to a series of friends.

In actuality, I married my husband because I acted assertively. We had met in March and had a very nice dinner at Lüchow's. He said, "I've got a series of speeches coming up, so I won't be able to call you for six weeks." He never called. The following November, I decided to give a big buffet and serve cassoulet, the French specialty involving hours of cooking and hundreds of ingredients. I didn't have enough single men, so I telephoned the man who had introduced me to Herb and asked, "Is that psychologist still around?"

The friend said, "Sure."

"Is he going with anyone?" I queried. "I'd like to ask him to the party. I need more men."

"Go ahead," counseled my friend. "You've got nothing to lose."

So, with much hesitation, I called and delivered the invitation. Herb was delighted to accept. He came to the party and thus started a romance which culminated at the altar seven months later. Subsequently, I asked him, "Would you have called me if I hadn't called you?"

"Probably not," he said with a smile.

6. *Make a deliberate attempt to expand your relationships with women.* Women together can serve as supporters because, due to similar conditioning, they can relate to and understand each other, be available in times of stress, remind each other of their rights, provide models and suggestions for change, and give positive reinforcement for each other's new attempts toward assertiveness.

a. *Don't fall into the "Queen Bee Syndrome."* Graham Staines, Carol Tavris, and Toby Epstein Jayaratne discuss this syndrome in a fascinating article in the January, 1974, *Psychology Today*, making the point that the true Queen Bee has achieved both professional and social success "in a man's world" while running a house and family with her left hand. She reasons that "If I can do it without a whole movement to help me, so can all those other women." She enjoys hearing that she is different from other women, ignoring the psychological evidence that people are products of their environment and socialization as well as the sociological evidence of economic and legal discrimination against women. She feels, "If I made it, anybody can." If you adopt this way of thinking, you fail to realize that women's assertiveness must begin with each other. From husbands, boyfriends, family, co-workers you may meet with resistance in your effort to change; from your female peers, who have experienced some of the same feelings of low self-worth and being second-class citizens, you can expect support.

b. *Ask for honest feedback from your female friends.* For example, you are new in town and know few people. Yet, a co-worker who comes from two thousand miles away has, in just a few months, developed a highly active social network. Ask her: "What can I do to meet new people?" ... "What do I do wrong?" Or you're a housewife with a humdrum existence. Yet your next-door neighbor manages an eight-room house, three children, and four volunteer activities with seemingly plenty of time for friends and fun. How does she do it? Why can't you? Ask her how.

c. *Practice assertion with your female friends*. In this situation which, for most women, is an easier starting point, you can learn and then be able to carry over your new behaviors to more complex situations with men and on the job. Says psychologist Andrew Salter, "Women who have trouble fearing rejection have trouble in relationships with other women. They let their girlfriends get away with things. For example, they lend books and clothes to them that they don't want to lend. As you get healthy with your own sex, you get healthier with men. What's involved with relationships with men is involved with relationships with women—plus extras that stem from the sex role department and getting along with men who have concepts of sex roles that differ from yours."

For example, you are having lunch with a friend with a rich father when suddenly she asks you if you would lend her $30 until she gets paid next week. You have the money, but were planning to spend it on something very important to you. Furthermore, you do not *want* to lend her money. She pleads, "Please lend me the money. I'll pay you back next week." What is your response?

Unassertive: Reluctantly you give it to her and seethe inside.

Aggressive: You respond, "Absolutely not. You still owe me $40. You're a leech and I've had enough."

Assertive: "No. I need the money. Better try someone else."

By doing this you will eventually be able to say to a male friend who asks you to perform a typing chore, "No, I'm annoyed. I type all day at the office and I feel that's enough. If it's an emergency, I'll help, but this constant asking isn't fair. Please don't ask me to type any more."

d. *Give yourself assertive assignments with women*. Sign up for an exercise class with a female friend. To another say, "Look, you've been here for dinner five times and you've never asked us once." Instead of daily telephone confabs with a long-winded cousin, cut her down to twice a week—or biweekly if that's what you'd like to do. In this way, you'll gain time for a new friendship with someone else.

e. *Form an Assertive Rap Group*. This is not Assertiveness Training but a chance for sharing and discussion of assertive problems. Some guidelines:

• Try for a group of eight to ten women. Homogeneity is not necessary. Members can vary in age, economic status, marital status, backgrounds, and professions. The problem of unassertiveness is universal among women, and, as the group goes along, you're bound to hear, "You feel that way too! I thought I was the only one." Meet once a week for ten weeks. Don't admit new members after the second session.

• Rotate the meetings among the member's homes. If you're initiating the group, start off at your home. Meetings should last for about two hours. Do not charge a membership fee. Each hostess pays expenses of any eating and drinking, which should be minimal. Rotate leadership from week to week. *Do not try to undertake therapy with anyone.* If therapy seems indicated, encourage the individual to seek professional help.

• Have a schedule. You might start by having each member give a brief biography including why she joined the group and in what areas she feels unassertive. Also, go around the circle and have each woman complete the sentence, "An assertive woman is————." In doing this, she should free-associate whatever words come to mind. In subsequent sessions cover the topics I've taken up so far in this book: role-playing of problem situations in impersonal situations, responses to criticism, setting of goals, giving of assertive assignments (and then the members report back at the next session), use of I-Talk to better communication, saying no. Then go on to social assertiveness (being assertive in meeting new people in new situations, learning to seek men out instead of always waiting for them to take the first step), business assertiveness, and assertiveness in close relationships.

Additional topic: You might ask the members to make up lists of all the rules and expectations for sex roles that they can remember from their parents, friends, relatives, or school experiences. They should add those they currently place on themselves. Then they can critically examine the ways they would like to change the stereotype.

In selection of topics, develop them progressively from

basic and nonthreatening issues (like returning items to stores) to more specific and threatening issues (like telling a close friend what bothers you).

By learning assertive methods that work for other women, you may be able to become more assertive yourself. It's a beginning.

7. *Entertain.* It's axiomatic that if you don't ask people to your home, they won't ask you to theirs. Have an active attitude about entertaining. Invest in the party props that make it possible—dishes, glasses, etc. Acquire from cookbooks or friends a few recipes that always work (I have three party specialties—paella, chicken Véronique, and pot roast of lamb—that I just keep alternating). Remember, if you don't want to entertain at home, you have alternatives. One young woman, who lives in a tiny studio walk-up, recently took over a room in a Chinese restaurant and threw a banquet for twenty. She says, "My apartment was too small, and these were people I wanted to know better."

8. *Reduce your anxiety.* It's all very well to say "call people," "go to parties," "talk to people," "join special-interest clubs." However, all these directives make the assumption that once you know what things you can do, you will go out and do them. By taking some form of definite action (picking up a man at an art gallery opening, going on a Saturday canoeing expedition, enlisting in a learn-to-ski weekend), you will receive delightful invitations and thus you will feel so good about yourself that you stop feeling tense and anxious.

It doesn't always work that way. Your fears may be so great that you never take the action and continue to sit home all alone by your telephone. Or you take action and pick up the man, take off on the canoe trip, learn to ski on the singles weekend, but with such anxiety that an unpleasant feeling becomes associated with the action, thus making it even harder for you to perform the next time.

Behavior therapists feel that one way to get people to learn something is through a process called modeling. Just as a picture is worth a thousand words, watching somebody do something is worth a thousand pictures. Scientists at major universities have proven that the powerful modeling technique can really help people overcome fears and can lead to behavioral change.

You don't have to have an actual person in front of you modeling a scene. You can do it through imagery. The following exercise, adapted from research done by Dr. Alan E. Kazdin of Pennsylvania State University, shows how you can use covert modeling to act more assertively.

EXERCISE IN COVERT MODELING

STEP ONE: Take a problem situation that calls for social assertion and create a scene in imagery in which a model behaves assertively in this situation. In devising your scene, follow two rules: (1) The scene must be something you can expect yourself to do with a little practice. If it's something you could never do, you won't learn from it. (2) As a result of the model's assertive act, there are positive consequences.

Sample scene: The model is at a party. Everyone else is busy talking, but she is alone. Then she sees a nice-looking man, also standing alone, but hesitates to go up to him and start talking.

The model does walk over and says to him, "I like the party, but don't know many of the people here. Are you a good friend of the hostess?"

He gives her a big smile and starts telling an interesting story of how he had met the hostess while on a Caribbean cruise. Soon the model and the man are deep in an animated conversation which other people join.

STEP TWO: Imagine this scene (or another one that suits your needs). It helps if you read it into a tape recorder, leaving a pause for imagery. The reading and the imagery should take thirty-five seconds.

STEP THREE: Over the course of the week you should imagine the scene at least four times, each time using a different model.

First time: Use a model who is very different from you. It can even be a man starting a conversation with a woman. But use the same phrases and imagery.

Second time: Use a model who is your age, but looks very

different. If you're tall and blonde, make your model short and brunette.

Third time: Use a model who is your age, similar in appearance, but who is not you.

Fourth time: Imagine yourself in the situation.

STEP FOUR: Vary your scenes. For example, if you are zeroing in on the problem of speaking to people at parties, you can change little details of the scene, imagining it taking place at a ski lodge, at a bar, or on a tennis court.

9. *Realize that other people have problems too.* You may feel you've been rejected when, in actuality, that's not the case. For instance, I had been very friendly with an editor at *Seventeen* magazine. Yet, after I left the publication, I did not hear from her. I felt terribly hurt and had all sorts of irrational beliefs: "How terrible I must be that after all these years of friendship she doesn't want to have anything to do with me because we don't work together any more." Finally my husband said, "Stop this. Call her and ask what's wrong."

I called and found out that (1) she had been forced to retire and was terribly depressed; (2) she had been flat on her back for three months with a slipped disc. I felt like a fool.

In another instance, I went to a cocktail party given by the Friends of the Music and Theater Collection of the Museum of the City of New York. I was supposed to meet a friend there at six o'clock. I arrived on time, but my friend didn't. So there I stood, glass in one hand, cigarette in the other, trying to look as if I belonged. Everyone was chatting in little groups, except me. I felt right back at a high school dance. So, I decided to be assertive. I went up to a plump, blonde woman who was also alone and made chit-chat. For a few minutes we talked about the museum's current exhibition, the new plays on Broadway, and how we each had "nothing to wear." Suddenly, I remembered my manners and introduced myself, saying, "I'm Jean Baer. "Hi, Jean," she said. *"I'm Shelley Winters."* She had been standing equally alone, glass in hand, obviously knowing no one.

Develop your conversational ability. Recently a young nurse in my AT group confessed, "Before AT I couldn't even open my mouth on a superficial basis. This was especially true in a one-to-one situation. With a man, if he didn't talk, there were deadly silences, and I'd think, 'What are we going to talk about?' I'd go into a panic."

Many women share this feeling. According to an experiment conducted by Dr. Cheryl A. Richey, women admitted that in group discussions they were quiet, reserved, cautious, afraid their comments would not be valid, low in self-confidence, tongue-tied. Other studies indicate that women are generally unassertive in verbal exchanges with men; they tend to talk less, offer fewer "attempted answers," engage in more "positive reactions" (agreement, praise, compliments), offer speeches of shorter duration and less elaboration, are more easily interrupted, and less influential. One study showed that when a male contributed an idea to a conversation, he was its primary supporter 75 percent of the time. Women supported their own ideas only 40 percent of the time.

How can you improve your small talk so that you feel more socially secure with both men and women?

1. *Prepare for conversation.* You can develop small-talk know-how in just the same manner as you perfect your skill on the job or at backgammon.

a. *Read news magazines so that you have a knowledge of what's going on in the world.* With some knowledge to back you up, you will find it easier to offer opinions about politics and world events, to say, "I agree" or "I disagree." If you can't think up your own ideas, crib them from columnists: "That reminds me of what Art Buchwald said" ... "Sylvia Porter had an interesting forecast on the economy last week." I've gotten through many an awkward social situation by paraphrasing Russell Baker, James Reston, and Tom Wicker.

b. *Learn to draw the other person out.* You do this not with offensive personal questions ("How much rent do you pay?") that will antagonize but with talk that will enable the other person to show something of himself or herself. Start with a statement like, "I'm not sure I like Governor————'s stand on————." Then follow with, "What do you think?" It also helps to remember small things about people. They like to know you have a special interest in them. Try lines like, "The last time I saw you you were reading————'s book.

Did you like it?" ... "How is your mother feeling after her operation?" ... "Did you enjoy your trip to Europe?"

   c. *Reveal something of yourself—but not too much.* In small talk you don't discuss your ten years of analysis or your innermost problems. You do talk about the film you saw last week, your most recent vacation, or what you thought of the best-selling novel *Ragtime*. It helps if you have some interesting anecdotes at your fingertips. I do very well with anecdotes about my travels—for example, how once, after two weeks of maddening experiences in the Soviet Union, I had hysterics in the middle of the Moscow airport and screamed, "It must have been better under the Czar!" It sometimes takes me awhile to work the conversation around to Moscow, but once there I'm off, and I've paved the way for the other person to talk about his/her vacation experiences.

   d. *Be prepared for lulls.* For conversational emergencies I use my game. It consists of asking people, "If you could pick any time in history to live and any person to be, what and whom would you pick?" The answers can lead to delightful, provocative conversation. For example, my husband would like to be a Polynesian fisherman on a South Seas beach. I would like to be a high-class courtesan in late-nineteenth-century France, earning my millions on my back.

   2. *Learn to initiate conversations.* If you don't learn, you may avoid social situations or go and end up speaking to no one. And your social anxiety will increase. Prepare. Have some phrases at the back of your head like, "I like your jump suit. Where did you get it?" or, "What a terrific blazer!"

Some women have special trouble initiating conversations with men. For example, Marian, a short, slim occupational therapist from a small, southern city, who now works at a large Manhattan hospital, found herself "awkward and insecure" at large New York mixers. As a result of Assertiveness Training, she made herself acquire a series of "openers" for such occasions.

   • To someone who looks as if he's not enjoying the party either: "You look as enthusiastic as I feel."
   • To someone who is tall: "You have an advantage over me—you have a much better vantage point."
   • At a summer lawn party in a resort area: "Do you

know the hostess or are you one of the four hundred people here who doesn't?" . . . "Do you have a house here?"

● To someone she knows very slightly: "I know this sounds like a funny line, but haven't I seen you at the hospital?"

● At a singles party she stands and waits for a situation in which she can use a small-talk "opener." For example, she sees a man she'd like to meet heading toward the punch bowl. So she heads in the same direction and ventures, "Such a big crowd—so many people in a cramped space."

During a week's vacation at Fire Island, another young woman who always felt uptight in groups decided to give herself the assertive assignment of initiating conversations with men. She restricted herself to "attractive men who were alone on the beach."

To Man One who was picking shells: "They're beautiful. Do you have a big collection?"

To Man Two: "Isn't it beautiful here during the week?"

To Man Three, who wore an Indian shirt: "What a great Indian shirt! Where did you get it?"

She says, "I used the same kinds of lines men use to approach women. And I got dates with all three men. I felt so good."

Incidentally, there's one line that through the years I have found invaluable at art galleries—whether the Prado, the Metropolitan, or the Louvre. It's, "I love the way he has used his white!"

You may know perfectly well how to initiate a conversation, but again your irrational beliefs and anticipations keep you from doing it. For example, you attend a concert and would like to make conversation with the man in the next seat, who is also alone. But you brainwash yourself with, "If I do, he'll think I'm pushy and that will be terrible." Counter your anxiety with:

A coping statement: "But if I don't try, I don't get a chance to influence what will happen. I need practice."

A pat-on-the-back statement: Even if you get rebuffed, reinforce yourself for trying. Say something like, "You tried. Nothing ventured, nothing gained. Sometimes you have to take a risk. I feel good because I tried. And what's so bad. A little rejection isn't the end of the world."

You may want to monitor how often you initiate conversations. If so, try the Bead Belt, devised by Dr. Cheryl A. Richey, which you can make for about sixty cents. Make a belt, about four and a half feet in length, out of black braided nylon string. On each end put a single one-foot strand of string with a knot tied in the middle of it. Above each knot place twenty-five small (one-eighth-inch) wooden beads. Each time you initiate a conversation, push a bead over the knot in the string. This is quiet, unnoticeable, and you don't have to drop your eyes to do it.

3. *Learn how to join ongoing conversations.* Use some practical assertive techniques: (i) Try to have an air of confidence. Says one young businesswoman, "I psyche myself up. I muster all my credentials. I say to myself, 'I'm terrific' and I go up to the group! The method has worked so well that it has become part of me." (ii) Try to be the first arrival or at least one of the early-comers at a cocktail party. The hostess will have time to introduce you to other guests. Later you can join these people in their conversational groups and won't have that petrified sensation that comes when you walk into a party at its peak and the hostess says, "Introduce yourself around."

In going up to a group, stay on the periphery until you get a chance to make a contribution to the topic the others are discussing. Unlike initiating conversations, this is not the time to ask a direct question. It may sometimes work as a conversational technique, but it's not apt to make you part of the group and more apt to be regarded as interference. Instead, try lines like, "You're discussing summer houses and that reminds me of the really extraordinary experience we had with our landlord in Maine," and then go on to tell about it. Or try, "I'm so and so, and I'm so interested in what you are saying about tennis camps. I spent two weeks at one last year."

4. *Take responsibility for conversation.* Learn to change a topic when it bores you. One young woman had a miserable time on a date with a dentist who spent the entire evening telling her about the latest in fillings and extractions. She listened dutifully, hating every minute. She could easily have

said, "You seem to enjoy your work so much. I like mine too and today I had a really wonderful thing happen to me . . ."

5. *Learn to end a conversation.* Some good basic sentences: "The hostess is finally alone; let's go talk to her" . . . "I hear them talking about the new school board over there; let's go listen" . . . "Will you excuse me? A good friend has just come in and I'd like to say hello" . . . "I'm going to circulate now. I'll run into you later." In dire situations excuse yourself to go to the ladies' room. It helps if you mix verbal and nonverbal behavior. Clutch your purse, move your body, and say, "It's really time for me to leave"—and go. You can always make another social stop en route to the door.

In determining to end a conversation, ask yourself two questions:

Am I bored? If you are, don't be so concerned about the other person's feelings that you stay right where you are and do nothing about moving elsewhere. You don't have to be rude. If you can't make your exit without feeling aggressive, wait until the other person pauses for breath, say something appropriate like, "That's really fascinating—I never knew that," and quickly follow up with, "Let's go and talk with Paul and Mary." Move fast.

Do I want to see him/her again? If so, you want to make sure of three things: (i) that the person knows your name; (ii) to offer information like, "I enjoyed meeting you—perhaps we can meet again"; this shows interest; (iii) to get information—his/her name, where he/she lives or works; this gives you a chance to follow up.

6. *Learn to answer the "What do you do?" query.* If you're a homemaker, do not respond with, "I'm just a housewife." Try, "I run a creative home." When asked this question—particularly by a man—many women still fear coming on brainy. One therapist says, "When I say I'm a psychiatrist to a man, he just shys away, so I don't say it." It's better to say it. If your degrees will scare him off, it may as well be before any relationship starts. Reveal your job, not in bare detail but in a manner that provides information. Say, "I'm a psychiatrist, but I don't analyze after six o'clock" or, "I teach autistic children," not "I teach." One young woman used to say, "I'm a social worker" until a date commented, "Why don't you be more assertive and say, 'I'm a psychiatric social worker'?"

Change your social network when you have a changed life situation. Perhaps you've gone back to work after sixteen years of being a housewife-mother. Your problem is now lack of time and a dissatisfaction with the members of your previous social network. Says one working mother, "I had to start selecting and rejecting. First, I made the decision that I would go only to parties where I wanted to ask the host and hostess back. Then I stopped asking anyone who would notice lint on the carpet and dust on the floor. Then I cut out anyone who couldn't adjust to my new time hours. I can meet a woman friend for a drink at 5 P.M. but that's no good for most of my old circle. That's when they're home 'resting.' So they had to go. Now I find I'm comfortable only with those women who work. No one else understands the pressures involved."

You may have spent your entire life as part of a social group in one town. Recently you moved (either through your own choice or because your husband has been transferred). Suddenly you find you must make the effort to meet new people, winnow out those you like and those you don't like, put down roots. Here again, follow the "special interests" dictum. The quickest way to get "established" is to follow your own enthusiasms, but be assertive enough not to turn everyone into a bosom friend immediately, no matter how lonely you are. Take your time. Good assertive technique: Somehow acquire letters of introduction before you move to the new community. Someone always knows someone else somewhere.

You may find that you are in new social circumstances because you have lost a spouse through death or divorce. Suddenly you're an unmarried woman, and you may find you have social hang-ups you never knew you possessed. This may be particularly true if you married very young and, in reality, have no knowledge of how to act on a date. In this case, you must form a new social network. Most of the friends from your married days aren't going to want you around as a single woman except in big groups. Three's not only a crowd, but competition. It's nonassertive to wait for these friends to do things for you; what happens to you will stem from their actions, which they might not take. Give yourself an assertive assignment: Look for friends in similar positions and organizations based on your special interests.

You must acquire the social skills I've outlined in this chapter or regain the ones you haven't used for a long time.

If you must do a makeover on your social life, just use all the previously outlined rules.

● Start from where you are at the moment.

● Formulate social goals and work toward them in a step-by-step manner.

● Constantly experiment with your social life and make sure that as you change, it does too.

Encourage the growing relationship with both sexes. "Going to cocktail parties and backyard barbecues is fine in its place," said one personable young woman. "But I want close relationships—with my friends, male and female, even my in-laws. I don't want to exist on a small-talk level." These pointers might pave the way:

1. *Pursue the relationship.* You can't get close to someone if you don't maintain contact or maintain it only by spasmodic correspondence and occasional phone calls. I have always been very timid about making the first social overture to anyone. There was always that fear of refusal. Yet when I finally asked my agent to dinner, she was delighted to come, and what had been a business relationship changed into a warm and close personal one. Don't stand on ceremony. Don't wait for paybacks. Keep those lines, "I'd like to see you next week for lunch," . . . "I'd like to see you next Sunday" in the forefront.

2. *Realize that just seeing someone a great deal doesn't automatically produce closeness.* You must deliberately show this person you want the relationship to deepen.

3. *As you move from the small-talk kind of relationship to growing ones, you must pick your people with greater care.* At first, if you know no one, you can't choose. You take whatever friends you can get to expand your social life. But once you have a social life, you have options. Would you like to join the Masquers Club or do you prefer another where the members are more on your wavelength? Would you like to get involved with Joe or keep him on a fellow-worker basis? Would you like to go out with Man One or Man Two on Sunday night or take yourself off to a ski lodge and try to meet Man Three? Are you now secure enough with new

friends to drop social remnants from your past who now bore you?

4. *Realize you have the right not to like everyone*. The question is, what do you do about it? Is it more important to have your husband's golfing partner, whom you dislike, to dinner or to refuse and make him unhappy? Is it more important to refuse a date with someone you've decided is a bad bet or to give in because you don't want to hurt him? Go by your feelings. You may make the assertive choice to have your husband's golfing partner to dinner because you care about your husband.

5. *Realize that the other person has the right not to like you*. Your overtures to closeness may get turned down. Take a hint. Remember, you may be dissatisfied with your female stereotype (passive, etc.) but you don't want to exchange it for an equally offending one of Annie Aggressiveness.

6. *Understand that as closeness develops, your fears, particularly of speaking up and rejection, may grow stronger*. These fears may be so powerful that you hide behind your emotional mask and prevent closeness from developing, rationalizing, "I want to be loved" ... "I don't want to get hurt." What you anticipate may be worse than what actually happens. You may not get hurt. And if you do, the experience may prove an enriching one that makes you more human.

If you act assertively in the feared situation, you can create greater closeness. You may also learn that a relationship which you viewed as close is not.

CASE

"Jack and I are getting married this August. Please come and be my bridesmaid." So began a letter to Evelyn Welch, a twenty-five-year-old copywriter at a Manhattan advertising agency, from her older sister who lived in Hawaii. Even though Evelyn was very happy at her sister's tidings, she did not want to go to the wedding: (a) She had made the costly flight to Hawaii just six months previously and had met the fiancé; (b) August was always the busiest time at the agency; (c) Short of cash because of the Hawaiian trip, she had planned to share a summer house with friends and save money.

When Evelyn communicated her thoughts to her parents, they were horrified. "What! Not go to your own sister's wedding. What will people think? You're so selfish!" Evelyn started to imagine her sister's reaction: "If you loved me, you'd spend the money. You just don't love me!" Evelyn felt under tremendous pressure from everyone to do something she did not want to do.

From Assertiveness Training Evelyn realized that if you try to solve all your problems at once, you end up solving nothing. She handled each problem separately.

The sister. Evelyn figured out that the best way for her to say, "I care so much—I know how disappointed you will be, but job pressures and money just keep me from coming" would be in a letter. She also thought through all the things her sister might say in a return letter or phone call ("How can you say no? You know how important it is for me to have you here") and tried to cover all the various points in the letter. She also offered the suggestion that they all meet the next spring in San Francisco. Evelyn needn't have been so apprehensive. By return mail she received a very feelingful "I'm terribly sorry but I understand" letter from the sister who thought the San Francisco idea was "just great."

Her parents. Evelyn thought up answers for the derogatory statements her parents had been making. She used I-Talk: "I feel bad because you're putting so much pressure on me and refuse to understand the position I'm in." This got through to the mother—so much so that Evelyn was able to say, "There's something that has been bothering me since childhood. I always felt you preferred my sister to me." This openness resulted in a frank discussion and greatly increased emotional feeling between mother and daughter.

With her father the I-Talk technique didn't work so well. He simply refused to listen. However, in her attempts to communicate with him, Evelyn realized her father was sending the message, "I don't care how you feel. Do it my way." She also became conscious that his real concern was not for her sister but for what neighbors and family would say about Evelyn's refusal to go to the wedding. Knowing this, her feeling of pressure from the father disappeared. He continued to act in the same way, but Evelyn didn't respond in the same way.

If Evelyn hadn't acted assertively, she would have been forced to do something she didn't want to do, added additional tenseness into her familial relationship and felt very bad about her own behavior. By switching her perspective from the "They shouldn't pressure me" approach to "How can I stand up for myself?," she saw more clearly than ever before the kind of person her father was, achieved greater closeness with sister and mother, and started to solve emotional problems that had bothered her for years.

Chapter 7

Coming of Age:
New Courtship Patterns
for Singles

Many single women forget that they have rights. They are
self-made victims of the "should" syndrome: "He should do
the calling" ... "He should earn more money" ... "He
should be the one to break it up." Because of their past conditioning, they don't pay attention to the fact that these are
different times; they don't realize that when you are properly
assertive, the man doesn't feel pushed, put down or hurt. Passivity and aggressiveness lead to distance. True assertiveness
leads to closeness. As an unmarried woman in today's society
you have the right to:

1. *Ask him out.* You don't have to have that old-fashioned
attitude, "If a man calls us, we're glad; if we call him, it
means we're pushy." Says one Assertiveness Training graduate, "If you're direct, it comes out as a request rather than
begging. I have the attitude that I don't expect a refusal, and,
if I get one, I say, 'Maybe another time' and don't fuss about
it."

The trick lies in the way you ask. Avoid the indirect approach or the wistful "When am I seeing you again?" that
puts him on the spot. By not stating a preference ("I'd like to
see you on Sunday"), you open the way for no response or a

negative one. In asking a man out, you should be specific, say exactly what you'd like to do, have a definite place in mind, and stop worrying about the consequences if he refuses. (In a study, Dr. Eileen D. Gambrill of the University of California at Berkeley found that 39 percent of the women queried wouldn't ask a man out again if they were refused the first time.)

Wrong way: "I'm a great cook. I make terrific spaghetti." And you wait for him to say, "When can I try it?" He may not say anything.

Right way: "I'm a terrific cook with pasta. Would you like to come for dinner next Friday and try my spaghetti *carbonara*? I'll ask the Joneses too." Don't dilute your message. Tell exactly what food you'll serve and who'll be there.

2. *Refuse a date*. Naturally your previous relationship with the man, or lack of it, influences the tone of your answer. Let's say a man whom you've dated once calls. You found him a bore and don't want to see him. You can say:

Unassertive: "Well, I'm not sure. I've a hectic week ... well, O.K."

Aggressive: "Look, take a hint. Leave me be."

Assertive: "No, Joe, I just don't share your interest in pursuing this relationship further."

When you refuse, don't say no with a big apology that says, "I can be convinced." And again, avoid indirectness. Instead of facing something, many women just cancel out. For example, Kay had made a Saturday night date with a guy who then told her he would first go to visit his family and would pick her up around 9:30 P.M. When Kay first heard this, she knew he wouldn't arrive until 10:30 P.M., and that, as a result, she'd be boiling. She decided to break the date. However, instead of having the courage to tell the man directly, she called his office on Friday and left an "I can't make it for tomorrow" message with his secretary. Kay says, "Before Assertiveness Training I would have kept the date, but even here I didn't have the guts to refuse the date in the first place and say why."

It helps to be honest and explain your refusal. For example, you've had a terrible day at the office and a man calls to ask you out for that night. Do you accept in spite of your fatigue? Alice Marks always did. But recently, after AT, when a male friend said, "I'd like to come over," she was able to answer, "Let's talk over the phone. I can't handle your coming over tonight."

Just because you're anxious doesn't mean you can't do what you want to do.

3. *Earn more money than a man and not feel guilty.* What can you say when a date feels upset because he learns that you get a larger take-home paycheck than he does? The following answers were suggested in an AT group:

"But I'm more valuable." (aggressive)

"They don't know your worth."

"How do you measure value?"

"Why do you think you have to be more valuable?"

"Hey, you really feel bad because I earn more money."

This last works best because it opens the way for an exchange of feelings. Through this exchange the man will probably agree you have the right to earn more money and you should not feel uncomfortable or unfeminine because you do. Remember, it all goes back to societal brainwashing attitudes: "He's a man" ... "He should win at tennis" ... "He should make more money than I do." Because you've been trained that way, you think of men as having fragile egos. Before you can fully develop yourself, you have to rid yourself of that complex.

4. *Ask for things you want.* Says Annette, "I have a feeling I have to cater to men. I never ask, 'What are we going to do?' I feel, they're paying. They should make the plans."

Says Marlene, "My guy is a great cook. His specialty is omelets. I hint around. I say, 'Are you hungry? What would you like to have?' I defeat myself. Then I say, 'Have some cold cereal.' I should say, 'I want you to make one of your terrific omelets.' "

You have the right to:

• Suggest a restaurant

• Say what kind of food you feel like eating

• Answer when he asks "What would you like to do?" instead of copping out with "Anything you want"

• Make suggestions about where you'd like to go—the new exhibition of Jane Austen's letters at the library, on an all-day hike and breathe fresh country air, to stay home and do nothing, say "I want to be alone"

- Have him take some responsibility in the apartment if you live together. Says Kathy, "If I don't buy food, we don't eat"
- Get emotional feedback
- Be frank about your needs and feelings

CASE

Terry had been dating a successful attorney who, in their six previous dates, had never taken her out for dinner. When he called for the seventh, she asked, "Is that for dinner?" He answered, "Oh, I've been sick and my stomach is still upset. Let's just make it for a movie." Terry said yes and brooded for days about the unfairness of it. What would have happened if, instead of "Is that for dinner?" she had been more specific with, "John, we've had six dates and not one has been for dinner. I'd like a dinner date with you."

CASE

Anne met a man at a beach party who wanted an intense relationship immediately—three nights during the week, all weekend. She says, "He was more enamoured of me than I was of him. I told him this. I wanted to be direct. I asked him, 'How does this make you feel that I can't return your exuberance? It makes me feel uncomfortable. But I do like you. It makes me feel good that you like me so much.' "

He told her, "I understand."

But some evenings later, he attacked. "I'm tired of giving and getting nothing in return."

Anne says, "I was enraged. Before AT I would have shriveled up. But I was able to say, 'That really is some kind of statement. I really want to discuss things.' We did. He had to learn that I couldn't love him in the way that he wanted me to love him."

The basic assertive rule is "What do I want?" Say it, and open the way for discussion. At the same time remember one of the best ways of sabotaging your romantic life is to be a spoiled brat or crybaby or have what psychologists call a "low frustration tolerance." A woman who is unable to bear frustration will normally demand that she have exactly what she wants—right now, pronto. And the man may well conclude, "She's pretty, bright, but who needs her?" Moreover, low frustration tolerance is one of the chief sources of goading aggressiveness, as distinguished from healthy self-assertion. The self-assertive woman asks herself, "What do I want in life and how can I go about getting it?" If blocked, she tells herself, "Too bad, I can't get what I want right now. Let's see, what I can do to get it later or how can I get along without it?" The aggressive woman asks, "How, by hook or crook, no matter whose toes I have to step on, can I immediately get what I want?" If blocked, she says, "I'll fix him. Now let me see how I can hurt him as much as possible so that he'll give me what I need and want."

Low frustration tolerance will often block your getting what you want.

5. *Say no to bed.* I'm not discussing occasions here where you want to say yes, but those situations that continually crop up where you want to say no but don't know how. As Dr. Herbert Fensterheim pointed out earlier, "This inability to say no is one of the greatest causes of unwanted promiscuity among young single women." Some lines you might use in response to undesired propositions or cracks like, "What's wrong—are you inhibited?":

• "You've got to be kidding" (when you get the invitation after ten minutes of chit-chat at a party).

• "No, I'm not inhibited. I'm just not going to bed with you."

• "With the right person I'm not inhibited" (in response to "You ought to let me loosen you up").

• "I'm not interested in going further with you. The evening has been very pleasant."

• "Look, right now I can't handle going to bed. There are good feelings and close feelings, but I'm not comfortable with the bed part yet" (where you don't want to cut off future possibilities).

• "I'm a coward. The risks are high" (when it's someone you date from the office and aren't sure how you want to proceed).

• "There's someone else."

• "I have someone waiting at home."

- "I don't know you well enough."
- "Wait a second. I've got to know you. This is too fast. I'm sorry." (This was the line used by a woman who went out for the first time after her divorce.)
- "Not yet. Let's wait a little while."
- "Look, I don't even know your middle name."
- "Look, you don't even know my last name."

6. *Date a married man.* Do you want this right? It's a decision only you can make. Today, in these days of urban renewal, Back Street has practically ceased to exist. The Other Woman is alive, well, and living everywhere from one-room efficiency to posh pad. However, unlike Ray Schmidt, the dependent heroine of Fannie Hurst's 1930 novel who gave her all for a Wall Street tycoon and ended up penniless at a Cannes gambling casino, today's OW may suffer some guilts, but she rarely becomes financially degraded, makes her lover the sole center of her life, or retreats from life waiting for an occasional moment of favor. Usually, she *chooses* to be the Other Woman. She does not consider herself immoral; she sees herself as a moral, self-respecting woman who is in the Other Woman situation.

Whether you are in the category of the young thing who chooses *not* to make a legal commitment, the divorcée who says, "I've got the perfect set up—I can put on cold cream at night, go to bed when I want to, have him when I want to," or the woman who becomes the Other Woman without premeditation ("We got involved because we worked at adjoining desks—now our affair has gone on for six years"), you might ask yourself these questions:

Can I stand the guilt of being the Other Woman? One OW who did marry the man says, "I've never had a happy moment. I keep thinking I took him from his wife and kids."

Will the pain be too much? Can I stand it when he introduces me to a business acquaintance by another name ... has a heart attack and I can't go to see him at the hospital ... when the wife hears about our relationship, writes my boss about it, and I face the chance of getting fired?

Can I bear it when my own child says to me, "Daddy says you are breaking up a marriage"?

Will I like doing all the little subterfuges I will have to practice—like never calling him at home, not buying him presents his wife might see, refraining from sending him love letters, eating at different restaurants from the ones where he takes her?

Can I tolerate the indefinite quality of the affair? In *The Affair* author Morton Hunt stresses that most affairs "endure on the order of several weeks to several years" but rarely past five. One survey showed that about one out of every ten unfaithful people married the person with whom they'd been having an affair.

Am I giving up too much? Will he be faithful to me? Jane, a divorcée, tells the story of how her husband asked for a divorce because he had fallen in love with a young fellow worker. "I promised it to him," she says. "I didn't want him to stay just because he had signed a piece of paper. Then one day the girl called me and wanted to meet me for lunch. She felt guilty."

At lunch the OW asked, "How do I know it won't happen to me!" Jane answered, "You don't."

With the humiliations and hurts, is it worth it to be the Other Woman? Successful ones, who accept the limitations or for whom the affair ends at the altar, say yes. For others, acceptance of the heartbreak of the Other Woman's life may seem the service of their own self-destructive needs (unassertive), a desire to destroy or hurt others (aggressive), and a pointless revolt against society.

In your individual case, only you can provide your own assertive answer.

7. *End the relationship.* It sometimes takes women years to get out those eight fateful words, "I don't want to see you any more." Just as they avoid other decisions in the dating game, women evade this one. You find women who are assertive in other social situations saying, "I wish he would make the move to break it up; then he could shoulder the guilt."

Says Dr. Herbert Fensterheim, "It's harder for a woman to break off an unsatisfying relationship than it is for a man. Women have been brainwashed for so long that they have to please a man, that they're lucky to have a man, that, if something goes wrong in a relationship, the woman feels it's her fault. Ending a relationship isn't a release for her; it's a confession of failure. So she often works harder than she should to make a relationship work."

It's not just female self-blame that lies behind the hesitation. Often it's a woman's subconscious longing to correct not just the relationship with the man but an earlier, primary one with one of her parents.

In my own case, before meeting Herb, I always dated difficult, hard-to-get men of the variety I call "uncommitted." No one could get any of them. They're all still on the loose or have been married briefly and just as quickly divorced. But, in retrospect, I realize they were all very much like my mother—critical of me. I could never make her love me. Maybe I could make these men love me. If I could change things with any one of them, I would right things with her. I would be exonerated from whatever I had done as a child to make her dislike me and make me feel so insecure.

In ending a relationship you should bear these thoughts in mind: When the negative feelings outweigh the positive and it seems it's always going to be that way, it's time to write *kaput*, no matter who did what, who's right and who's wrong. You should get out of it as intact a human being as you can be.

a. *Before actually taking action, you might try to improve the conditions.* One woman in Assertiveness Training had this problem: For two years she had been dating a man from out of town who told her he loved her but flew into town to see her very infrequently. Feeling the relationship was going nowhere, she gave herself the assertive assignment of making a speech which went like this: "Listen, Gerry, this has been going on for too long. There has been no improvement or change in our relationship. There's no point in continuing. It's unfair to me. If we continue, you'll have to change. You'll have to see me at least once a month. You've been talking about changing jobs. You don't like the one you have and you have the chance of one in town here. Give it a trial. If you won't, I can't continue." The man did take the job in her city and the relationship exists on a better basis.

b. *Don't leave the entire responsibility to the other person.* It's indirect to try to make him be the one who says the exit line. For example, Sue had been dating a man for eight months and felt dissatisfied with the status quo. However, she couldn't get out the words, "I'm through." One night the man invited Sue to dinner at his apartment. It was a cool May evening and as Joe hung her wrap in the hall closet, Sue noticed a heavy lumberjacket hanging there. In her eagerness to have Joe take the responsibility for breaking off the affair, Sue gave him his cue with, "I guess I won't be seeing that jacket this fall!" Joe said nothing. The affair dragged on. By that October Sue had had three months of AT. She did manage to say, "This isn't going to work. We both want different things. Let's end it." Sue's prophecy was right. She didn't get to see Joe in his winter lumberjacket, but she didn't care. She felt good because *she* had taken the action she had wanted to take for so long.

You can't play that passive little-girl role forever.

c. *Use just one criterion in the way you handle the actual writing finis: Will this action increase my self-respect?* That should be your concern, not worry about being lonely or that other people might think, "Poor thing—she has failed again." How you end the relationship depends on what will make you feel good. Do you leave a note, write a letter, or discuss it with him? Make your decision not on the basis of what he will think of you but what you will think of yourself. Remember, doing what's easiest and most comfortable is usually not doing what will give you the greatest feeling of self-esteem.

Sometimes using the technique of the bottom line helps: "What I want is this . . . What I want to do is this . . . My bottom line is this. I've had it."

One woman found she was able to end a "destructive relationship with a bad guy" by making up a list of his pros and cons. It went something like this:

Pros	Cons
Smart	Won't share anything
Fun to be with	Spy-oriented ("He asked too many questions about my personal life")
Good-looking	
Likes to travel	
Successful	Won't talk about feelings

Never takes me out
with his friends

Doesn't like
spending money

Can't say
"I love you"

She says, "The list helped me make up my mind and I started to date other men. I got involved with a new man and suddenly realized that a man can give. My new man can say 'I love you.' He doesn't feel saying it makes him sound like a phony."

There is the special case where you love a guy who's a bastard. Every night you cry yourself to sleep with, "He's destroying me, but I love him."

Says Dr. Herbert Fensterheim, "A love relationship that destroys you as a person is something you have to break off. Once you've made the decision, sharp, abrupt surgery is necessary. It doesn't work if you drag it on. And like any surgery it's going to be a shock and hurt like hell. There's going to have to be a recovery period. Be strong and do what you have to do."

d. *Be prepared to deal assertively with the emotional aftermath of the breakup.* Again we get back to the coping statements I mentioned earlier. Dr. Eileen D. Gambrill suggests a woman train herself in the behaviorist technique of "anxiety management skills." You translate feelings into mental statements and use negative statements to trigger thoughts. For example, the minute you find yourself thinking, "I shouldn't have broken up with him," you use that thought as a cue to say to yourself, "I have a perfect right to want things different in my life." Or, if you find yourself thinking, "Gee, things were so good with him," you use that as a cue to say to yourself, "No, things were really miserable. It's good to be through with it."

Some assertive acts when a relationship ends:
• Take a vacation while you've got the chance
• Rediscover pieces of yourself you've given up for him—clubs, women friends, job advancements

• Throw a party and invite people who aren't part of the old you

In this way you can become happy enough with yourself so that you don't have to grab at the first guy who comes along.

Chapter 8

Getting Closer in
the Close Relationship

W. H. Auden wrote:

> "Private faces in public places
> are wiser and nicer
> than public faces in private places"

Many women fail to achieve true closeness with men because they hide behind the veil of their "public faces." As wives they play roles, ranging from the servant or the flatterer to the briber or the power behind the throne. They may play these parts because they feel vulnerable. They want so much to be loved that they conceal any trait—like hostility—that may mar that image. Or, from years of deferring to and taking a back seat to men in general, they are intimidated by their husbands. Their low self-esteem causes them to view themselves as second-class citizens and they don't speak up when they feel most offended, put upon, or hurt. Conversely, they may speak up too much, always expressing anger and rarely love.

Often these same women believe their difficulties *à deux* are caused by outside events—bad luck, a mean mother-in-law, some fancied health problem. Actually, they are in trouble because they seek human response from lovers and spouses without revealing their real thoughts, feelings, selves. Because they are emotional conservatives, they create a *closed* relationship, not allowing for growth, instead of a *close and open* one.

If you get in touch with your true feelings and express them assertively and appropriately, you can change marital interactions and consequences.

THINKING THE
RELATIONSHIP THROUGH

Determine Your Problem Area

Do you play any of the following roles, often chosen as "parts" by women?

1. *The unfulfilled woman.* You're competent and have a strong desire to achieve, but you've been brought up to believe that if you are successful—whether on the job or in the community—your husband will be jealous and view you as competitive. You feel you have no rights of your own and that your need for success should be satisfied by your husband's accomplishments. Often he doesn't have the same ability or capacity for accomplishment and he doesn't achieve. Or, if he does, it's not in the area you want, and dissatisfactions multiply. You're angry because you expect him to do what you should do for yourself.

2. *The manipulator.* Whether you use tears, whining, tantrums, or the "Darling, you do it so well" approach, essentially you get your way by maneuvering your mate rather than stating what you want in a direct way. You have ulterior motives which differ from the ones you express. For example, you look around your living room and say sweetly, "There's a vacant space there," instead of, "We need a chair for that space." You may even use your children to accomplish your ends: "Janie, I'm tired; go ask Daddy if he'll buy

us Chinese food for tonight." And "Daddy" resents being played like a violin.

3. *The dwarf.* As your husband becomes more successful, you become increasingly threatened by his professional and economic advancement. You realize that you do not fit in with your new life-style, but you do nothing to change yourself. Instead you continue to behave the same way you did as a young bride and to talk about things in which your now mature mate has no interest.

4. *The child wife.* Your refrain is "Poor me—I'm so helpless." You like playing helpless. It puts you in a position to make demands and control your mate ("If I knew how to put in a storm window, I would have done it already"). Eventually you become helpless. Because you're so busy playing games rather than saying what you think and feel, real intimacy becomes blocked.

5. *The emotional blackmailer.* You make deals. You use lines like, "You behaved so terribly at the party that I can't bring myself to have sex with you." Your favorite line: "If you really loved me, you would do this."

6. *The get-even girl.* To get your own way, you use indirect aggression. Instead of expressing anger or annoyance, you just "happen" to forget to put gas in the car tank, or when your husband asks you to buy film, you say, "Yes, I will" and don't do it. It's far better to directly communicate your resentment ("I feel it's a burden to get your film developed") than to embark on a program of subversive sabotage.

7. *The nag.* Nothing is ever your fault. Instead you're always on the lookout for what your mate did wrong. You constantly criticize ("Why did you get cigarettes at the drugstore instead of the discount place?") and check up ("Did you get the insurance for the car?"). By concentrating on how he should be "better-richer-stronger" and blaming him for all your problems, you bury any feelings of tenderness. This is as much a lack of assertion as too much passivity.

8. *The egotist.* You're essentially concerned with your own needs, whether comforts, pleasures, or money. You feel put upon when your mate has any expectations of you. Often, you are unwilling to give things—whether emotional or physi-

cal—to your husband. At other times you give him what *you think* he wants rather than what he actually wants.

9. *The servant.* The "docility training" you received in childhood, enabling you to please Daddy, who wanted you to be "feminine," gets transferred to wanting to please your husband. You're the slave. He's the master. You give little attention to your own needs. Sometimes you feel your needs should matter, but you don't disclose them.

10. *The disciple.* You follow your mate's leads, taking no responsibility for planning the present or future of your mutual lives. You give your mate no feedback. Sometimes you don't even answer when he expresses a thought. Or you may say, "Tell me your hopes, dreams, fears" and to yourself you say, "But I won't tell you mine."

11. *The woman with health problems.* You constantly don't do what you can or should do because you suffer from some ailment (tension headaches, ulcers, etc.)—often psychosomatic. Whether psychosomatic or real, you use your health as an excuse for not doing.

Set Your Marital Goals

So many marriages are unhappy. The partners exist in a relationship of falseness because they refuse to share feelings. The goal of the intimate relationship is to maintain what closeness already exists and to move still closer. In the Assertiveness Training approach to closeness, the word "closeness" means an ever-increasing ability to *share* more and more of your personal feelings, fantasies, thoughts, ideas, and, concomitantly, a similar ever-growing ability to *act* in such a way that your partner is able to share more and more of his personal feelings, fantasies, thoughts, ideas. You and your husband trust each other and like to be with each other. At the same time both of you feel free to be a "self" and express your own individuality.

Says Dr. Arnold A. Lazarus, professor of psychology at Rutgers University, "In marriage, the continuously close physical proximity and all the shared burdens and responsibilities dictate the need of some degree of emotional privacy. Whereas the ideal friendship is an A-to-Z relationship, the ideal marriage should proceed no further than A-to-W. Marriage is not ownership. Each partner is entitled to his or her individuality, emotional privacy, and considerable freedom of psychological movement. The only proviso is that when exercising freedom of movement and individuality one must take care not to encroach on the partner's rightful territory."

He offers the following diagrams of marital relationships.* Note figure two, which should be your goal.

This depicts a poor marriage relationship. There is very little togetherness or common ground.

This depicts an excellent marriage. There is about 80 percent togetherness but also sufficient separateness to permit individual growth and essential privacy.

This represents the romantic ideal where two people merge so completely that they become as one. In practice, were this possible, it would probably result in emotional suffocation.

Here is a reasonably good marriage in which each partner has an independent interest or relationship which in no way interferes with or threatens the marriage as it occupies only each one's own individual territory.

In this figure, one of the partners has an interest or relationship which not only occupies some of his or her own territory but which also intrudes into their (the marriage) territory as well as encroaching upon the other partner's individual zone.

*From *Behavior Therapy and Beyond* by Arnold A. Lazarus, Ph.D., 1971. Used with permission of McGraw-Hill Book Company.

How Good Is Your Marriage?

Do you have 80 percent "togetherness but also sufficient separateness"? The following Marital Happiness Quiz may help you to think through your satisfactions and dissatisfactions.

MARITAL HAPPINESS QUIZ

STEP ONE: In your Female Assertiveness Notebook draw a scale:

0	10	20	30	40	50	60	70	80	90	100

STEP TWO: Answer the following questions, each time rating your percentage:

1. How certain are you that you want to remain married to your husband?
2. How committed do you feel your husband is to this marriage?
3. What percent of making this a good marriage rests on you alone?
4. What percent of the time that you spend with your husband could you really call pleasant or happy?
5. How much do you think your husband or marital situation itself allows you to be really you?
6. To what extent do you think you are *allowed* to make your home a truly happy one?
7. How certain are you that twenty years from now it will be a good marriage?
8. To what extent is any specific area—sex, fighting, children, etc.—so bad that it disrupts your entire relationship?
9. During sex with your husband how often do you have fantasies about another man?
10. To what extent do you and your husband share activities?
11. To what extent do you do activities on your own?
12. To what extent do you feel your marriage is a subjugating experience for you as a woman?

What Would You Like to Be Different in Your Marriage?

Try to pinpoint your own specific goals. In the Assertiveness Training approach to working out marital goals, participants realize that specific behaviors involved in the marital contract may have many different meanings at many different levels—conscious and unconscious—but rather than getting caught up in the meaning, husbands and wives try out this behavior and that behavior until he satisfies your needs and you satisfy his. Whatever your individual goals, essentially you want to consider three major areas: communication, decision-making, and behavioral change in specific areas.

A BEHAVIORAL CHANGE PROGRAM FOR MARITAL HAPPINESS

Improve Your Communication

Nowhere is frank transmission of ideas and feelings more important than in the close relationship. Yet many women rationalize their lack of communication with "I'm afraid to say no to him" ... "I don't want to hurt him" ... "If I say what I think, he'll think I'm pushing him."

But if you wear your "public face" in the "private places" and don't speak up, you don't know what the real problems are. Because you don't share feelings, you can't develop an ever-deepening relationship with your partner. Because of the lack of communication, resentments, misunderstandings, and limited closeness develop. You may even feel you live with a stranger.

How well do you communicate with your mate? The following questionnaire, adapted from one done by Dr. Richard B. and Freida Stuart, may help you to evaluate this:

COMMUNICATION QUIZ

	Always	Almost Always	Occasionally	Rarely	Never
a. My mate understands what I want to communicate					
b. I feel I understand what my mate wants to communicate					
c. I give positive feedback to my mate when he does things for me					
d. My mate gives me positive feedback when I do things for him					
e. I feel free to ask my mate to do things for me or things I want done					
f. My mate feels free to ask me to do things for him or things he wants done					
g. I pay attention to my mate when he talks and express interest in the things that concern him					
h. My mate pays attention when I talk and expresses interest in the things that concern me					
i. I feel free to disagree with my mate					
j. My mate feels free to disagree with me					
k. I feel free to have a knock-down drag-out fight with my mate					
l. To get anything accomplished I must manipulate the conversation so that my mate thinks my idea is his idea					
m. I enjoy spending talk time with my mate					

What can you do to better communication? Here is a three-point program:

1. *Correct your conversation so that it is assertive and appropriate.* In every Assertiveness Training group there is usually one woman—and often several—who complains, "My husband doesn't talk to me." Do you feel that way? What do you do to keep him from talking? How can you improve your own conversation with him? What kind of things can you do to help him improve his conversation with you?

a. *Speak up about trivial matters.* It's when you *don't* say, "We always go to the movie you want to go to" or, "I wish you'd talk to me at breakfast instead of reading the paper" that marital problems start to develop. By speaking up about trivia you: (i) avoid gunnysacking—when marital grievances are toted along quietly in a gunnysack for any length of time, they make a dreadful mess when the sack finally bursts and everything spills out at once, (ii) begin to set the pattern of openness in your marriage; (iii) hopefully resolve the problem to the satisfaction of both. Remember, you have a right to your feelings. You own them. When he asks, "Do you want to see *Gone with the Wind*?", and you don't, you have the right to say, "I'd rather see *Love and Death*."

In my own case, Herb always used to steal my stories—not little experiences that had happened to me but anecdotes I had collected from exhaustive research—and tell them at dinner parties as if he had done the research and with no credit to me. There we would be at some dinner. The talk would turn to France and I would hear him say "You know the courtesan Caroline Otero earned thirty million dollars on her back and died cooking rabbit stew in a furnished room in Nice." *I* was the one who had spent two years studying the *grands horizontals* of Paris 1890 for a possible book on *La Belle Epoque*.

Incidents like this went on for years, but I hesitated to say anything ("He's so busy. How can I bother him with something so trivial?"). Then one day, as we were being interviewed by a newspaperwoman, I heard him tell *my story* of how Havelock Ellis, the British sex authority, had been impotent all his life and through his first marriage until his later years when he finally established a beautiful sex life with a

Françoise de Lisle. I had finally acquired Mlle. de Lisle's memoirs after writing to *thirty* British second-hand book sellers.

I was furious, and this time I didn't act like silent dumb Dora. To the reporter I said calmly, "I'd appreciate your not using that story. I plan to use it in a book." When she left, I said, equally calmly, to Herb, "I don't like what you did this morning"—and went on from there, telling him all my resentments about his lifting of my painstakingly acquired anecdotes.

His reaction was unexpected. Far from being angry, he was extremely apologetic, saying, "I just thought they were good stories. It never occurred to me what my telling them might mean to you."

Remember the basic rule: It never is a question of *should* you speak up, but *how and when.*

b. *Stop using that rationalization, "If I say something, I'll hurt him" as an excuse for avoidance of communication.* Many women have the erroneous concept that men have fragile egos ("My husband is like a little boy; I must protect him"). For example, Marilyn says, "My husband gave me an expensive shirt for my birthday. He knows I don't like it because I've never worn it. But I can't take it back. I'm afraid of hurting his feelings. When your husband gives you a gift, you take it and say thank you—that's what my mother taught me. This silly little shirt is causing a strain in our marriage."

Your partner is a grown man, not a "little boy"; he does have feelings. How can you reveal your feelings without getting his defenses up? One way is the "We have a problem" approach: "George, we have a problem. I appreciate your giving me the shirt but it looks terrible on me. Can we take it back and will you help me choose another?"

c. *Make sure you send the right message.* There are two parts to a message: (i) the part you send; (ii) the part your partner receives. Even if you send a clear message and the receiver doesn't understand, you may have to find another way of sending it. And sometimes your message may be unclear and you expect your partner to be a mind reader.

d. *Use conversation as a way of expressing your real feelings, not as a device for attack.* For example, you ask your husband to pick up a loaf of bread at the store. He comes home minus bread. You start in with, "You never do what I want." He counters with, "If you'd make better meals, I'd remember," and you're off. When people feel hurt, rejected, or unloved, they frequently attack instead of saying, "Look, what you've done makes me feel uncared for." How much better when he says, "If you'd make better meals . . ." to answer, "Look, I'm not saying you're a terrible person just because you forgot the bread but just that you made me feel bad." And if he counters this with, "You're too sensitive," try, "That makes me angry. You're rejecting my feelings." Again, you have the right to your own feelings. And what is feeling if you don't communicate it in a way that leads to resolution?

e. *At all times express your own feelings honestly, directly, and appropriately.* It is dishonest to ask a question when you have already formulated the answer. For instance, it is honest to ask, "Do you want to eat Chinese food tonight?" when you really want to know, dishonest when you have already made the restaurant reservation. If you are aware that your spouse dislikes spareribs and lemon chicken but you feel a passionate longing for them, it is more honest to say, "I really would like to eat Chinese food tonight. Would you be willing?" That way he doesn't have to go along feeling resentful and manipulated. Asking a direct question is as important as asking an honest question. You may ask your mate, "How do you like my new coat?" What you want to know is, "Do I look pretty?" You get mad when he answers, "I think you look younger in red than black."

If you have conversational problems in the close relationship, you might try these two exercises:

TALK-TIME EXERCISE

Schedule talk time. Turn off the TV. Take the phone off the hook. Put down your book. Talk. Do this with your mate for fifteen minutes once a day. You ask him questions about what he did that day, and he asks you. You both talk about mutual interests you have or plan to develop. You both say what's on your minds. Experiment with this technique and you won't need it for long.

EXERCISE IN GUT-LEVEL COMMUNICATION

Aim: To show a deeper level of yourself and get your mate to show a deeper level of himself

STEP ONE: Take an important emotional experience (it can be happy, sad, or traumatic) that happened to you during your formative years. Tell it aloud or into a tape recorder. It should be something that has real meaning to you (the time you beat a boy at chess in junior high and experienced tremendous guilt, the feeling of rejection you had at a prom when no one asked you to dance). Listen to how you sound. Think through how you can make the story more emotionally revealing.

STEP TWO: Tell it to your partner.

When I tried this, I told Herb a story I had never dared tell anyone before. For ten long years my mother had died painfully of cancer. As a teen-ager I had had responsibility for the household and two younger siblings. During the last year before her death she was hospitalized. My brother and sister were away at college. I had no social life. Every day I commuted from my house in Mount Vernon to my job in New York City (by then I was working). At lunchtime I went to the hospital and at night came home to cook for my father.

One morning at 7:30 A.M. my father called me from the hospital, to which he had been summoned in the middle of the night, and said, "Your mother just died." When I hung up, my first reaction was that I no longer had to bear all those burdens. I went into the bathroom, locked the door even though no one else was in the house, and screamed aloud, "I'm glad she's dead." For years my guilt over that statement has haunted me. When I told the story to Herb, expecting to hear what a "dreadful person" I was, he said simply, "How hard it must have been on you to keep this bottled up all these years. Why do you feel so terrible because in a tragic moment you had an outburst? After all, for ten years you did everything." He really understood. It was one of our closest moments.

2. *Increase your expression of tenderness.* Many wives base their lives on avoiding marital unpleasantness ("If I say anything, he'll yell at me") instead of giving attention to doing things for the sheer pleasure of it. These same women, often falling in the nag or shrew category, may have little trouble saying, "I don't like what you did." They forget that they will feel happier if they show tenderness in a gesture designed purely to please.

a. *Tell your mate what you like about him.* The following exercise may aid you in verbal expression.

TENDERNESS EXERCISE I—PLEASURE INVENTORY

STEP ONE: In your Female Assertiveness Notebook list five things your mate does which please you.

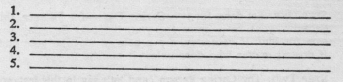

1. _____
2. _____
3. _____
4. _____
5. _____

STEP TWO: Ask your spouse to make out a similar list. Here, as an example, is the one Herb made out about me.

1. "Your fierce loyalty—I know that no matter what happens you'll be with me."

2. "Your zest for living—the way you get so excited over a new dress or being with certain favorite friends."

3. "Your curiosity—the way when I use a technical word like 'ontogenetic' that you don't know, you run to the dictionary, look it up, and then use it yourself two days later."

4. "Your genuine concern about people and their problems—the way that even when you're on deadline for a book, you'll spend hours every night talking to a friend about her romance."

5. "The way you always have warmth and tenderness when I need it."

STEP THREE: Discuss your respective lists. Give each other positive reinforcement. I felt so good when I read Herb's list. It sounds naïve, but I really didn't know he thought so highly of me. I thought he loved me because I was so competent and organized.

b. *Start a program of Caring Days.* This is a technique, based on recognition of the fact that many couples place the emphasis on what they don't like in their mates, that I heard Dr. Richard B. Stuart describe at a recent convention of the Association for the Advancement of Behavior Therapy. The aim of Caring Days is twofold: (i) to make each partner aware of what *pleases* the other rather than what annoys him/her; (ii) to form the habit of doing things just for the sake of pleasing, thus making the relationship more rewarding for each.

TENDERNESS EXERCISE II—CARING DAYS

STEP ONE: Set dates for two Caring Days—for instance, this Saturday your mate cares for you, the next Saturday you care for him. If necessary, flip a coin to see who goes first. It doesn't matter who does unless it matters to you.

STEP TWO: The Caring Person (and let's say in this instance it's the wife) makes a list of some fifteen to twenty small, reasonable, doable things that she might be able to do for her mate on that day. When you compose the list, make sure they are small, trivial behaviors. If they're complex, they don't belong on the list. Remember the list's purpose: to train you to think in terms of what your partner might like.

STEP THREE: On your Caring Day, do the things. Check off each item as you do it.

STEP FOUR: That evening, or sometime soon after, talk about it. Tell your partner the things you enjoyed doing and the ideas you've gotten for the future. Your partner then tells you what he enjoyed. You may be as surprised as I was. My agenda was full of services: "Bring Herb breakfast in bed" and "Straighten Herb's sock drawer." He didn't want "so many things"—he wanted more "spontaneous affection" and "a backrub in the bathtub." Actually, instead of thinking what would please him, I had thought about what would please me if I were he.

STEP FIVE: Your partner goes through the same process on his Caring Day. Again you evaluate reactions.

STEP SIX: After each of you has done one Caring Day, schedule another pair for the near future. Continue these alternate Caring Days as long as they give you pleasure.

Says Dr. Stuart, "Often a man and wife want the same things, but each defensively holds back. With a Caring Day you demonstrate that caring with the purpose of building trust in the other."

c. *Remember, nonverbal communication is just as important as verbal in expressing tenderness.*

Combine touch and words. Kiss him and tell him that you love him. You can also practice nonverbal speaking up by creating special projects that say things without words. On those occasions when my husband has an emergency patient and must work until 10 P.M. before having dinner, I hand him a strong scotch and water as he walks in the door. It is my way of saying, "I know how tired you must be—I care."

3. *Learn to fight to gain intimacy.* In the book *The Intimate Enemy* authors Dr. George R. Bach, founder and director of the Institute of Group Psychotherapy, Beverly Hills, California, and Peter Wyden, write, "When partners don't fight, they are not involved in an intimate relationship; honest intimates can't ignore their hostile feelings because such feelings are inevitable."

You can't have a mature relationship without having it out. The technique: speak up, find out what's the matter, and negotiate for realistic settlement of differences. The existence of conflict and airing of hostility don't signify lack of love. It is when neither love nor hate can move a partner ("I couldn't care less what he does") that the relationship deteriorates. Remember, a fight between intimates is not like a tennis game with strangers where there's only a short-term goal of quick victory. The only way to win an intimate confrontation is for both partners to win. You win by clearing the air, sharing feelings, finding a solution, gaining greater understanding.

A Good Fighting Guide

Make an appointment to fight. In this way you can organize your thoughts before the confrontation so that your argument will be cogent, the fight will confine itself to one issue instead of ricocheting all over the marital arena, and your partner will be able to come up with counterproposals. By setting an appointment you avoid the situation where you open fire when your partner is in an inappropriate frame of mind, about to leave on a long-distance business trip, or is finally getting down to some long-delayed chore. You should engage your partner just as soon as possible after an issue presents itself. With Herb I use the line, "There is something that bothers me—I'd like to talk to you about it right after dinner."

Prepare for a fight. Ask yourself questions:

- Should I really fight about this or that?
- How afraid am I of being rejected by my partner?
- Am I willing to be honest and tactful in this fight?
- How well will I tolerate the tensions of the fight?
- If my partner tries to duck it, will I give in?
- Am I sure that I have identified the real issue ("The way he put me down in front of my friends at the party on Saturday") and am not about to do battle about a trivial matter that really camouflages another, deeper grievance?
- Am I ready to follow up my beef with a specific demand for a change in the status quo ("I want you to get home in time for dinner and not stop off for two drinks at the Biltmore every night")?

Try to be "unisex" in your fighting. Men and women have different fighting styles, taught to them as children ("Boys don't cry" ... "Cry and then you can get him to do what you want him to do"). You don't have to use tears or "feminine wiles" as a fight tactic. These are excuses for not bringing conflicts out into the open. When women use tears during an intimate battle, it's a signal that they feel too abused, defeated, frustrated, or hurt to continue the battle. If you fight in a unisex way you make it harder for your partner to use his culturally induced stiff-upper-lip or strong, silent technique.

Set ground rules that allow for fair fighting.

● No physical violence.

● Each must provide information or there can be no settlement of differences.

● Both have to be ready to listen as well as talk.

● Each partner must doublecheck her/his interpretation of what the partner has said so that there is no misunderstanding ("Are you angry because I deserted you at the party or because someone else did something?").

● The fight should be about something your mate has done—not the kind of person he is. To attack with, "You are a horrible person" or, "You have an oedipal complex" won't change anything.

● Don't dismiss trivia as "not worth having a fight over." If you suppress all minor frustrations in the interests of domestic harmony, there is eventually bound to be a major explosion—perhaps over something far from trivial.

● Don't attack his Achilles heel. If your husband has lost his job, you don't say, "What kind of wage-earner are you?" It took me a long time to stop saying to Herb, "How could you have been so dumb as to have married that woman?" about his first wife.

Avoid uncontrolled fights. The pointless recurring fight that never gets anywhere . . . the "Vesuvius" where one partner steams over an issue that has nothing to do with the two of you . . . the fight where you fight over everything but the issue . . . the no-limit where you bring up every hurt and grievance that's on your mind. Also avoid lines like, "Get off my back" . . . "I love you but you don't know what love is" . . . "You don't love anybody but yourself" . . . "You don't know how to give, only to take." Do use lines like, "Come on, what's really eating you?" . . . "I do wish you wouldn't do————" . . . "You've got to stop ignoring me" . . . "It drives me crazy when you————."

Have an agenda for your fight.

● You state your beef and tell why it bothers you.

● Your partner gives feedback. He articulates what he thinks you're saying. If necessary, he corrects your statement to bring the issue into sharper focus and to launch a counter-offensive.

● More discussion. Then maybe an intermission that can last anywhere from an hour to a week.

● Resume the dialogue. You advance your own cause.

A good fight might go something like this: Situation: husband and wife go to bed, but he notices she seems rather withdrawn.

HE: What's eating you?

SHE: Some days ago I found a handkerchief with lipstick on it on your bureau. Then I thought of how many times you've been coming home late from the office recently. But I didn't say anything.

HE: But you were thinking things. You just brought it up so it obviously bothers you.

SHE: It did bother me because I know you had that affair three years ago.

HE: But it's your handkerchief. Look at it. You kissed me on the cheek when Ralph was coming for dinner the other night, and I wiped it off, took a new handkerchief, and left the stained one on the bureau.

SHE: You're right. (*Pause.*) I'm glad we can talk about things like this.

Being able to "talk like this" had brought it out into the open, kept the incident from festering and kept her from arguing about something that had no bearing on the incident.

Review the fight. After it's over, quiz yourself.

● What did I learn from the fight?

● Was I hurt badly?

● Did I hurt my partner?

● Was the fight valuable in that both he and I let off steam?

● Did the fight prove useful in revealing new information about me, my partner, and the issue in dispute?

● Am I satisfied with the conclusion?

With acquaintances, bosses, or dates, a bad fight can spell the end. But true intimates want to maintain a continuing relationship and rarely enjoy making their partners miserable for any length of time. With constructive fighting you stop playing games and move toward closeness and increased understanding.

Take Assertive Action to Improve the Decision-Making in Your Marriage

Many marital problems arise over day-by-day decisions in every area from social life to sex. Sometimes you feel you have to decide everything. One woman told me, "My husband can't make decisions. I make them all and feel domineering." You may feel you don't get a chance to make any decisions. Another woman said, "My husband takes the responsibility for everything."

You may have been so conditioned that you automatically make all decisions in the areas that are supposedly "feminine." For example, when Herb and I were about to get married, we signed a lease on an apartment which we took "as is," meaning we assumed responsibility for painting, rewiring, and any structural changes necessary to make it function as a combined office-home. Brought up to believe that the house is "a woman's responsibility," I took over. I did fine with the merging of two sets of furniture and the paint colors, but made a complete mess of the plumbing and wiring.

Herb asked, "Why are you doing everything?"

I explained, "I'm *supposed* to handle everything."

He said, "You're forgetting that there are two of us. Obviously, you can't handle the plumbing and electricity. Stay out of those areas. I'll make the decisions there."

There *are* two of you. You want to find a way to make decisions in a way that satisfies both of you.

1. *Evaluate the way you currently make decisions in your marriage.*

DECISION-MAKING EXERCISE I—EVALUATION QUIZ

STEP ONE: In FAN fill out the following chart,* reprinted from the *Marital Pre-Counseling Inventory* by Dr. Richard B. and Freida Stuart. Your partner should also fill out the form separately.

*Copyright © 1973 by Richard B. and Freida Stuart, Behavior Change Systems.

The following questions relate to the way in which important decisions are made in your family. Please be certain to answer every part of both questions.

1. In your family, whose responsibility do you think it usually is now to make decisions in each of the following areas? Please answer by drawing a circle around the appropriate alternative.

	Almost always husband		Shared equally		Almost always wife	Does not apply
a. Where couple lives	1	2	3	4	5	—
b. What job husband takes	1	2	3	4	5	—
c. How many hours husband works	1	2	3	4	5	—
d. Whether wife works	1	2	3	4	5	—
e. What job wife takes	1	2	3	4	5	—
f. How many hours wife works	1	2	3	4	5	—
g. Number of children	1	2	3	4	5	—
h. When to praise or punish children	1	2	3	4	5	—
i. How much time to spend with children	1	2	3	4	5	—
j. When to have social contacts with in-laws	1	2	3	4	5	—
k. When to have social contacts with friends and relatives	1	2	3	4	5	—
l. When to have sex	1	2	3	4	5	—
m. How to have sex	1	2	3	4	5	—
n. How to spend money	1	2	3	4	5	—
o. How and when to pursue personal interests	1	2	3	4	5	—
p. Whether, and if so, which church to attend	1	2	3	4	5	—

2. Now please look back over the way in which you think decisions are now made in your family. Use an X to indicate how you think decisions should be made in your family.

STEP TWO: Compare forms and discuss.

STEP THREE: Choose an area to work on. This should be one where you have the greatest chance of succeeding. This will spur further success. Then move on to another area.

2. *Practice making decisions.* In this way you'll learn your hang-ups and weaknesses.

DECISION-MAKING EXERCISE II—THE MOON GAME

STEP ONE: Pretend you are an astronaut. You are a member of a space crew originally scheduled to rendezvous with a mother ship on the lighted surface on the moon. Due to mechanical difficulties, however, your ship was forced to land at a spot some two hundred miles from the rendezvous point. During landing, much of the equipment aboard was damaged and, since survival depends on reaching the mother ship, the most critical items available must be chosen for the two-hundred-mile trip. Below are listed the fifteen items left intact and undamaged after landing. Your task is to rank them in terms of their importance for your crew in allowing them to reach the rendezvous point. Place the number 1 by the most important, and so on through 15 (the least important). Also, put the reason why in the space headed "Reason."

Reason	Items	Rank
_____	Box of matches	_____
_____	Food concentrate	_____
_____	Fifty feet of nylon rope	_____
_____	Parachute silk	_____
_____	Portable heating unit	_____
_____	Two .45-caliber pistols	_____
_____	One case dehydrated Pet milk	_____
_____	Two 100-lb. tanks of oxygen	_____
_____	Stellar map (of moon's constellation)	_____
_____	Life raft	_____
_____	Magnetic compass	_____
_____	Five gallons of water	_____
_____	Signal flares	_____
_____	First-aid kit containing injection needles	_____
_____	Solar-powered FM receiver-transmitter	_____

STEP TWO: Your husband should do the same thing, independently, rating his priorities in the same way. Allow fifteen minutes for each of you to complete the task.

STEP THREE: Sit down together and discuss your respective lists. It helps if you tape-record your discussion. Then come up with one list. In your discussion guard against viewing differences of opinion as a hindrance rather than a help in your decision-making.

STEP FOUR: Look at the answer sheet in Appendix II of this book for the sample answers.*

To illustrate the efficacy of the "Moon Game" as a decision-making technique, Dr. Barry Lubetkin of the Institute for Behavior Therapy, New York, tells the story of Mary, a twenty-four-year-old teacher, and Bob, a twenty-eight-year-old graduate student, who had problems communicating about decisions. When she had to decide anything, Mary would be indirect, often whimper, play her "little-girl" routine. Then Bob would become demanding and domineering, and Mary would resent this.

When they played the "Moon Game" in Dr. Lubetkin's office, Mary followed the same routine she always used. As they tried to agree on items to take along with them she used lines like, "Oh, you know much more about mechanics than I do" ... "You're so much better at games" ... "Men are astronauts anyway." On the few occasions when she did make a decisive statement, she followed it with a laugh.

Dr. Lubetkin taped the session. Mary and Bob listened to the playback. As a result of this one session, Mary realized how she defeated getting her own preferences by laughing and ceding to Bob the power of decisions he didn't really want to make on his own. She put him in the position of saying, "I know better." When she finally protested, it was too late. She felt angry, but she had already signaled him he could take the power role.

On their own at home Mary and Bob kept playing different versions of the "Moon Game." When Mary would go back to her old tricks of pouting, lowering her head, and saying,

*Special permission for reproduction of the "Moon Game" is granted by the author, Jay Hall, Ph.D., and publisher, Teleometrics International. All rights reserved.

"You know better" over decisions about money and entertainment, Bob would remind her, "Remember what we learned from the 'Moon Game.' "

Says Dr. Lubetkin, "The 'Moon Game' was important because it gave them feedback and illustrated to them the way in which they could work out all-important household decisions together. Mary is typical of many women who often hold back and let the man take the lead. The 'Moon Game' can be important in Assertiveness Training because through it many women learn how indirect they are and come to realize how counterproductive this indirectness is to their needs."

3. *Try a marriage contract as a decision-making aid.* More and more couples are discovering that modern marriage contracts, as yet nonlegal, that detail caveats of communication, division of labor, and what will happen in case of divorce serve a twofold purpose: (a) by spelling out possible areas of difficulty, they act as a "preventive tool"; (b) they help couples of all ages overcome their problems about decisions.

More and more these contracts are finding increasing use—by newlyweds, nearly-weds, long-term marrieds, and unmarried couples living together. They run the gamut in length and provisions. Some are thirteen-page documents, including everything from rights, expectations and limitations to sexual, financial, household and parental responsibilities. Others consist of a terse vow that at the end of five years "We will remarry with a new set of vows." Some take the form of promissory notes ("I promise to send you through graduate school"). And some people simply make verbal contracts.

Even though these modern marriage contracts will not stand up in court in most states (though legislation is pending), the very act of drawing them up has its own benefits, making people think things through, clearing up possible areas of conflicts in expectations, enabling couples to deal with changes in themselves through renegotiation, and affecting children through new definitions of roles.

HOW TO WRITE A MARITAL DECISION CONTRACT

Think through your statement of intention and the areas you want to cover, individually at first, then draft the final form in tandem. Your areas might include:

1. Provisions over where to live, whether or not to have a child or children, the education of the children, whether or not to use birth control, what kind, who uses it. What happens if the wife gets a good job offer she wants to take that requires moving to another city? If remarried, does the stepparent have the right to make decisions over the children or does only the biological parent have this right?

2. Household responsibilities and division of labor. Some couples alternate division of household tasks on a monthly basis, others do the chores each likes to do.

3. Social interaction—relationships with in-laws and friends.

4. Use of time. One couple contracted for ME time (to do things alone), YOU time (giving it to the partner when he/she needs it), and US time (doing things together).

5. The wife's right to use her maiden name. If she does, what name will the children bear? Sandi Gelles married Dennis Cole and took the name Sandi Gelles-Cole. Their contract specifies their children will use the last name Gelles-Cole. When lawyer Marc Fastau married feminist attorney Brenda Feigen, he combined his name with hers to create their new name Feigen Fastau.

6. Financial arrangements over present property, earnings, savings, expenses. Some couples agree that all property "gained once the marriage is licensed shall be considered community property," thus insuring that a non-wage-earning partner will have an equal share in family income. Others prorate expenses according to respective incomes. Others pay expenses from pooled incomes and divide any surplus.

7. Sexual exclusivity—or not. Many contracts opt for monogamy. Others spell out that "sexual freedom heightens the relationship."

Whatever decisions you put in your contract, be sure to set times to renew, reevaluate, amend, and possibly renegotiate it. Many couples do this yearly over anniversary champagne.

Choose Specific Behaviors for Change

Concentrate on actions you like, not actions you don't like. Remember, you want to change the relationship from one where the thrust is to keep unpleasant things from happening to one *where each of you attempts to please the other.*

• Identify the behaviors you must change to improve your relationship.

• Start a specific program to acquire the behaviors you want to acquire.

• Realize that the only way to get your mate to change is to change your behavior to him. You do not say, "He should be different." You do say, "What am I doing to make him act the way he does?"

• Remember that Assertiveness Training does not concentrate on the *why* of what you want—for instance, a loving kiss from your husband when he walks in the door at night. You don't have to try to probe whether this kiss serves as a symbolic means of attaining the affection you failed to receive from a parent. Instead you just accept the fact that you crave the kiss; it has meaning to you, and that in return you are willing to do something that has meaning for your mate.

According to Dr. Richard B. Stuart, "If you change your behavior, your spouse will change. Then your thoughts and feelings will change. Behavior change is the technique through which thoughts and feelings change. That is the ultimate goal."

1. *Pay attention to the behaviors you want to increase.* The following exercise, adapted from Dr. Richard B. and Freida Stuart's *Marital Pre-Counseling Inventory*, may help get you started.

MARITAL CHANGE PROGRAM

STEP ONE: Fill out the following three forms in FAN.

a. Please list three things you would like your spouse to do *more often.* In answering this question and the next two, please be specific and positive. For example, write "During dinner ask me how I spent the day" instead of "Be less preoccupied with yourself during the time we are together" (vague and negative). In answering this, think through the importance of each thing to you and also note how often your spouse did each of these things in the last week.

1._____   It was done   Do you consider it:
            _____ times in   ___very important
            the last week   ___important
                                    ___not too important
2._____   It was done   Do you consider it:
            _____ times in   ___very important
            the last week   ___important
                                    ___not too important
3._____   It was done   Do you consider it:
            _____ times in   ___very important
            the last week   ___important
                                    ___not too important

b. Please list three things which your spouse would like you to do more often, again being specific and positive. How often have you done each of these in the last week?

1._____   I did it _____   My spouse asked me
            times in the last   to do this ___ times
            week   in the last week
2._____   I did it _____   My spouse asked me
            times in the last   to do this ___ times
            week   in the last week
3._____   I did it _____   My spouse asked me
            times in the last   to do this ___ times
            week   in the last week

c. Please indicate aspects of your own behavior you would like to change.

1. _____
2. _____
3. _____

STEP TWO: Your spouse fills out the same forms.

STEP THREE: You and your mate exchange lists. Each of you explains what you mean by each item. For example, when Herb and I discussed the item on his list, "When I cook, pay attention to whether my trout baked in sherry is good rather than to wondering why I took so long to cook it," he said to me, "You don't recognize the fact that I have a different style from you. I like to take a long time in the kitchen. It's relaxing."

Note: The items on each list should be things the partner can reasonably be expected to do, and isn't dead set against doing (for instance, when Herb and I do a joint writing project, he refuses to type and insists on writing in longhand. I've given up on the possibility of that behavior change). Discuss any disagreements. If your partner absolutely refuses to do one specific thing, substitute another.

STEP FOUR: Each of you should keep count of how often *the other* performs the desired behaviors. For instance, you want your mate to "talk to me about me for a half hour every day." Every time he does, put a check next to that item on the list. Or use a graph. At preset times, perhaps just before going to bed, communicate the count to each other, discussing each episode and your reaction to it. In this way you work toward getting the behaviors that please your partner, and he works toward the behaviors that please you.

This AT technique really works.

CASE

I have a close friend, Anne Summers, who all her life has felt unjustifiably insecure about money. She is the mother of two teen-age boys and has been married for seventeen years to Peter, a highly successful business executive, but Peter and Anne have grown increasingly apart. Caught up in her own neurotic fantasies about "being poor someday," she concentrates most of her waking hours primarily on saving pennies. She has lost sight of the goal: to make a happy marriage. On his part, Peter has accepted a situation he basically doesn't want.

Recently Anne telephoned me from a pay phone. She sobbed hysterically, "I'm sure Peter wants a divorce." She was on the way to the bank to get all his bearer bonds out of the vault and put them in a new safe deposit box to which she alone had the key!

I said, "Anne, have you ever thought you might be doing something wrong? I'm sure Peter doesn't really want a divorce. Did he say so?"

In a weak voice, she answered, "He said he 'might want one someday.' "

Thinking of the Marital Change Program, I counseled, "Listen, I'm surprised he hasn't left you already. You give him hamburgers and canned peas every night for dinner. You talk only about the boys. And you never go out alone together. Now I want you to do just one thing as an assignment: You ask him to take you out to dinner."

She said, "He won't do it. He hates going out to dinner."

I said, "Do it. Say, 'I want to go out to dinner alone with you.' And when you go, don't talk about how much everything costs. And make your food choices from the top of the menu—not the bottom."

She agreed to give it a try. The next day she reported, "He was delighted. We're going to a new French restaurant on Friday night. Jean, you were so right. He said, 'I'd love to on one condition—you must promise not to talk about how expensive the food is.' "

They went. They had a good time. It was the first of several similar steps in the right direction. It worked because:

• Anne tested reality in a way that was meaningful to her. She found out that Peter didn't act the way she thought he'd act and that divorce wasn't really on his mind.

• For the first time in years she paid attention to what might please Peter and strangely enough found she enjoyed it too.

• She changed her thinking to "What can I do to make this marriage a little better?"

The uninitiated frequently wonder about such a formalized and programed approach to solving marital difficulties. They say, "It's so unromantic" or, "This way there's no spontaneity." But if you learn the skills of behavior change, spontaneity will develop. As the late Frederick (Fritz) Perls pointed out, "It's very peculiar that we become spontaneous only by utmost discipline."

2. *Ask yourself, "What do I do to reinforce the very behaviors in my husband that I don't want?"* Unknowingly many a woman sets up just the situation she doesn't want. Here are five examples that came up over and over in my Assertiveness Training for Women groups.

a. *Complaint*: "He's so distant."

Situation: You want your second husband to be of some help with your children from your previous marriage. But when he comes home and asks, "What happened with the kids today?" or, "Can I do something for the kids?" you respond, "That sounds so phony; don't say it if it's not from the heart" or, "I don't believe you mean that." Thus you reinforce his distance.

Right way: "I'd be glad of some help on————. This and that happened today." Thus you reinforce his interest.

b. *Complaint*: "He talks about his day. I never get a chance to talk about mine. I'm entitled to some courtesy too."

Situation: Every night your husband comes home from the office and true to that societal directive "talk about him," you start in with the questions: "How was your day?" ... "What did the boss say about your report?" ... "Did you have lunch with Joe?" You talk about what you think he wants to talk about, perhaps feeling "I'm not entitled to take talk time for me." Inwardly you resent that all the concentration is on him.

Right way: Practice self-revelation. Good opening line: "I had a hard day today. How was your day?" After he answers, tell what went wrong for you. In my AT groups almost all the women role-playing this situation constantly fed questions to their mates and never mentioned their own feelings. Say something about what you feel.

c. *Complaint*: "He won't help around the house."

Situation: You both work. One day your husband scrubs the kitchen floor and comments, "Someone has to do it." You reply, "You don't do it very well" or, "I know I'm a bad housekeeper." With the first sentence you patronize and the second you go on the defensive. Neither encourages the behavior you want.

Right way: "Joe, I can't tell you how much I appreciate your doing this. It's such a help."

d. *Complaint*: "He never wants to visit my family."

Situation: You want to visit your parents but you're sure your husband doesn't want to go. You discuss the matter in such a way that you virtually force him to say, "No, I won't go. I've had enough of your family."

Right way: Don't get caught up in this self-fulfilling prophecy. Just say directly, "It would mean a lot to me if we could visit my folks either this Sunday or next."

e. *Complaint*: "He never says nice things to me."

Situation: Your husband says, "I love you." You respond, "You can't really mean that because of the way you acted at the Joneses last night" and go off into a whole tirade about his "terrible social performance."

Right way: Return his tenderness with some of your own and hold off about the Joneses.

3. *Try a Behavior Exchange Contract.* In the Marital Decision Contract, you both contract to make certain mutually satisfying decisions. In the Behavior Exchange Contract, you contract for a change in certain specific unsatisfying behaviors to avoid the situation "I carry the whole burden and my mate gives me nothing in return."

RULES FOR BEHAVIOR EXCHANGE CONTRACTS

a. Each partner gets something he/she wants from the other. For instance, you contract "to wear a nice robe in the morning instead of that torn one." He agrees to "come home for dinner on time instead of drinking with the boys." You start with simple behaviors and progress to more complex ("She should initiate more sex" ... "He should kiss me more").

b. Each of you must be willing to accept the specific responsibility in return for the specific reward.

c. Try to exchange behaviors that are positive (again, stress the behaviors you want to increase rather than those you want to decrease), specific, and countable ("I will spend all day Sunday with you," not, "I will spend more time with you").

d. Whenever possible, keep track of the target behavior with graphs, charts, points, or tokens.

e. Avoid disagreements about the contract by writing it out. Keep it in a spot where you both can see it easily. Many couples put it on the refrigerator or bedroom door. When you effect one Behavior Exchange Contract to your mutual satisfaction, go on to another.

CASE

Dr. Herbert Fensterheim told me of the following case, involving Lenore and Alan White, a childless couple in their thirties, who felt their marriage was growing emptier and emptier. Both of them wanted to do something about it and also to stop their respective extramarital affairs. The core of the difficulty seemed to be that while Lenore and Alan were both highly verbal people and always discussed work, politics and ideas, they rarely talked about feelings. Even their sexual interaction was mechanical.

In working out a Behavior Exchange Contract with Dr. Fensterheim, they zeroed in on exchange of feeling expressions and personal communication. Their assignment:

One partner would have to use I-Talk expressions ("I like what you said" . . . "I don't like what you said"; "I like what you did" . . . "I don't like what you did"; "I want you to . . ."; "I don't want you to . . .") for two weeks. During that time the other partner would have to tell three stories each night: (a) a sexual fantasy (even if he/she had to make it up on the spur of the moment); (b) a personal reminiscence of something meaningful that had happened during the growing-up years; and (c) one experience, preferably current, where he/she had strong feelings about someone with whom he was in contact.

Lenore took the I-Talk assignment for the first two weeks while Alan took the stories. At the end of two weeks they switched.

They taped their conversations and brought them to Dr. Fensterheim's office for replay. Then both Dr. Fensterheim and the other partner would offer counsel: "You could have elaborated on that story" . . . "Notice how many feeling verbs you used," etc.

At home Lenore and Alan started coaching each other. Alan told Lenore, "That would have been the perfect opportunity to say, 'I like what you said.' " And when Alan had trouble thinking up stories, Lenore would say, "You once mentioned you were on the track team in high school. Did anything happen there?" Thus she helped him recall a story he could share. When he had particular difficulty coming up with sexual fantasies, one day she brought home a batch of magazines like *Playboy* to help trigger him.

Says Dr. Fensterheim, "This went on for two months and at the end of that time there was a definite loosening up. The extramarital affairs stopped. Before they were wondering 'Where is this relationship going?' Now they knew they were on the right track."

Guard Against Falling into Certain Traps in the Close Relationship

1. *Don't feel guilty as you start to change.* Women have been so conditioned to play the patsy-martyr role that when they do start acting more assertively the marital relationship improves, but they react, "I really shouldn't speak up so freely" ... "My mother would turn over in her grave if she knew Joe cooks all our weekend meals" ... "My husband says it's fine if I go to work and put the kids in a day-care center, but none of my neighbors work. What will they think of me?" It's what you think of yourself that counts. If you operate on guilt, it's self-defeating.

2. *Watch out for the Compassion Trap.* Women in the Compassion Trap always place more emphasis on other people's needs than their own. The assertive woman feels free to act on her own behalf. She chooses when to be compassionate.

Do you see yourself as a Red Cross nurse on twenty-four-hour duty? Do you feel you must always be compassionate? Would you like to get out of the Compassion Trap?

In the close relationship you do not have to:

- Exist only to serve your husband.
- Be the one that bears all the responsibility for his sick relatives.
- Take sole responsibility for "keeping the family together."
- Confine yourself to the *Kinder, Küche, Kirche* (children, kitchen, church) role advocated by Hitler in Nazi Germany and still firmly rooted in the minds of many women.

• Always push aside your own creative work to take care of someone else. For instance, for years my husband used to ask me to "take care of the wife" when a male professional colleague came visiting. I must have seen the Empire State Building thirty times. But recently when I was on deadline for an article, I asserted myself to Herb with, "Look, I'm busy. I don't ask you to take the husbands of my out-of-town friends sightseeing." He saw the point and the particular wife involved on this occasion had a very good time lunching with an old school friend.

If you want to do these things, you do them through choice, not dictatorship.

Writes Margaret Adams in her article "The Compassion Trap" in *Woman in Sexist Society: Studies in Power and Powerlessness*, "The primary imperative for women who intend to assume a meaningful and decisive role in today's social change is to begin to perceive themselves as having an identity and personal integrity that has as strong a claim for being preserved intact as that of any other individual or group. This attitude will require women to develop an explicit sense of the value of their own concerns and, at times, to insist that they take precedence. It will also compel them to abandon the role of compassionate sibyl at everyone's beck and call, because being permanently available to other people's needs hinders women from pursuing their chosen avocations with the steadfast concentration that is essential to their successful completion."

3. *Don't be litigants.* Many couples are like two lawyers in court. They give lists of what the other has done wrong with all sorts of evidence, involving themselves in argument and counterargument with the goal of proving "I'm right and you're wrong." As lawsuits often do, this adversary relationship leads to antagonism and bad feelings. You become sensitive to what's wrong with your adversary and not what's right. You lose sight of what you can do differently. You spend a lot of energy in terms of winning and losing at the expense of communication.

4. *Don't have the erroneous idea that by being assertive you will always win.* Your husband has the right to be assertive too. For example, my husband refuses to have one particular friend of mine in the house. She is a friend from

grade-school days. I like her. He detests her. I have spoken up most feelingly about this, but he still says, "Have her—only I won't be here."

Sometimes you may lose in the whole relationship. Often there are hopeless situations. According to Dr. Alan Goldstein of Temple University School of Medicine, "Marriages are no longer made in heaven. Sometimes it's better to cut the cord. You may have to say to yourself, 'Look, I'm entitled to a better place.' Sometimes optimizing the life experience may be better than patching it up."

5. *Don't think that it's always assertive to speak up in the close relationship. Sometimes real assertiveness is saying nothing.* Recently "our ex-wife" brought a court action against my husband. I felt the whole thing was so unfair (particularly since it involved a subpoena regarding all financial records on a book which *I* had initiated, sold, and which we had written *together*) that I was literally like *The Madwoman of Chaillot* with rage. For weeks before the hearing I planned what I would say ("Judge, I get up at 5:45 A.M. to work so that his minor child can go to private school. Have you asked *her* what time she gets up?"). In my fantasies I imagined myself addressing the packed courtroom, and at the end of my moving oration, the entire audience would break into wild applause. I also had more aggressive fantasies—for example, one in which she slid into a manhole filled with bubbling hot oil. I kept all this up until Herb told me, "Stop acting like Bette Davis in a 1940 movie. You're not the star here."

The hearing began. We spent two days in court. I made a brief appearance in which my knees knocked so loudly that they could have been heard on the West Coast. I guess I must have been pretty good; her lawyer waived cross-examination. At the conclusion of the second day, our lawyer, at the suggestion of the judge, moved that Herb be allowed to see his daughter Ann, whom he had seen only once in five years. Ann was ordered to appear in court the next day.

That night we went out for dinner. Everything in me wanted to sound off—about the humiliation of having to appear in court (it turned out to be a tiny chamber, not a vast, packed courtroom), to boast, "Boy, you sure are lucky to have married me. She wouldn't do what I do." But I saw his face—so dear, troubled, worn, nervous about what would happen the next day. I took a deep breath and said, "Herb, I know what you're going through. Now, let's not talk about the court case tonight." And I forced myself to be entertaining.

The next morning as he prepared to go off to Family Court, I again wanted to make cracks but held back, saying simply, "Good luck. No matter what happens, I'm with you." Much as I wanted to, I did not go with him, feeling he would be freer without my tense presence.

Three hours later Herb burst into the house, exulting, "I'm seeing Ann next Saturday. The judge ordered it. That's all I care about." Then he put his arms around me and said tenderly, "You helped so much last night and this morning, Jean. I was able to speak very freely and feelingly to the judge about Ann today because you were so feeling and understanding with me."

I felt so good. By keeping my big mouth shut, I had behaved in a really assertive way. I had *chosen* to keep quiet. Suddenly all my aggressive and hostile feelings toward his ex lessened, and I felt freer to be a warm and loving second wife. I didn't have to play Bette Davis any more.

Chapter 9

The Sexually Assertive Woman

Just as you can learn to make the assertive social request "I want to go out to dinner tonight," you can learn to communicate your desires in the sexual area. Good sex may be only part of the good life, but it is far too important for any woman to wait for it to happen.

But many women *do* "wait for it to happen." Why?

Societal brainwashing has had a severe effect in the sexual area. Many women still believe the "old wives' tales" and taboos: "Masturbation is bad" ... "Men need more sex than women" ... "It's the woman's fault if the man is impotent" ... "Grin and bear it" ... "Sex is a woman's duty."

Says Dr. Beverly Hotchner, executive director of the Center for Human Concerns, a sexuality resource center in St. Louis, Missouri, "Women are now at the stage of talking more openly about sex, but for most of them things haven't changed. Women are trained from Day One to be passive. The early injunctions are so potent and pervasive that it's difficult for women to have different behaviors as adults."

Some women feel they don't have the right to sexual pleasure—that's a male prerogative. They are brought up to be pleasing, to stifle their own wants. Asking for what they

214

need in bed would be "unbearably selfish and "unladylike." So they spend years suppressing desires and faking orgasms to make their partners "happy." Meanwhile this pretense makes them angry, and inner resentment builds until it stifles their ability to relax during sex.

According to Dr. Helen Kaplan, clinical associate professor of psychiatry, Cornell University Medical College, and head, Sex Therapy and Education, Payne Whitney Clinic, The New York Hospital, "The woman who enjoys sex has always been looked down on. Women are considered whores if they get pleasure from sex. Yes, the cultural climate is changing and today many very young girls are at ease with their own sexuality—but many more women still are not."

Says Dr. Alan Goldstein, associate professor of psychology and psychiatry at Temple University School of Medicine, "Despite the so-called 'new morality,' the societal pressures are still there. The woman's role isn't like the man's—she isn't encouraged to sow her wild oats. Many women still feel they should be nonsexual in their actions. Studies show that men reach their sexual peak in their late teens and early twenties and that women don't reach it until their thirties. I'm not sure this is physiological. To overcome their early 'hold back' conditioning, women have to go through years of positive conditioning."

Other women don't communicate their real desires to their partners because they automatically assume there's no need to do so. Because they have the partner's erection to guide them during lovemaking, they make the mistake of thinking he is as aware of their state of arousal as they are of his. Neither realizes that, in contrast to the male, the female's responses are largely "cryptic and internal." They mistakenly depend on the male to orchestrate lovemaking—and then feel angry when he proceeds solely on the basis of his own cues, not realizing that his apparent indifference to her needs stems from ignorance rather than callousness.

As Masters and Johnson have said, "The most unfortunate misconception our culture has assigned to sexual functioning is the assumption by both men and women that men by divine guidance and infallible instinct are able to discern exactly what a woman wants sexually and when she wants it.

Probably this fallacy has interfered with natural sexual interaction as much as any other single factor."

Some women suffer from one, some, or all of a series of fears.

SEXUAL FEARS

Fear of hurting him. If you say or do anything that appears critical, you'll hurt that tender male ego. And you can't do that. "Better to suffer in silence," you rationalize.

Fear of being thought unfeminine or aggressive. You think you'll end up in the "bitch" category if you make such statements as, "You do not always satisfy me sexually" or, "There's something you do that bothers me."

Fear of rejection. For example, if you delay your partner's ejaculation by asking him to prolong foreplay or make him "work" by indicating you want to be stimulated clitorally or if you do not reach orgasm on coitus and *let him know,* you will be compared to others who don't make such "excessive" demands and will be rejected in favor of a more generous and less bold partner.

Comments Dr. Kaplan, "Women who fear rejection may find it less anxiety-provoking to suppress their own sexual needs and wishes, to simulate arousal, to *silently* and passively let the man retain full control of sex. It's safer to signal the end of foreplay when she senses *he* is ready for intercourse, or when she feels *he* is getting impatient and tired of waiting for her to become sufficiently excited or when *he* signals that his sexual urge is compelling. On the other hand, this type of transaction is not likely to result in her own sexual fulfillment."

Fear of total abandonment. If you give yourself completely, you really make a commitment. Some women can't do this. For example, Dr. S., a thirty-eight-year-old physician and his twenty-nine-year-old wife had been married for three years and had one child. They came to see Dr. Kaplan because of Mrs. S.'s growing reluctance to have intercourse. It turned out that although she seemed to attach great importance to her family, actually she was in conflict about her commitment to the marriage. To her, marriage represented a kind of bondage. In return for being taken care of financially, she felt she had to "service" her husband, devote herself to his well-being and give up any active creative goals of her own. Unconsciously she viewed total abandonment as a final surrender of her rights as an individual.

In the course of treatment Mrs. S. was able to make the decision to improve her sex life which she no longer equated with a lifelong irrevocable commitment to the "bondage" of matrimony. The couple worked out a mutually arousing and satisfactory style of lovemaking and Mrs. S. was able to resolve the conflict between her need to be independent and her desire for a close relationship—she enrolled in graduate school and hopes ultimately to embark on an academic career.

Fear of competition. If you have a desirable man and a fulfilling sex life, other women will try to hurt you, to take him from you. Thus, you reason you "mustn't have this good life so that this dreadful thing will not happen." Often this irrational belief is purely a rationalization for doing the things you've been trained to do.

Says Dr. Kaplan, "Even today sex is still associated with shame or danger, and this association has had a much stronger adverse effect on female than on male sexual behavior. Thus, women who have been taught from an early age to consider compliance and passivity a virtue are likely to react to their impulses to assume a more active role in sex with guilt and shame. Men, on the other hand, do not usually fear rejection and censure if they actively seek out sexual stimulation and pleasure; on the contrary, such behavior is considered a sign of virility."

What are the characteristics of the sexually assertive woman?

• She knows her own body. She understands it well enough to know her sexual wants.

• She is comfortable with her own body. This doesn't mean you have to be twenty-one years old or possess 34-24-34 proportions. It does mean you feel proud and confident about your appearance. You *know* men find you attractive. Says Dr. Kaplan, "People's emotions are transmitted. A man can tell if a woman feels sexy."

• She takes responsibility for her own sexual well-being. She feels the gratification of her own desires is just as important as the pleasure of her partner. Says Dr. Kaplan, "Women have had the feeling for so long that a man must be the aggressor. But if a woman and man don't have sexual autonomy, there are bound to be sexual problems. It's important for a woman to become more important in the sexual act, to learn to communicate her own needs in a gentle and nondefensive manner. A man with self-esteem will enjoy a woman who wants to participate and not just lie there like a vase. The idea that a man should have sex out of the house and the woman should cook and bake is out of date."

• She is not bound by the sexual dictates of her parents, relatives, friends, culture. She believes, "If it makes me feel good and I like myself for doing it, it is O.K."

• She can communicate her desires to her partner— gently, openly, appropriately, and in a nondefensive manner.

• She is willing to take risks—of judgment, criticism, possible rejection. She is always willing to try new things that may make her a more sensual person and provide increased fulfillment.

How can you apply the principles of Assertiveness Training to your own sex life?

A PROGRAM FOR THE SEXUALLY ASSERTIVE WOMAN

Take Your Sexual History

However you now feel about sex, the sexual values that you have come from a multiplicity of life experiences. The following questions are designed to enable you to know yourself. Fill in the answers in your Female Assertiveness Notebook. This will take thought and honesty.

SEXUAL HISTORY QUESTIONNAIRE

1. How did your parents relate to each other?
2. How do you feel your parents got along sexually?

3. What attitudes about sex did your parents communicate to you?

—Were your questions about sex answered freely?

—Were you brought up to "Look pretty" ... Don't get sexually involved" ... "Keep the guys from taking advantage of you" ... "Lead them on to marriage"?

4. Do you recall playing any sex games as a child? If so, were you ever punished for this?

5. At what age did you first experiment with masturbation or with any kind of solitary activity which produced a "genital" feeling of pleasure?

6. When did you start to menstruate?

—Did you consider the onset of menses as something to be anticipated or dreaded?

7. What is your first explicit sexual memory?

8. Where did you first learn about sexual intercourse and what were your feelings about it?

9. Where did you first absorb "appropriate" sexual behavior for men and women?

10. Where did your first sexual experience occur?

11. Have you ever experienced orgasm? Yes——No—— —Under what conditions?

12. Do you think it's acceptable for the female to initiate sex play? Yes—— No——

13. Do you think it's acceptable for *you* to initiate sex play? Yes—— No——

14. When you have sexual intercourse, do you always expect to have an orgasm? If not, how do you feel when you don't?

15. If married, what were your expectations regarding sex, lovemaking, intercourse, etc., before marriage?

—Were these expectations fulfilled during the first year of marriage?

—If not, describe.

16. Are you satisfied with the frequency of your orgasm? Yes—— No——

17. Are you satisfied with the frequency of your partner's orgasm? Yes—— No——

18. Does your partner often desire sexual activity when *you* do not? Yes—— No——

19. Do you often desire sexual activity when your partner does not? Yes—— No——

20. When you are not sexually aroused, do you act as if you are to please your partner? Yes—— No——

21. Do you tell your partner or lover what pleases you most sexually? Yes—— No—— What displeases you? Yes—— No——

22. Do you feel comfortable undressing in front of your partner? Yes—— No——

23. Who usually chooses the time for lovemaking? Are you content with this?

24. Which of the following represent your most frequent reasons for using body contact?
—Affection or desire for affection
—The need to be "recognized" by partner
—The desire for reassurance
—Solace or comfort
—The feeling of belonging
—Sexual gratification

25. How do you react when your expressed desire for body contact is ignored?

26. What are your favorite ways of masturbating? Do any of them make you feel guilty?

27. Which aspects of your sex life would you change?
—Increase frequency of intercourse
—Enjoy more of the things your partner enjoys
—Increase ability to achieve orgasm
—Increase ability of partner to delay orgasm
—Variety (position, time of day, etc.)

28. Let the following be a scale of desire: 1 2 3 4 5 6 7 8 9 10 (much desire). Where do you think you fit?

29. What is the current state of your feelings toward your partner?

30. If you don't have a current partner, do you feel a sense of worthlessness?

31. Do you feel attractive at this point in your life? Yes—— No——

32. Do you have sexual fantasies that you would like to put into action? Yes—— No—— Do you put them into action? Yes—— No——

33. Have your sexual attitudes changed in recent years? How?

Taking this quiz should enable you to think through your current attitudes about sex and see how past influences contributed to them, assess your pleasures and displeasures about sex, and help you judge your sexual assertiveness. The quiz should also help you to set sexual goals.

Get Information About Sex

To achieve fulfillment you must have sexual knowledge. Some women just don't realize how little they know. Others have highly rigid ideas about what is normal and allowable.

1. *Read.* The emergence of new data has completely changed certain sexual concepts. By reading you'll learn that masturbation, which used to be regarded as a neurotic and guilt-producing activity, is now seen as the first step to better sex ... that there aren't two kinds of orgasm—that all orgasms stem from the clitoris ... that all women are capable of orgasm provided they are not suffering from "a serious neurological, endocrinological, or gynecological disease which has destroyed the physical basis for orgasm" . . . that with two consenting adults there is no such thing as "abnormal" sex. It's "normal" if you both choose to experience whatever act it is and the act doesn't become compulsive or get out of control.

Many excellent books exist. To expand your sex life, read *Woman's Orgasm* by Georgia Kline-Graber and Benjamin Graber, *The Joy of Sex* by Alex Comfort, and *Sexual Stimulation* by S. G. Tuffill. For dysfunctions, read *The New Sex Therapy* and *The Illustrated Manual of Sex Therapy* by Helen Singer Kaplan and *Human Sexual Inadequacy* by William H. Masters and Virginia E. Johnson.

2. *Talk to other women.* This has two advantages: (a) you may hear more of those old wives' tales but you may also gain new knowledge; (b) the very tradition of women's sexual oppression may enable you, once you start doing it, to speak up more honestly about your sexual feelings—*you* don't have to pull the *machismo* routine that men feel they must. Because you can admit to ignorance and don't feel you have to be the female equivalent of Don Juan, you can share

your real feelings more openly and hopefully get some frank answers in return.

Think Through Your Sexual Bill of Rights

Before you can take effective action, you have to know what you want. What do you feel are your sexual rights? Some typical ones:

- I have the right to understand my body.
- I have the right to orgasm.
- I have the right to enjoy sex whether I have an orgasm or not.
- I have the right to refuse sex when I'm not in the mood.
- I have the right to ask for things more than actual sex (like tenderness or love talk).
- I have the right to get involved for the sake of emotion.
- I don't have to go to bed with everyone.
- I have the right to express commitment.
- I have the right *not* to express commitment.
- I have a right to determine the conditions of sex (time, place, etc.).
- I have a right to ask for what I want and if I don't get it, to say how that makes me feel.
- I have the right to be treated like a mature woman—not a passive child or demanding female.

Using the above as a guide, work out your own sexual bill of rights. Write them down in FAN.

Says Dr. Beverly Hotchner, "Developing this sexual bill of rights gives you a support system. There are three rules. First, you work out your bill. Second, you must feel it—not just write it out or say it. Third, translate it into behavior."

You have the right to be assertive in the sexual area, just as you have the right to be socially assertive at a cocktail party, but knowing and acting upon your rights does not mean a "me first always" attitude. In a satisfactory sex relationship *a major right is the freedom to have the desire to please the other person. It becomes a problem when the pleasing is not a matter of choice—when you're forced to please him.*

Learn About Your Own Body

It's difficult to ask for what you want if you don't know what will make you feel good. You may have the attitude that "He's just using me for his own pleasure." In actuality, it may be that *your partner doesn't know what will give you pleasure because you don't.* Take the guesswork out. Get in touch with yourself. When all is said and done, men are turned on to women who are turned on to themselves.

A Sexual Enhancement Program

1. *Look at yourself nude in the mirror.* Regard your body as if you are seeing it for the very first time. What do you like? What don't you like? Think about your body and its effect on your life. Ask yourself, "Has my body made a difference in the way I have lived my life?"

2. *Run your fingers over your body from head to toe.* As you do this, what thoughts come to your mind? Nothing? A sense of self-consciousness? Pleasure? Does anything feel unfamiliar? Where would you like to linger? Try to catch all your thoughts and perhaps put them down on paper.

3. *Spend time walking around nude.* To learn to feel comfortable with yourself completely naked, give yourself one nudity assignment a day. You might start out by making the bed with no clothes on, then progress to spending a half hour daily reading a book while nude.

4. *Take a long, hot, luxurious bath.* As you lie in the tub, use your body—stretch out, arch your back, wiggle your toes. Pour your favorite body lotion (which you have previously iced in the refrigerator) over your breasts and abdomen. Close your eyes and massage it into your skin. As you do this, allow yourself to focus on a sexual fantasy. Let your imagination go.

5. *Practice using your pelvis.* Your pelvic area is the source of the movements and energy of your sex life. Proper use of your pelvis can increase sexual enjoyment for both you and your partner.

Pelvic exercise: Put on a record that has a fast "rock" beat. Kneel in front of a full-length mirror. Put your hands on your hips or stretch them out to your side, whichever feels more comfortable. Now, move your pelvis as if you were dancing to the beat, hitting first to the left, then to the right, or back and forth. Once you get control, you can do "bumps and grinds" with your pelvis just like a burlesque star.

6. *Take a hand mirror, lie down on the bed, and look at your genitals.* Arrange for privacy. Try to be alone in the house; if this is impossible, lock the bedroom door. Use a diagram of your "genital anatomy" (there is an excellent one on page 16 of *Woman's Orgasm* by Georgia Kline-Graber and Benjamin Graber), and carefully examine the clitoris, labia, vaginal opening, and perineum (the area between the vagina and rectum). How does this make you feel? Good? Guilty? Ashamed? Anxious? Repeat this procedure every day until you feel comfortable with it. You must be familiar with your anatomy before you can enjoy it.

7. *Do "Kegels."* The exercises, originally invented by the late Dr. Arnold Kegel, a California gynecologist, have the advantage of being able to be done lying down, sitting, standing, on the phone, at a bus stop, in a restaurant. Their purpose is to strengthen the muscles around the vagina. Dr. Kegel found that after doing them for a time, orgasmic women developed a greater capacity for orgasms, and his nonorgasmic patients began experiencing climax.

The primary muscle involved is the pubococcygeus (PC) that underlies the vaginal mucosa and which, when exercised, increases sensation in the vagina. To find the PC muscle, squeeze your buttocks together and draw the pelvic area in; the clenching sensation you feel is a PC contraction.

- Contract the PC muscle
- Hold for three seconds
- Relax for three seconds
- Squeeze again
- Do this in sets of ten three-second squeezes at three different times during the day. Build up to twenty three-second contractions, done, if possible, more than three times a day.

8. *Think and voice sensual thoughts.* The greatest sexual enhancement comes from freeing the mind. In the course of a day you can have many sexual thoughts, but most women

tend to close them out. Don't. Practice spinning sexual thoughts.

● When you go to the supermarket, don't think of it as an errand. Squeeze a tomato. Think how it feels—soft, round, succulent. What does it make you think of?

● Be a crotch-watcher. On the street, look at the men wearing tight knit slacks and zero in on the penis. Don't be like some women who take a glance and then avert their eyes.

Reading erotic books can spur new feelings of sensuality. You can seek them out on your own, but you might try *Lady Chatterley's Lover* and *Women in Love* by D. H. Lawrence, *My Life and Loves* by Frank Harris, *Fanny Hill* by John Cleland, *Crazy Ladies* by Joyce Elbert, *My Secret Garden* by Nancy Friday, the *Kama-Sutra* of Vatsayana, the founder of the Hindu, or crafty, school of sex.

9. *Masturbate.* I'm not going into a dissertation about the benefits of it, but in the newer sex therapies teaching a woman to masturbate often proves a major step to better sex. It's the most accurate way to learn about your own sensuality. Masturbation workouts will teach you what kind of manipulation in the clitoral area gives you the quickest and most satisfying response, what your multiple orgasm pattern is. (Must you stop for a minute before going on or are you able to continue manipulation and go immediately to the next orgasm?) You'll also learn how many orgasms you can have in a single session before tiring.

It is your choice to make the assertive decision about whether or not to masturbate, but you should consider how masturbation may help you to become more sexually assertive. You might read *For Yourself* by Lonnie Garfield Barbach and "The Role of Masturbation in the Treatment of Orgasmic Dysfunction" by Dr. Joseph LoPiccolo and W. Charles Lobitz in *Archives of Sexual Behavior*, Vol. 2, no. 2, 1972.

Identify the Specific Problems You and Your Partner Have in Communication and Do Something About Them

Says Dr. Kaplan, "Nowhere is open communication more important than in the sexual area. Nowhere is it harder to do. If you can communicate openly, many problems will disappear."

COMMUNICATION CUES

1. *Identify your fears about communication.* I pointed out some typical female fears earlier in this chapter. Do your fears concern your partner? Are you afraid that if you speak up in any way about your mutual sex life, he will judge you "unladylike"—or find someone else? Do your fears concern yourself? Would you feel "unfeminine" if you expressed a sexual need?

- Finish the sentence "I am afraid to say————." Can you imagine sharing this sentence with your partner?

- Take a page in your Female Assertiveness Notebook and write down a list of anything you have felt like saying or doing in the sexual area that you haven't done—for example, "You come too quick" or, "There are some new sexual techniques I'd like to try. I'd like to————." Then go over your list and for each item say to yourself, "If I had said that, my partner would have said . . ."

- Examine your fears to see if they are irrational (remember the irrational beliefs I discussed on pages 145ff. In Chapter 6). Try to substitute a rational belief for the "terrible" irrational one. For example:

Irrational belief: "If I say anything about our sex life, he will think of me as low, base, lewd, common, insatiable."

Rational belief: "If I say anything about our sex life, he will be very surprised because I've never spoken up about this before. He may not like it, but that will not destroy me."

Follow the techniques I outlined in Chapter 6 for disputing your irrational beliefs. Why must the consequences be so terrible? By disputing the irrational belief and substituting a rational one, you will feel less anxious.

2. *Use the nonverbal approach to communication.* If you have trouble articulating what you want, show him. One couple, who were married for fifteen years and who had a "good loving relationship," came to see Dr. Barbara Hogan, a New York psychologist on the faculty of the Mount Sinai School of Medicine. There were two problems: (a) the wife was getting turned off by sex and (b) the husband had premature ejaculation. The frequency of their sex was diminishing. Because she feared rejection, the wife was very self-conscious about saying what she wanted—which was oral sex. She was afraid to say the words. So Dr. Hogan encouraged her to guide her husband nonverbally. This she did. During their next lovemaking Mrs. Jones pulled her husband's head down. Both enjoyed the experience, something she had craved during those fifteen years of matrimony but had always been afraid to ask for.

3. *Metacommunicate.* This psychological term means "talk about talking." This technique can overcome shyness and get you started talking about sex. For example, you say, "Look, every time we get started talking about sex, both of us get embarrassed and we get off on all sorts of tangents. So, let's not discuss sex. Let's talk about why we have so much trouble talking about sex. I guess I do because my mother told me a woman should never discuss the subject. But you're a man. You weren't brainwashed. Why do you have trouble?"

4. *Practice gradualism.* Don't start off talking about a big sexual problem ("You don't satisfy me") where you feel any discussion will create enormous tension. Build up to it gradually. You might start by talking about sex in general. Then you might discuss any sexual difficulties you feel you might have. This sort of self-revelation about your own problems might relieve some of your partner's doubts about his own sexuality and decrease some of the tension. Gradualism is especially useful if you and your partner experience difficulty sharing deeply felt emotions.

5. *Schedule a "sex talk" session at which you and your partner will both talk freely about your problems.* Because sex is an area of such vulnerability, most people don't do this. Instead they give in to the temptation to ward off a real talk,

refuse to engage in any discussion, deflect any possible accusation by casting blame first.

a. *Pick the right moment.* Make sure the talk takes place out of bed. Don't talk when either of you is tired, preoccupied, in a hurry to get to an important appointment, or has had too many cocktails. Some women always choose the wrong moment because, consciously or unconsciously, they want the talk *not* to take place. Before you start to talk, ask yourself: Is this the right time? Is this the right place? Am *I* in the right mood to begin? Is *he* in the right mood to begin?

b. *Be prepared.* Before you have your talk, you should have thought through your satisfactions and dissatisfactions in various aspects of your sexual life. Use the following questions to trigger yourself so you know what you want to say:

• Am I satisfied with the way we decide to have sex?

• Am I satisfied with the time of day we have sex?

• Am I satisfied with the length of time spent in foreplay?

• Am I satisfied with the variety of activity during foreplay?

• Am I satisfied with the variety of positions during intercourse?

• Am I satisfied with my partner's expression of affection and interest during intercourse?

• Am I satisfied with the length of time spent in intercourse?

• Am I satisfied with my partner's expression of affection and interest after intercourse?

• Am I satisfied with the frequency of our intercourse?

• What new sexual activities would I like to experience?

• What do I see as the sexual problems in my present relationship?

c. *You might start the discussion by asking your partner the question "What can I do to turn you on more?"* Listen to what he says. And then, you can tell *him* what will turn *you* on more. Says Dr. Helen Kaplan, "I've never met a man who wouldn't like to be a good lover. You have to get feedback. A secure man will love this. He wants to learn. An insecure man might say, 'I can't make love if I'm told what to do.' Some men can't be told. Some women can't. But the average, heathy, open person welcomes criticism if it's done positively."

d. *Use I-Talk.* Don't say, "You don't do such and such." Do say something specific and positive like, "I'd like my toes sucked" or, "I'd like it if you'd spend time kissing the back of my knees" (often women get quite excited by having supposedly nonerotic parts of the body caressed) or, "I'd like to———. Will you?"

In the sexual area almost everyone has trouble saying "I want." Getting those words out is like plunging into icy water. You must make the conscious decision to take the risk and do it. If you start your sentence with the word "I," you have a better chance of coming out in a positive way.

e. *Don't use psychiatric jargon.* You are talking about how each of you can improve the sexual act, not your respective psyches. Attacks like, "You're still working out the oedipal relationship" leave the other person feeling hurt and do nothing to improve the situation. You don't get what you want by hitting below the belt (literally).

f. *Make your aim the substitution of one behavior you do like for another behavior you don't like.* You can do this in a gentle, noncritical way. For instance, you say, "It really turns me on when you kiss my breasts. I like it so much more than when you kiss my ears."

The very fact that you want changes may lead a man to think his lovemaking is less than perfect. Because he feels threatened, he may attack. If he does, you should realize that (i) sex is a sensitive area to him just as it is to you; (ii) maybe you did attack him in the way you voiced the sentence or wish. Try to keep the conversation going with sentences like, "I feel discouraged because you're putting me down. I meant to do something to make our sex life more interesting. Can't we discuss it?" Or, "My intentions were so good. Did I hurt your feelings in some way? I didn't mean to. Let's discuss how we can make our sex life better." Keep right on like a broken record.

Warning: If you don't speak up, you may ruin the relationship anyway by an unsuitable outburst at the wrong time. One young woman had a long relationship with a man who used to blow on her mouth between kisses. She hated it, but

never said a word until one night she exploded, "I can't stand
it when you do that." Shortly afterward, he left her apartment—for good. Now she says ruefully, "I wouldn't have lost
him if I had just spoken up sweetly at an appropriate time."

6. *As an aid to communication, try these "Resent-Appre-
ciate" exercises which Dr. Hogan uses in her sexual therapy in
the Human Sexuality Program at Mount Sinai School of
Medicine, New York.*
Resent Exercise. The idea is that you will tell your partner,
"I resent you because————." In his answer to your statement he does not get defensive but shows he understands
what it is that you resent. He plays your thought back to you
with explanation. For example:

YOU: I resent it when sometimes you initiate sex at two in
the morning.
HE: Oh, you're talking about Tuesday, I understand why.
You had to get up terribly early for an appointment on
Wednesday morning.

Appreciate Exercise. This uses a similar technique. You
say, "I appreciate it when————." In his answer your partner shows that he understands just what it is you appreciate.

YOU: I appreciate it when you want to know what turns me
on.
HE: I remember that you said you like to be slowly warmed
up and I tried to do it.

Before you do these exercises, explain them and their purpose to your partner. You may want to let him have first
turn.
7. *Give yourself assertive assignments in sexual communication.* Eleanor Smith, a woman in treatment with sex therapist Freida Stuart at the Family Service Organization of Nas-
sau County, New York, discovered she liked to have her pubic
hair stroked. Mrs. Stuart asked, "Would you like your husband
to do it more often?" "Yes," responded Eleanor. "Did you tell
him that?" queried the therapist. "No," said Eleanor. So sex
therapist Stuart assigned Eleanor to make a *minimum of
three sexual requests that would be pleasing to her* before she

reported for her next treatment session. Try this technique yourself. Again, in this way you accent the positive.

8. *Don't expect your partner to be a mind reader.* If you want to be tickled, pressed, or licked in a certain way, say so. Conversely, if you don't want to be tickled, pressed, or licked in a certain way, say so. If you don't, you're taking too little responsibility for yourself.

By speaking up, you not only clarify the problem but may eliminate it. One couple went into treatment with Dr. Helen Kaplan because as the husband got older, he started to have a potency problem. He panicked and became totally impotent. The truth of the matter was that for the twenty years of their marriage the wife had always much preferred clitoral stimulation to actual intercourse, but for these same two decades she had been afraid to say anything. Once she managed to tell him, the pressure was off. In just one month not only did his erections return but, says the wife, "My speaking up has resulted in a great sex life—for both of us."

Good sex requires language. As Dr. Arnold Lazarus, professor of psychology at Rutgers University, puts it, "I can't feel what you feel. You can't feel what I feel, but we can do what no animals can do—we can tell each other. We can show and describe and keep each other in the picture the whole time." He adds, "Talking can make the doing so much better."

Speak Up About Your Rights

1. *You have the right to share responsibility for sexual decisions.* Says Dr. Goldstein, "Frequently women feel that the man is in charge of all decisions about when to have sex. But the spouse may feel quite differently."

A frequent problem in decision-making is who initiates sex. Suggested assertive assignment: You initiate sex on odd days; your partner on even. Or make it even more specific: you initiate it at 10 P.M. on Wednesday. He initiates it at 9 P.M. on Thursday. Says Dr. Goldstein, "This sounds mechanical, but if you set up enough structure, you reduce anxiety."

2. *You have the right to keep your sexual actions to yourself.* If a friend, co-worker, relative, or parent asks, "Are you having an affair?," your response should follow your own desires, needs, and style. You have a right to answer ("Yes, I

am and I'm so happy" or, "Yes, I am but I don't wish to discuss it") or refuse to answer ("That's a very personal question and I really feel you don't have the right to ask it"). Just as you have a right to ask questions, others do too. But you also have the right to take the Fifth Amendment. Your love life is nobody's business but yours.

3. *You have the right to avoid pregnancy.* You don't have to take all the responsibility, but you'd damn well better take care of yourself and use some kind of contraception if you don't want a child. You're the one who's going to get pregnant—not he.

4. *You have the right to say yes—and no.* Many women are polarized. Whether or not they want to have sex, they comply. Then they feel angry and resentful. They're afraid of the consequences if they say no. Others feel being "liberated" means they have to go to bed with every man they meet. But that's not "liberated." Liberated is seeing that you have a choice and options.

As I pointed out early in the book, many single women are afraid to say no to a man because they think they'll lose him. Often they do lose him by saying yes. For instance, one divorcée in her early thirties was out on a date with a successful lawyer. After the movies, they went to her apartment. She wanted very much to see him again but did not want to sleep with him. Unable to say no, she gave in and went to bed with him, but, resenting the situation, behaved coolly and passively. He got the message, and never called again.

If you're involved in a close relationship, you can say no, even though getting out this two-letter word to the man you love may seem as difficult as blocking a two-ton Mack truck. Most women protest weakly and then capitulate because of a whole series of fears: "It would be too cruel—I'd unman him in his most vulnerable spot" ... "He'd get the idea I'm too liberated" ... "If I say no to him, when will he start saying no to me?"

How can you say no without making your partner feel you are rejecting him?

• Don't use sex as a weapon. If you say, "Uh, uh ... when are you going to speak to your boss about a raise?" your partner would be right to see this as a rejection. It is.

• Be honest. Express your own personal feelings just as

you do when you say, "I don't like Dick and Mary Jones. I don't want to go to their party." You can also say, "Look, I can hear your parents right in the next room and that means they can hear us. It makes me feel uncomfortable."

• Make it clear that you are saying no to sex on this particular occasion—not forever. Use lines like, "Tomorrow when we get back home" or, "As soon as the kids have gone to bed" or, "Let's plan a weekend out of town when we can really be together." Sentences like these not only relieve your partner's anxiety; they show you want him too.

• Offer an alternative to sex. At the Center for Human Concerns, St. Louis, Executive Director Beverly Hotchner offers Assertiveness Training in *Emphatic Responses*. The idea:

> You state what you feel.
> He states what he wants.
> You listen. You restate.
> For example, take the following dialogue:

HUSBAND: I'm horny tonight. I want to get it in.
YOU: I hear your need. But I've had an overstimulating day. I can't handle more. Let's take a bath together and massage each other. That would be good for me.
HUSBAND: That might be good for you, but I'm horny.
YOU: I understand how you feel, but you have to understand how I feel tonight. Let's take that bath and see what happens. [or] Can you suggest something which considers the way I feel tonight?

• Learn to see your own moods in the context of the situation. When a man feels insecure, he often tries to prove his virility. In this case, maybe your sympathy should overcome your reluctance. A good relationship always involves compromise. Sometimes you may want to ignore your mood for the sake of your mate. Just as you expect him to do for you.

• Examine why you want to say no. Perhaps he wants you to try a particular sexual action and you are reluctant. To say no after you have tried a sex act is one thing but to refuse without experimenting often makes a partner resentful. If you have tried this particular sex act and *know* it is not to your liking, you have the right to refuse. You are lovers bent on *mutual pleasures*. You have the right to say no, and, feeling that, you may also feel freer to say yes.

● You have the responsibility on occasions to explain your negative response. You can't refuse sex forever. For example, one woman had a husband with the problem of premature ejaculation. She got into the habit of saying no (what she meant was, "I am not pleased with the way you do it, so why bother?"). He became timid. When they finally talked about the problem, she was able to voice the fact that his premature ejaculation meant, "You don't love or respect me." The free communication also paved the way for her to say, "Look, I'm afraid of what will happen, but let's try." She made the shift from interpretation of his motivations to her own feelings. It took the onus off.

Learn to Act Assertively in Awkward Social Situations

Naturally new sexual problems occur among the rapidly burgeoning number of singles, men and women who have lost a partner through death or divorce, and couples living together minus wedding band. Some would have baffled Emily Post. Here are suggested solutions to those.

SITUATION ONE: You're a divorcée with a very bright little boy of eight. You have lots of dates who spend the night, but you don't want your boy to know about them. You're always in a dither for fear the guy won't leave before your son gets up.

Wrong way: You do nothing and keep on stewing.

Right way: You tell the guy how you feel and set the alarm for the time you want him to depart.

SITUATION TWO: You've invited a male friend from out of town for the weekend. He arrives with a bulging suitcase and announces, "I thought I might as well stay for a week—I've got lots of things to do in town." How do you handle it when you don't want him to stay?

Wrong way: You let him stay (unassertive) or you attack with, "You've got a lot of nerve" (thus probably ruining the weekend for both of you).

Right way: You say, "I'm so delighted to see you, but I do have plans starting on Monday. Shall I help you find another place for then?"

SITUATION THREE: You've spent the night at a divorced man's apartment. At 1 P.M. on Sunday he says to you, "You have to go home now—the kids will be here at two o'clock."

Wrong way: You leave docilely but feel resentful.

Right way: You say, "John, I'm happy you're seeing your kids, but I wish you had told me they were coming. You make me feel as if you're throwing me out and I don't like it. In the future please tell me."

SITUATION FOUR: You see a lot of a certain man. Friends of his, a couple with children, invite both of you for the weekend. You want to sleep in the same room.

Wrong way: You wait until you arrive to voice this fact—and then find yourself in separate rooms.

Right way: They're his friends. He should call up and point out the sleeping arrangements you both want. If the hostess says, "No, because of the kids," respect her wishes. Either stay at the house under her conditions or go elsewhere. If the friends are yours, you make the advance call.

Try to Keep Sex from Being Routine

1. *Vary the location and time of sex*. Change your pattern. If you always have sex at night, try love in the afternoon. Shift locales. Locate a lover's lane and use it. Make a motel date. On your own turf, you can start by sexually christening each room in the house and then go on to the front and back yards (this may take some doing if you live in a development). Remember, there are forests, beaches, trails (complete with bugs), mountaintops, canoes, and friends' country houses. It's a good idea to tie in sexuality with other love messages. A Thursday luncheon date can improve Friday sex. A telegram with a short "I love you" can open floodgates of feeling.

2. *Use words that arouse you and him*. Because women have been so brought up on that "be a lady" routine, using supposedly "dirty" words can prove a turn-on. They don't

really have to be obscenities. You can use four of the com-
monest terms without offending anyone merely by writing
them backwards or sideways: *cuff, werks, kirp,* and *tunc.* The
German word *fikken* means "to beat" much like the Arabic
dok which means to "pound like a pestle in a mortar." Many
people substitute the word "go" for "come." Others assign
names to parts of the anatomy (Brenda and Cobina for
breasts, Robin Hood for the penis). You can use like-sound-
ing, made-up words in place of real things—during *cogitus,*
the male's *vector* has to break the *hyphen!*

3. *Adopt the attitude that you are not trying to have an orgasm with your partner to please him but to please yourself.* I
reiterate the point: A woman often doesn't know what to do
to her partner or what to have him do to her. Being ignorant
of both how to give pleasure to herself or how her lover can
pleasure her, she depends on him, thus perpetuating her lack
of knowledge and preventing successful sex. The following
two exercises, suggested by Georgia Kline-Graber and Dr.
Benjamin Graber in *Woman's Orgasm,* are starters in increasing "your ability to communicate directly and concisely your
sexual/sensual likes and dislikes and to take active responsibility in discovering what you like."

COMMUNICATION EXERCISE

STEP ONE: Take a bath together. Using soap and water,
slowly and gently caress your partner's body, trying to feel as
much as you can while you do the washing. Wash each other
simultaneously if you like. Keep the conversation limited to
explaining feelings about what you are doing. Then he does
the same for you. If the bathtub is too small for two, one of
you might sit on a stack of pillows next to the tub, and wash
the other. Then dry each other.

STEP TWO: In another room, sit facing each other, without
clothes and in comfortable positions. Take your partner's
hands in yours, and starting at the head and working down-
wards, show him exactly where and how you like to be
touched. Your partner should tell you that he understands
and at the same time demonstrate with his hands. If he is not

doing it the way you like, reexplain and show him again until he does.

STEP THREE: As soon as you are both satisfied that he understands how you like to be touched, switch roles. It's his turn.

STEP FOUR: Continue alternating back and forth until all the nongenital areas of your bodies have been touched. Then do the genitals.

STEP FIVE: Immediately upon finishing the exercise, share all your feelings. Start with the negative feelings first. Try to say what you *would have liked,* not what you didn't like. Finish up with what you did like. You've completed the exercise when both you and your partner feel you have sufficient information to begin using it in lovemaking.

FACIAL AND BODY CARESS

STEP ONE: Decide who will be the giver and who the receiver.

STEP TWO: In comfortable positions, using some oil or lotion, one touches the other slowly and lightly, while making solid contact with the other's skin. If you're the giver, imagine that his face is made of velvet. Use your full hand, your fingers and especially your palms to caress his face. Let your fingers and hand travel all over. Find the ears, the mouth. Go inside the lips with a finger. Touch the gums and the insides of the cheeks. Feel the wetness. Then let him direct your hands to the places he wants touched, indicating what kind of pressure he wants.

STEP THREE: Switch roles and repeat, preferably on a different day.

STEP FOUR: Do not go on to additional sexual contact at the end of the facial caress, but at a different time do a body caress without genitals (the same slow touching on every inch of his body) and then switch roles and he does this to you— preferably on a different day. As the next step use the same technique to try a body caress with genitals.

STEP FIVE: After each exercise, you share your feelings with each other about what you would have liked, and what you did like.

4. *Share fantasies.* This is one of the safest, least expensive, and handiest aphrodisiacs. If you have fantasies that are sadistic (you are dressed in sequin bra and shorts whipping fifty men who cringe at your feet), masochistic (you are raped by fifty Neanderthal types), or even homosexual (you and your female lover in ecstasy on a deserted Greek island), you probably think, "My God, what does this say about me!" What it says is that you're human. Just because you have a homosexual fantasy doesn't mean you're a lesbian.

Fantasies can add spice to sexual experiences. You can simply talk them out or translate them into action. One woman used to imagine herself as a prostitute. Encouraged by her husband, she donned a blonde wig, flashy make-up and strutted around like her idea of a whore. She loved it. So did he. Some popular female fantasies: being raped, starring in a porno movie, being smuggled into an all-male prison and being passed from cell to cell, working as a madame in a brothel, servicing an entire shipload of sailors, meeting a handsome bisexual who gives up his male lovers for you. One woman always fantasizes that her father-in-law is in the next room.

Some fantasy pointers:

• If you have trouble reaching orgasm, switch to fantasy. According to Dr. Kaplan, a "fantasy can be a tranquilizer. It is difficult to be in fantasy and be anxious at the same time."

• If you don't have fantasies and would like them, you may want to assemble a collection of fantasy aids—for examples, pictures from *Playgirl* and *Viva* or take your own picture of your favorite man in a pose that is provocative to you. Or give yourself a fantasy assignment: Make up one a day. At first your fantasies may be wooden. Try to develop creativity. Rate yourself on a SUE scale (Subjective Units of Excitement). Zero is no turn-on whatsoever; 100 stands for as sexually excited as you have ever been in your life. The 50–75 range is usually satisfying.

• If you feel anxious about sharing your fantasy, ask

your partner to tell you his. Then you may feel freer to reveal yours.

● There are two purposes to telling fantasies: (a) reassurance—you want to be told, "You're O.K. with me, kid; you're normal"; (b) to make the fantasy part of sex play itself. But your fantasy belongs to you. You don't have to tell your partner a sexual fantasy about his best friend. You tell only what increases intimacy.

5. *Arrange with your partner for a sexual weekend*. Dr. Joseph LoPiccolo of the State University of New York at Stony Brook and Vinnie Miller of the University of Oregon have developed a program to improve the sexual relationships of "normal couples." A typical program brings together three couples and a male-female leadership couple for three three-hour sessions over a weekend. The group then meets again for a follow-up session two weeks later. Here is an adaptation of this sexual weekend which you might use to improve your sex life.

THE SEXUAL WEEKEND

The purpose of the weekend is primarily and exclusively for sex. Ground rules: no drugs, alcohol or socializing with other people. With the exception of food and perhaps very brief walks, the only activity is sex.

Go to a hotel or motel. There carry out the following program.

a. Part of the time you or your partner (or both simultaneously) is completely nude. The remainder of the time each of you dresses "sexy" by your partner's estimation. Let him give you ideas.

b. Talk "dirty" as much as you can to set up the condition of *verbal disinhibition*. Use familiar words or simulations of words.

c. Don't fight. Don't complain. Use willpower. Save any disagreements for another time.

d. Make suggestions to your partner for things he can do or do more of. Give effective feedback. Don't say, "Stop, I don't like that." Instead say something like, "Just a little slower and lighter is better for me." Your partner also gives feedback to you.

e. Until Saturday evening there is to be no attempt to achieve climax in any way. Take turns using sensate focus on each other. This is the Masters and Johnson technique in which you massage and touch each other to find areas in each other that are pleasurable. The person to whom it's being done concentrates only on his/her feelings. The person doing it actively tries to find things that please the partner and pays attention to his/her feelings in giving the pleasure. In addition you might try the bath exercise I noted earlier.

f. Toward dinnertime, look over the collection of erotic books and magazines which you should have brought with you. Scan them together and discuss what turns you on and off. Have a light dinner and during it talk only about sex. Tell each other what you enjoyed doing during the day and the kind of things you'd like to do with each other that evening.

g. That evening try some new sexual techniques and, again, give each other feedback. The point of this evening is not to have a "fantastic" sexual experience but to enjoy experimentation, free from the pressure of results.

h. The next morning talk about what you did, what you enjoyed, how you might make sex better. Write out a two-week plan in which you make sex a high-priority activity rather than the last thing you do before falling asleep. At this point you should also deliberately schedule another sexual weekend for two months to ten weeks hence.

Watch Out for Sexual Traps

In trying to become the sexually assertive woman, there are things to guard against:

1. *Don't be the controlling woman.* It is very important for you to take responsibility for yourself. You must allow your partner this same right. If you have the attitude, "I will hug or kiss him in such and such a way because he's still such a little boy that he can't tell me what he wants," you are taking *magical responsibility for him.* Sex is for both of you.

2. *Don't be manipulative.* Because for so long women have had so little power, they have tended to use what they do have in the sexual area. Remember Lysistrata who led the women of Athens in a sexual strike ("We must refrain from

the male altogether") until the men would stop making war and come to terms of peace. Women particularly often barter sex with such lines as, "If you don't do this, I won't do that" (the idea here is to provoke the partner into wanting sex and then denying him until he gives in to her wish, like a Paris vacation) ... "You're lousy in bed" (actually you're belittling him because he flirted with a pretty blonde at a party) ... "I'm going to look for someone else" (threat).

The worst thing about sex as a payoff for good behavior is that you're really saying, "O.K., he wants it and gets all the pleasure out of it, and I'm not really doing it for myself but for him."

If you want to make a deal, do it openly. At the Institute for Behavior Therapy, New York, Drs. Barry Lubetkin and Steven Fishman used a sexual behavioral contract to openly deal with the problem of a woman who held back on sex because her husband "did so little around the house." Says Dr. Lubetkin, "They exchanged one need for another. She wanted the work done. He wanted sex." The contract worked on the token system. The husband got tokens for performing various household chores; the wife received tokens for initiating sex and various sexual actions. Use of the contract eliminated many of the sexual stabs perpetrated by both in the past in an indirect way and greatly helped "the tone of the marriage."

3. *Don't allow yourself to have an "open" sexual experience—and then be vulnerable.* The experience may not have the same meaning for the man that it has for you. Says Dr. Helen Kaplan, "The average woman becomes vulnerable. If you're like that, don't have sex unless you have a relationship you can rely on."

4. *Realize that asserting yourself may bring about rejection.* As Dr. Kaplan says, "A woman's reluctance to express her needs is not always based on cultural paranoia." You may run a real risk of displeasing your partner if you become more assertive sexually. Some men are actually repelled by such behavior and regard women who attempt to assume a more active role in sex as aggressive, "ballsy" females. It's particularly difficult to switch from submissiveness to assertiveness in marriage, where you've already established a pat-

tern. It's slightly less difficult when you don't know the man well.

However, if you want to be assertive sexually, you should be. The man who will feel threatened, turned off, and run away won't be the man you will want to be involved with on a long-term basis. Says Dr. Goldstein, "Inevitably the women who sacrifice themselves feel so much resentment that in the long run they lose interest in sex, and the very thing they fear happens—they lose the man. It's better to speak up."

5. *Don't hide your real self.* If you are naturally assertive, act that way. For instance, when one successful career woman meets a man, she always plays the bright-but-demure role. At first she's all loving passivity. Then, as the relationship progresses. she becomes herself—a gutsy person who isn't afraid to say, "I want." The guys leave, saying, "You're not the woman I first met."

6. *Know that as you feel free to want more, you may end up being the rejector.* He may not be able to give you what you want.

Learning to Become the Sexually Assertive Woman May Not Be Enough: You May Have to Take the Active Step of Seeking Professional Help

Masters and Johnson have estimated that more than 50 percent of American couples suffer from sexual dysfunctions. The new therapeutic methods for treating sexual dysfunctions (vaginismus, frigidity) are relatively brief and have a high record of success. *Why suffer when you don't have to?*

In writing this chapter I found two quotes that have significance for me and would have, I believe, for every woman.

One is from Dr. Kaplan: "The best aphrodisiac is still being in love with someone."

The second was written by Abigail Adams in a letter to her husband John in 1776: "Men of sense in all ages abhor those customs which treat us only as the vassals of your sex."

Chapter 10

Assertion and Children

Marian Rogers sits in her suburban living room and fights back the tears. She has just driven her fifteen-year-old daughter to school and received a long list of directives: "Iron my skirt" ... "Pick me up at three to take me shopping" ... "Return my library books." Resentfully Marian thinks, "She's such a boss. She should be running General Motors." But just as she follows the commands of others in her effort to "make everyone love me," Marian will do as daughter bids. This passive pattern has produced a rebellious, headstrong teenager who stays up until 3 A.M. reading, is always late for school, scoffs at her parents and tyrannizes the household. ("We'll go where *I* want to go on vacation or I won't go!")

Two thousand miles away Claire Martin has an equally aggressive fifteen-year-old daughter. But Claire's parental pattern differs greatly from that of Marian. Each day Claire voices long lists of things her daughter has done wrong: "Why didn't you get 100 instead of 90—that math course isn't difficult" ... "Why are you friendly with that Smith girl—why not be friendly with so and so?" She thinks that by saying words she communicates. In actuality she sends her daughter the message, "I am contemptuous of you. You do

243

nothing to please me." This critical, angry pattern is much the same as the one she uses with friends under the pretext of helping them. Interpreting her mother's aggressive behavior as "I wish you'd drop dead," the daughter has given up on her mother and on herself. The only way she can establish any kind of self-respect is through rebellion, so she stays out late, responds to her mother's continual injunctions either by yelling back or withdrawing, and is now threatening to run away from home.

In this case both the overindulgent mother and the abusive one have produced an aggressive child. According to Dr. Arnold Lazarus, professor of psychology at Rutgers University, "An inhibited parent can produce an inhibited kid or a little Hitler. An aggressive mother can produce an inhibited kid or a little Hitler. But assertive parents almost always produce assertive kids."

When you assert yourself with your children, you affect the kind of adults they will become. By modeling an assertive way of behavior throughout their childhood, you enable them to grow up with that sense of self-esteem that you desire so much for yourself.

Many women realize this intellectually. Why then do so many mothers have such difficulty being assertive with their children?

• Consciously or unconsciously, they don't want to stir up the same kinds of arguments and disagreeableness that came between them and their parents and left them feeling tense and guilty. They confuse "peace" with closeness.

• They want to live vicariously through the child. They see him/her as an extension of themselves, not as an independent human being. They expect the child to fulfill all the fantasies they had for themselves.

• They feel powerless and helpless in most life areas. Only with their children do they feel any power. They then use this power to the detriment of other goals—like raising a happy child.

• They have never learned to act assertively. They are not sure of their own rights and they do not know how to stand up for them. They cannot appropriately express their own feelings, let alone encourage the child to share his/her own feelings.

• They have not learned the skills of parenting. One common error: They pay attention to the child only when he does something they feel is "wrong." Thus they train the child to do just the things they don't want him to do.

• They lose sight of their goals with their children. For example, instead of the goal of a cooperative interchange, they set competitive goals. They see only win-lose approaches. When there is conflict, they try to resolve it in their favor so that they win and the child loses. Others, fewer in number, constantly give in to their children out of fear of conflict or of frustrating their child's needs.

• They fail to change as the child changes. They attempt to deal with the adolescent by using the very same habits they established when the child was two years old. Throughout the growth period they fail to see that to change the child, they themselves must change what they do and the way they do it.

Goals of the parent-child relationship. As with any assertive approach, you must formulate your goals as to where you want to go and keep them constantly in mind. Besides the obvious ones of caring for their health and basic physical needs, in general, there are usually two goals concerning children: (1) to help them grow into independent, happy and productive individuals, capable of functioning in our complex society; (2) to share love and tenderness with them always—even when they mature and become independent.

AN ASSERTIVE GUIDE TO DEALING WITH CHILDREN

1. *Assess your own behavior with your children.* Are you passive, aggressive or genuinely assertive with them? The following questions may help you to think this through.

• Am I always the winner?
• Is my child always the winner?
• Do I ask too much from my child—more creativity, intellect, achievement than he/she can do realistically?
• Do I ask too little from my child?

• Do I deliberately train my child to be independent (for example, to resolve his/her own difficulties with friends)?

• Do I hold back from giving any directives because I can't stand the thought of my child's tantrums, tears, or sulks?

• Do I encourage my child to stand up for his/her rights with others?

• Do I listen to and really try to understand what my child has to say?

• Do I tell my child the feelings he/she should have?

• Do I say yes more than I say no to my child?

• Do I say no more than I say yes to my child?

• Do I allow my child to disagree with me (about friends, importance of grades, spending of free time, concepts of what's right and wrong)?

• Do I overprotect my child (not wanting her to take up fencing because she "might get her eyes knocked out")?

• Do I allow my child privacy?

• Do I allow my child the chance to participate in decisions which affect the whole family?

• Do I want my child to grow up in my image?

• Do I openly express love for my child?

2. *Be the right kind of model.* If your child sees you acting with self-respect, standing up for yourself, communicating honestly, directly, and appropriately with salespeople, friends, spouse, he will learn to do these things. If you are the female reincarnation of Caspar Milquetoast or, conversely, the pushy mother, no matter what words you use with your child or what directives you give, he will be passive or aggressive, rather than assertive. Some cautions:

a. *Lead a full life yourself.* Then you are less apt to live vicariously through your children and set impossible standards for them.

b. *Be aware that you and your child are separate individuals.* One common problem among unassertive mothers is to filter everything that happens to the child through their own low self-esteem. If you are unassertive or lead an isolated existence, you are apt to take the things the child does or that happen to him (for example, he is not asked to a party) as a bad reflection of you.

c. *Realize that you not only provide a model but your*

assertive behavior influences your child's own perception of himself. For example:

SITUATION: The teacher calls you in and says that your six-year-old son doesn't pay attention to work, behaves terribly in class and this is due to the fact that "you have brought him up in an undisciplined way."

Unassertive response: You say, "Yes, you're right. He does need more discipline at home. Send us a note every time he misbehaves. Meanwhile we'll forbid him to watch TV at night." That night you yell at John, turn off TV, brush aside his attempt to explain and send him to bed without supper. And you lie awake all night. In this case John has learned that his needs or feelings don't matter. He feels either that he is "bad" or the world is unfair. In either case he is being taught to be helpless.

Aggressive response: You say, "You just don't understand my son. From the things I've heard I think you're a terrible teacher. I'm going to talk to the principal about this and get John transferred to Miss Jones's class. She has the reputation of being a good teacher." You do talk to the principal and John gets transferred but you say nothing to John. John learns that he has no say over what happens to him, that his needs and feelings are irrelevant. He begins to feel he lives in an unreasonable world.

Assertive response: You say, "That's strange. It has never happened before. What do you think is going on? Let me talk to him about it, and next week I'll come by with some ideas." That night you have a long discussion with John (and your husband). You learn that a boy in John's class had bullied him, and, as a result, he felt upset. You go back to school, report the facts to the teacher and discuss what can be done. Because of your assertive action, John learns that what he feels and thinks have importance to others and that he can influence what happens. He also has the model of constructive communication and the working out of a problem with you.

    d. *Avoid sexual stereotypes.* Children learn values and ideas within the family context. If your daughter hears you say, "I just can't fix a fuse," she may well elect to be mechanically inept. On the other hand, if your husband assumes what was once thought to be "woman's role" and cooks, vacuums, or does the dishes, your son can identify with his behavior. Says Dr. Lee Salk, professor of psychology and pediatrics, Cornell University Medical College, "Teaching children that men are capable of cooking isn't as good as a father who actually cooks." The aim is to have the child grow up with a flexibility and with the combined strengths or both roles.

3. *Learn to stand up for your own rights.* Some women believe they have no rights; they feel in order to be good mothers they must be at the complete beck and call of the child. Others feel they have the right to do housework minus interference but lack the right to be left alone to read. Others question the right to go to work even if they have made adequate arrangements for child care.

a. *To act on your rights you must first determine them.* Take assertive action by making a list of the rights that should obviously be yours. Do you have the right to get a babysitter once a week and take the afternoon off? Do you have the right to chat with a close friend on the phone for half an hour without interruption? Discuss these rights in a rap group, with friends, within the family. See what other women do. Formulate your own decisions and revise your list. After you've worked out your list, see how well you stand up for yourself in each area.

One way to make clear to yourself that you have the right to have rights is through the *reductio ad absurdum* method. Says Dr. Lazarus, "In my practice when I treat overdutiful mothers—the kind who feel 'I don't have the right to an hour to myself'—I paradox them. I blow up the situation to an extraordinary degree. I say, 'I don't think you have the right to a meal. Maybe your child wants your food.' ... 'Maybe you don't have the right to a glass of water. The tap may run dry and your child may need what water is there.' I blow it up until they laugh and see the absurdity of the situation."

For example, Dr. Lazarus treated a forty-five-year-old working mother who used to get up at 6:30 A.M. to get lunch ready for her fourteen-year-old daughter. She said, "It's my duty as a mother. She wants me to make her school lunch."

Using the *reductio ad absurdum* technique with such questions as, "Do you have the right to have friends? Shouldn't you give up everything and spend all your time with or doing things for your daughter," Dr. Lazarus enabled the woman to see that she had the right to sleep an hour later and that "not making her lunch doesn't mean a reduction of my love. I can show her I love her in some other way." You answer: Does this woman have the right to expect her fourteen-year-old daughter to make her own lunch?

b. *Start standing up for your rights.* Some techniques that help:

● Discuss the "hows" with your spouse or friends. Your husband may help you to stand up for your right to practice the piano without interruption. A neighbor may tell you, "I refuse to serve dinner at three different times," and then you may feel better about saying, "I'm not a servant. If you don't eat when we eat, fix it yourself."

● Send I-messages. This is an appropriate way of standing up for your rights and simultaneously increasing the exchange of feelings. The technique, a modification of I-Talk or "feeling talk," is described in detail in an excellent book, *Parent Effectiveness Training,* by Dr. Thomas Gordon, a California psychologist. An I-message has three parts: You tell directly what you feel, what the child has done to elicit these feelings, and explain how and what the child has done to intrude on your rights and create a problem for you.

SITUATION ONE: A four-year-old smears peanut butter all over the kitchen counter.

Wrong way: "What a dirty bad boy you are."

I-message: "I feel so discouraged because you're smearing peanut butter all over that counter just when I spent so much time cleaning up. Now I have to clean it all over again just when I want to make an important phone call.

SITUATION TWO: A six-year-old keeps asking questions and just won't stop.

Wrong way: "Shut up. You're driving me crazy."

I-message: "I feel so annoyed because you keep asking me questions when I'm trying to write copy that is due at the office first thing tomorrow morning."

At the moment you may not be able to send I-messages to stand up for your rights. Either you take the unassertive keep-quiet or the aggressive yelling approach. You can learn the I-message technique. Practice and rehearse.

Determine the behaviors that keep you from sending I-messages, and deliberately train yourself in a behavior that is incompatible with this unwanted behavior. For instance, if you can't send an I-message because you constantly yell at your kids when they do something you don't like, train yourself to deliberately relax everytime you become aware you are yelling. It's hard to relax and yell at the same time. Once you've controlled the yelling, then deliberately send an I-message.

If you did not send an I-message when you should have, think what you could have said. Imagine saying it. Say it with your spouse. Enough practice should enable you to send on-the-spot I-messages.

Be aware of one point: If you cannot phrase the last part of the message—the part about how it interferes with your rights—you may be dealing with matters of taste, style, or values where the child has his own right to differ from you. In that case, check the appropriateness of your own feelings so that you don't inhibit the child from forming his own individuality.

4. *Exercise your right to be a parent.* If you don't, in the long run everyone loses. You should apply to your parental role all the assertive ways of handling things that I've outlined in this book.

a. *Use self-disclosure.* Express your feelings. Don't say, "You come home at midnight or else." Do say, "I want you home by midnight because I get anxious. At your age you need your sleep."

b. *Don't generalize. Be specific.* Don't say, "You always contradict me." Do say, "You contradicted me when I told Mary about my new dress, and I wish you wouldn't do that."

c. *Attack the behavior, not the person.* Don't say, "You're a selfish and inconsiderate girl." Do say, "That was a selfish and inconsiderate thing you did when you stayed for dinner at Joan's house and didn't even phone and tell me where you were."

d. *Don't mind-read. Deal with the obvious.* Don't say,

"You are obviously feeling guilty." Do say, "I think you may be feeling bad because you took the car without telling me."

e. *Be firm*. Sometimes you have to make a decision and stick to it. Firmness in saying no is an example. Says Debora Phillips, director, Child Therapy Program, Department of Psychiatry, Temple University School of Medicine, "The mother has to say no when she means it and stick to it. She has to have the attitude no means no—I will not change—and refuse to let herself be wheedled. And she doesn't have to spell out why."

You don't have to offer all sorts of reasonable explanations. Assert your parenthood: "No, you cannot play in the road" ... "No, you cannot put a hairpin in the electric socket . . . "No, you cannot use a skateboard into oncoming traffic."

In actuality, many children feel comforted and cared for when parents say no. When my husband's daughter Jane was four, she had a bad upset stomach. When she finally stopped vomiting, she complained of feeling thirsty and asked for a drink. He told her, "No, you'll get sick again." She kept insisting. Finally, he couldn't bear the tears in those blue eyes, so he gave her a little water. Immediately, she got sick and told him reproachfully, "You shouldn't have given me the water." He was apologetic and said, "Jane, you kept insisting." Then she said firmly, "You should have said no."

f. *Speak up*. You do this to:

• *Teach your children to respect the rights of other people*. This respect for the rights of others is an important aspect of assertion. It helps the child to differentiate between aggression and assertion and it helps him to crystallize his own rights and demand respect for them. You say, "Stop it immediately" when a child writes all over your freshly painted white walls with a Magic Marker. Or when your five-year-old wants to eat steak with his hands and you've got a crew of dinner company, you should say, "If you want to eat that way, go eat by yourself." This kind of behavior infringes on the rights of others.

You can also do this with older children. One mother found herself extremely annoyed by the political ideas of her daughter's boyfriend. She didn't interfere with the girl's right to date the boy, but she did feel she had the right to have a pleasant dinner at her own table. So one night she announced, "Let's declare a moratorium on all political talk at the table. Discuss it among yourselves later."

    ● *Set standards of behavior for the household.* For example, Mary and Dick Davis recently decided that Susie, their fourteen-year-old daughter, was old enough to sit for the two younger girls. One subsequent Saturday night they went out to dinner and when they came home found Susie ironing clothes in her bedroom as a boyfriend sprawled on the bed. Susie immediately shrieked, "We weren't doing anything." That night Mary made the rule: "No boys on the second floor at any time." She says, "This mattered to me. I have certain standards of how this house will operate."

    g. *Use the "We have a problem" approach.* Sometimes your needs and rights and those of the child may be in conflict. The "We have a problem" technique leads to a negotiation wherein the rights of both are considered. For example, your son, a seventeen-year-old high school senior, has a date for a dance and insists on the family car. You and your husband also have a date for a dinner party, four miles away. You can treat the situation aggressively ("No, we need the car. Your father earns the money for this house. When you get a job, you can get your own car"), unassertively ("Sure, we'll figure out another way to get there"), or take the assertive "We have a problem" approach. Try something like, "It is a problem. Is there some other way you could get to the dance? Could you go with a friend? Why don't you check and we'll check too. Maybe some other people from this neighborhood are going to our dinner. If not, we'll work out who goes by cab."

    5. *Teach your child to be assertive.* Just as you can learn specific techniques, your child can too. However, if you are going to teach him this, you have to learn to be a good teacher. Here are some of the skills:

    a. *Show respect for babies.* According to Dr. Salk, "Children who are forced to cry for long periods because no one respects their needs go off to sleep. That's their response to a stress situation. But if you respond to the crying with talking, listening, and giving time to the child, the infant learns to relate to people and later become an independent, assertive person. Most people make the mistake of thinking that if you satisfy the need of the crying child, you'll spoil him and he'll always be a baby. That idea is incorrect and damaging. In actuality, it's the other way around. If you don't respond, you frustrate him and keep him passive and dependent."

b. *Give approval.* Showing attention and approval (giving positive reinforcement) to the behaviors you want to increase is the most effective way of changing behavior. Too often, we fall into the trap of trying to change behavior by attending to and punishing the behaviors we do not want. Not only is this less effective but it also brings about a number of undesirable consequences (such as an unpleasant family atmosphere). Don't hesitate to praise, approve, encourage. Look for opportunities to do so. Be honest about it. Also remember that it does not always have to be with words: a smile, a tender pat, a loving hug are very effective signs of approval.

c. *Offer options to children so they develop the ability to make choices.* Say, "Would you like to wear the red, orange, or green slacks?" In this way you simultaneously provide guidance and set limits. If your daughter picks out the slacks you like least, say, "This isn't what I would have picked," but accept her choice. Do not say, "Pick out whatever you want"; by doing that, you take an "I don't care" attitude. Let the child know her individuality at the very beginning. Give her a chance to take an assertive decision-making step.

d. *Early on, train your child in assertive behaviors.* Says Debora Phillips, "The therapist can't be there on the spot to model assertive behavior, so at the clinic we train the mothers to do it." Two of the behaviors she works on are:

• *Learn to take the risk of being wrong.* Let's say you have the instance of a fearful child who does not volunteer in class. In her therapeutic sessions Ms. Phillips has the child ask the mother difficult questions. The mother tries to answer, but when she cannot, she does not get anxious. Finally the mother says, "Not knowing isn't the end of the world. I'll go to the library and look up the facts so that I can get the information you want." Then Ms. Phillips uses the same technique with the child, gradually working up to questions the child cannot answer. Says Ms. Phillips, "The idea is that you take the child into the arena. Also you praise the child if he laughs when he has guessed wrong on an answer. The mother should say something like, 'Good guess. You came close.' "

• *Change aggression to assertion.* Children have to learn to appropriately express their angers. Among young children particularly, many are all too quick to come out punching and kicking. Says Ms. Phillips, "When the child is ready to punch, try one of two methods: (i) the line 'Tell me what is wrong' or (ii) offer an alternate behavior. You might say, 'I know you're angry but let's pat ... clap ... tickle.' The important thing is for the child to get out that expression of feeling."

You can also offer an alternate behavior by the behavior rehearsal technique. For instance Amy, my then thirteen-year-old niece, telephoned one day and said, "My friend always takes babysitting engagements and then at the last minute decides she has to study and makes me take them. She wants me to take over for her today, and I don't want to. I'm angry with her, and we're going to have a big fight." I offered Amy an alternate response which we rehearsed. As a result, Amy was able to get out this sentence to her friend: "No, I have my own homework. I can't take over for you."

e. *Be an askable parent.* Encourage questions by paying attention to them. Try to use phrases like, "I'm busy" or, "You're bothering me" only when it interferes with your rights in an important way. Says Dr. Salk, "Children become assertive individuals if you nurture their curiosity."

f. *Allow the child to work out his own problems.* Respect your child's right to have his/her own problem, and don't make it yours. You can try to help, but he must resolve it. One technique of encouraging independent thought: the You-message, a method derived from the noted psychologist Carl Rogers which Dr. Gordon calls "active listening."

In using a You-message, you:

• Invite the child to share his feelings. You use phrases such as, "Tell me about it" ... "Tell me more" ... "Keep on. I'm listening" or simply, "Uh huh." In this way you are saying that you are interested, that you consider his feelings are important but that you are not taking over. It is the child who decides where to go, what to talk about, even though you are with him every step of the way.

• Act as a sounding board. For the moment set your

own feelings and thoughts aside. Just try to catch the child's feelings or thoughts and simply reflect them back to him. If he senses an incorrect message or you misunderstood the message, he will correct it. In this way you help the child to realize that it is his problem not yours.

YOU-MESSAGE

ELLEN: Roger called today. He said he'd call back at nine. I think he wants to drop me.

MOTHER: That would be very upsetting to you.

ELLEN: I'd die, particularly because I think he'll start dating Alice.

MOTHER: That's why you're upset—you think he'll start dating Alice.

ELLEN: Yes, all the boys like her. So I guess Roger will fall for her too. She knows how to treat men. I don't. I don't have anything to say.

MOTHER: You wish you felt more at ease with boys the way Alice does.

ELLEN: Yes, I'm not popular. I guess I'm too nervous that I'll do something wrong.

MOTHER: You want so badly to have boys like you that you're afraid you'll make a mistake—and that they won't.

ELLEN: Yes, that's it. So I stand around like a wallflower.

MOTHER: You feel you're worse off now than if you talked and said the wrong thing.

ELLEN: Yes, I'm a mess. I guess it would be better to go talk to the boys and not sit on the sidelines.

Notice that in this dialogue the mother does not use "I," correct the child, or suggest solutions. But Mother's You-messages help the girl to uncover the basic problem, encourage problem-solving on her part, and eventually help her to consider making a change.

In using "active listening," there is a caveat: Don't expect to come to any solution, get results, or, if there are results, to find out what they are. The purpose of the procedure is, through your attitude, to understand and reflect the child's feelings, allow the child to accept responsibility for his

problem and go his own way. You may never know the outcome.

g. *Respect the fact that your child has certain inalien-
able rights.* These include the right to his own values (which
may be similar to or completely different from yours), to
choose his own clothes, achieve at his level of competency,
choose the subject he wants to concentrate on in school and
his own career. Says Dr. Lazarus, "It's the child's choice to
elect whether or not he keeps his room clean. I can impose
sanctions on my own room or other rooms in the house but
not on my child's room unless it becomes a safety hazard."
Remember, your job is guidance, not dictatorship. You
should not coerce a child into a decision (like a profession or
selection of college) that represents your needs, not his.

By respecting his rights, by allowing him to set his goals
and overcome his own obstacles, he begins to develop feelings
of strength, competency and self-worth. Says Dr. Salk,
"Everybody needs a sense of self-worth. If you've learned
how to pursue a goal and cope with the obstacles, you can
get a high from achievement. But some kids haven't learned
how to solve problems. The parents have protected them, or
they come from a subculture where others look down on
them if they struggle to get out. If you can't get a high from
assertive activity, you may try to get a high chemically.
Drugs give you a false sense of self-esteem. When this happens, it's a failure that has actually taken place much earlier.
The early experiences have a tremendous impact on later assertive behavior."

*Warning: Allowing your child to resolve his own prob-
lems, respecting his rights, does not allow you to abdicate
your responsibilities as a parent.* Your child does not have the
right to interfere with your rights. Nor does he have the right
to destroy himself. This is particularly true of adolescents
who have neither the experience nor the maturity to make
certain decisions regardless of consequences. At these times
you must step in.

Under these conditions, there are times when no amount
of discussion or reasoning does any good and you must actually become a benevolent despot.

Says Dr. Lazarus, "With adolescents one reaches the
point where, as a last resort, you must be the benevolent dic-

tator. You must say, 'I want you to do this because I tell you to.' If that doesn't work, you institute consequences—no car, new coat, late hours, etc. If you lack control and don't utilize consequences, you don't have power."

6. *Change as your child changes; dealing with the adolescent.* During the early formative years the parent has enormous power and influence over the child. She controls the child's food, friends, total environment. As the child grows older, this power and influence lessen. Your child has other models available in the form of teachers, peer friends, relatives, and all the people he watches on TV. Also you no longer have the same control over his environment.

Because of this change in the power balance, the methods you may have used for years will no longer work. To insist on them leads to disaster. *You* must change and find new methods for discussion and negotiation.

Some behavior change techniques for dealing with adolescents:

a. *Try a Family Council session to improve faulty parent-adolescent communication.* The council can be held biweekly and can be extended to include—in addition to adolescent and parents—other immediate family members and even grandparents or surrogate parents. Establish the following rules, adapted from a paper on "The Family Council: a Segment of Adolescent Treatment" by Debora Phillips, at the first session and abide by them.

• Each person may speak about any issue or problems concerning himself or his relationship with members of his family.

• No one may interrupt him.

• No shouting. Voices must be kept at a moderate level.

• No "dumping." "Dumping" is direct criticism in the form of judgmental statements such as, "You're awful" . . . "You're sloppy" . . . "You don't care about anyone but yourself" . . . "You have no consideration for your mother" . . . "You irresponsible teen-ager" . . . "You goddamn lousy alcoholic" . . . "You have never provided for your family."

• Each person tries to express himself in terms of his own feelings by using sentences beginning with "I": "I feel tired and resentful when I pick up dirty socks from the floor"

... "I feel rejected and neglected when your schedule leaves us no time for dinner together."

• Stress accurate reiteration. At any point during a session, a family member may be asked to reiterate what another member has just said. The point: to teach family members careful listening. Often a parent's own viewpoint can interfere with accurate understanding of an adolescent's statement. For instance, the following dialogue took place at one of Ms. Phillips' sessions:

JON (*the son*): I smoke marijuana infrequently at parties with my friends.

THERAPIST (*to father*): Would you repeat what Jon has just said?

FATHER: He smokes that dangerous weed with those loafers he hangs around with.

THERAPIST: Jon, would you please repeat your statement?

JON: I smoke pot at parties sometimes.

THERAPIST (*to father*): Do not represent your own feelings or opinions at this time.

FATHER: O.K. Jon said that he smokes pot once in a while.

THERAPIST: That's fine.

• No grudges. Nothing said within a session can be held against anyone after the session is over.

• Right of veto. If someone does not want to discuss an issue in the session, that is his right, at least temporarily. For example, if a sixteen-year-old boy asks his parents about their marriage and they do not feel ready to discuss aspects of it with him, it is their right to say so. At a later date they may feel more comfortable discussing this.

• Any family member may request the temporary exclusion of another family member to discuss a particular issue with greater ease.

• Participants must talk directly to each other. Use eye contact. Parents and child should face each other and not turn chairs to avoid eye contact.

• No person can speak for longer than one minute at any one time. This prevents rambling or domination by a single family member. Family members take turns being "referee" (mirroring the role of a therapist). When emotionally charged issues like drugs, dating, or sexual mores come up, it is crucial that the "referee" remain impartial unless "physical or emotional hazards are involved."

Conducting a Family Council is difficult, but it has proved effective in many cases. Usually it works best when parents and children have had some exposure to family therapy.

b. *Try a parent-teen Behavior Exchange Contract.* This is another version of the Behavior Exchange Contract which I outlined for couples in Chapter 8. Most adolescents do want things from their parents and are willing to admit they have certain rights. These are starting points for negotiations.

● The purpose of the contract is to balance rewards and responsibilities. To get what he wants, *each* party must take on the responsibility of giving the other something in exchange.

● Start with what is most negotiable. There may be some things where there is just no chance for negotiation at this point. To insist on these is to fail in the entire project. However, if you have had a series of successful negotiations on other matters, you may eventually come to some agreement on the more difficult ones.

● The responsibilities and rewards should be described in terms of specific, observable behaviors. For example, the contract might state, "Earn a C grade or better on the weekly quiz" rather than "Do better in class" . . . "You can stay out until 10 o'clock" rather than "You can stay out later."

In a paper, "The Family Contracting Exercise," Drs. Lawrence Weathers and Robert Paul Liberman list reinforcers which can be traded by teen and parent.

Reinforcers which can be offered to teen	Reinforcers which can be offered to parent
1. Stop nagging you about_____	1. Do____minutes homework nightly from____to____
2. Let your son/daughter stay out longer, until _____on weekdays, and _____on weekends.	2. Make my bed and hang up my clothes before I go to school.
3. Let your son/daughter	3. Clean my room, which

go out another night
per week.

4. Give you $_____ per week
allowance

5. Buy you a_____

6. Let you watch TV more.

7. Let you use the family
car to_____.

8. Stop going through your
things.

9. Stop listening in on
your phone calls.

10. Stop being critical of
your clothes, hair,
friends, etc.

11. Let you get a driver's
license.

means_____.

4. Less talking back or
arguing when_____

5. Bring my friends to meet
my parents. Friends are
_____.

6. Improve my grades in the
following:
Pass_____to_____
Pass_____to_____
Pass_____to_____

7. Attend_____classes at
school every day with
less than_____tardies
per_____.

8. Not run away from home.

9. Not smoking (at)_____

10. Help with chores around
the house such as_____.

11. Ask parents' permission
to go out.

12. Be home by_____weekday
nights and_____weekend
nights.

13. Get up in the morning
without a hassle, which
means_____

14. Babysit for younger brother
and sister when_____

15. Play my stereo/TV/radio
more quietly when_____

16. Not fight with my brother/
sister when_____

Parents frequently ask, "If I negotiate a contract like
this, isn't it bribery?" An answer to this might be, "No, it is a
reward. A reward is payment for doing something socially acceptable such as the salary you get for working. A bribe is
payment for doing something illegal or immoral such as
being paid to steal something."

As with all Assertiveness Training, there is no guarantee that you will win them all. You do the best you can; that's all you can do. You may have to accept the fact that there are certain behaviors you cannot change: heavy make-up, drinking, associating with certain kids, smoking pot, premarital sex. Parents object. They say, "It's my responsibility to see that my daughter doesn't sleep around" ... "I must use my authority to see that my daughter doesn't associate with those dreadful kids from bad homes" ... "I'm not willing to sit back and see him smoke grass. I must do something." All a parent can do is be a model, an effective consultant, and try to develop a good relation with the child. If the child is bent on such behaviors, ultimately the parent will not have the power to prevent them.

Comments psychologist Andrew Salter, "Can you be mentally healthy in every area and not be mentally healthy with your kids? No. Can you be mentally healthy with your kids and still have kids that give you headaches? Yes. Children are victims of things over which their parents don't have control. If parents have handled the kids in a healthy way, the children will come out of it every time, but there may be an interim period that will drive you to your wit's end. The resolution of the interim period is primarily determined by the way the children were before they entered it and by parents keeping contact with the children during it. The parents who say 'Why me!' needlessly castigate themselves."

Chapter 11

Getting Where and
What You Want at Work

When the founders of a medium-sized publishing company had a fuss with the new corporate management and walked out, Lois, their right-hand aid and close personal friend, was left with a limited chance of survival under the new regime. Within eight months Lois took three steps. Each time she asked herself the same question, *"What would be the assertive thing to do now?"*

STEP ONE: She decided not to quit in a huff but to stay and see what would happen. To show the new president her loyalty to the company, she immediately sent a lengthy memo detailing work in progress and how she planned to follow through. On every possible occasion she also offered him her help.

STEP TWO: She adopted "the psychology of a top person." Since no one replaced her former superior, who had been editor-in-chief, Lois automatically assumed many of this person's editorial duties. She says, "I just acted as if I were the top acquiring [of manuscripts] editor there—and as a result I became it. All the agents called me."

STEP THREE: In the spring Lois saw that, despite her efforts, the pressures from management were such that she could not find satisfactory solutions to problems. She decided to leave "on my own terms." Wanting to find a job while she still had one, she started an intensive campaign. She recalls, "With interviewers I didn't sound hungry. I sounded sure of myself and successful." Lois started looking on June 18. On August 5 she landed a job with a prestigious publishing company at a sizable increase.

She told me, "It was the concept of assertiveness that helped me. Without it, when my friends quit, I once would have felt, 'I will surely be fired' or, 'I must quit too.' Instead I assumed that I was smart and that the firm would keep me, and it did. When things subsequently went wrong through no fault of mine, I didn't wring my hands and say, 'Oh, dear, what should I do?' I said, 'I'm going to get out.' Once I would have waited until they put me out. I might have gotten severance and unemployment insurance that way, but that wasn't what I wanted. Assertiveness breeds success. People admired what I did. I had my choice of three jobs."

Are you sitting in a dead-end job?

Do you fail to utilize your capabilities at work?

Do you talk about going back to work—and do nothing about it?

Do promotions and raises go to others who are, in actuality, no brighter or more talented than you?

Do you fear success, thinking it will make others— boyfriend, parents, husband—view you as "unfeminine"?

If you answer any of these questions in the affirmative, whether you are single, married, divorced, widowed, have children, belong to a women's group, even if you are making an effort to think, feel or be independent, you are still acting dependently. You may be a passive dependent—you do nothing to change the situation. Or you may be an active dependent—you complain and wring your hands or you do a great deal for the company but fail to think about what's good for the most important person in your professional life—you.

Failure to be an assertive person in the work area affects not only your earning capacity but your attitude toward yourself. This lack of job assertion can take many forms. You can be unassertive because you:

Have never learned to call attention to your own accomplishments.

Procrastinate or daydream away the 9-to-5 hours. Your poor work habits prevent promotion. You constantly expect to get fired. Often you are.

Gripe constantly about your "terrible job," "the awful working conditions," "the waste of my talents," but you never think of any constructive action you can take. You make your complaints to people who aren't in a position to do anything about them rather than those in power.

Can't say no. By saying yes to virtually every request, you can't get the things done that should be done.

Push too hard. Your superiors and co-workers don't like your aggressiveness. Your bull-in-the-china-shop approach also hides the fact that your actual work is very good.

Fear taking risks. Your insecurity makes you tell yourself, "I'm lucky to have the job I have."

Fail to ask yourself, "Is this job giving me what I want from it?"

To different people the job means different things, but any woman who wants to make it in the working world should be aware of certain psychological and practical facts of life.

1. *There is a difference between being assertive on the job, in superficial social relationships and in close relationships.* The goal of the superficial relationship is to make things interesting for you and the others involved. Whether on a date, at a party or ski weekend, you want to share ideas and interests, show something of yourself, and invite the other person to reveal something of himself/herself. In the close relationship the goal should be an ever-increasing sharing of feeling, fantasies, thoughts, emotions. However, on the job the assertive emphasis is on action rather than on feelings or interpersonal growth. Your goal: To achieve your career objectives, keeping your relations with others sufficiently pleasant and smooth so that you can accomplish this goal and *always acting in a way which you yourself respect.*

2. *More and more women are entering the job market—* mainly because of economic necessity but also through choice. However, unlike men, most women get their jobs by

chance. Men are conditioned. They have been raised to believe that all their adult lives they will be working and supporting a family. Thus they view working as a long-term commitment, which is something most women don't do. Women must realize that there's a need for them to be prepared to be independent, that working might not always be something that is fun, fills time, or provides clothes and family vacations. They have to ask themselves what will happen in the job area if I never marry, my husband dies suddenly, or if I get divorced.

3. *There's a female generation gap*. The under-twenty-fives feel a "woman can do anything." The twenty-fives to thirty-fives think, "A woman can do almost anything." But according to management expert David McLaughlin, principal of McKinsey & Co. and author of *The Executive Money Map*, "The bulk of women from the mid-30s on have been terribly conditioned by 100 years of discrimination in American industry to think in narrow terms. They show this by their aspirations. They never assume they can become president of a company. They think, 'I don't have to remain a secretary,' but they don't think big. Men do. Women also aren't as sophisticated as men about money. They tend to think of pay as a salary check. And they usually lack the ability to function as part of the power group. It's the women who have been working for a while who really show this societal conditioning."

4. *Things are changing, but even in business the double standard still exists*. Thousands upon thousands of men are incapable, unwilling, or reluctant to concede that women should have the same privileges, rights, and freedom they have themselves. A man may remind a woman that she is not an equal member of the group with, "Let's hear from the lady first." He may deliberately hire an incompetent woman, so that, when she fails on the job, he can say, "I told you it wouldn't work." He may assume that any female answering the telephone is a secretary. He may pat a woman on the head when he is pleased with her and comment, "You're a real doll." He may not only refer to his gray-haired and competent secretary as "a girl" but as "my girl."

The myths still exist. Here are some of the most prevalent, as noted by Edith M. Lynch in the book *The Executive Suite—Feminine Style*:

- Women can't take heavy responsibility.
- Women ask for special privileges (You need just one special privilege—maternity leave).
- Women cry too much—they are too emotional.
- Women are terrible bosses and men don't like to work for them.
- Women are terrible bosses and other women don't like to work for them.
- Women use dirtier tactics than men to climb up the ladder.
- Women can't do two jobs well—either home or career must suffer.
- Women in management have lost their femininity.

5. *Women perpetuate these myths.* Often they are their own worst enemy. Says Dr. Elizabeth Mintz, a New York psychologist, "A woman feels she has to choose between being a woman and being a success." Many women discriminate against themselves. For instance, after Assertiveness Training, one woman realized that at her weekly department conference, where she was the only woman, she automatically took a seat at the salt end of the table, separating herself from the others. She did not consider herself a full-fledged member of the group. Other women fear that success will make them social outcasts with their friends and family and arouse hostility in both male and female co-workers. They have learned the lesson all too well, "Women are taught not to compete—and if they compete, not to win." The lesson is that you won't be popular if you win, and many women are sure this is true. As one female executive points out, "We have met the enemy and it is us."

To be assertive on the job, you need to learn these two "lessons":

- Be action-oriented—not passive, dependent, diffident, docile, or aggressive.
- Realize that self-assertion is vital to any job situation.

AN ASSERTIVE PROGRAM FOR SURVIVAL, SUCCESS, AND GROWTH ON THE JOB

Take Inventory of Who You Are, Where You Would Like to Go, and What You Can Do to Get There

You should do this whether you're thinking about getting a job, leaving a job, have a job you hate or one you love.

1. *Before you even start to think about career objectives, get rid of the biases with which you have been brought up.* Don't blame "the system" for what you are now. You have to eliminate certain traditional attitudes on your own: that there's a conflict between femininity and assertiveness, the fear of working for a female or having a man work for you, in short, all the things I've talked about in the book so far. By understanding why you think the way you do, you can re-think where you're at and take the steps to become the professional person you want to be.

2. *Assess your strengths and weaknesses.* Periodically you should take a reading of both your good and bad points. There are several assessment methods you might use.

a. *Find out how strongly motivated you are about having a career.* Here is a quiz* used by Edith M. Lynch in her book *The Executive Suite—Feminine Style.*

JOB MOTIVATION QUIZ

1. What do I really think of my own talents?
2. Am I willing to make the most of my talents?
3. Do I resent the fact that men seem to have the best jobs,

*Reprinted by permission of the publisher from *The Executive Suite—Feminine Style* by Edith M. Lynch. © 1973 by AMACOM, a division of American Management Associations.

the best chances of promotion, and the most exciting challenges?

4. How am I trying to improve my own position—more education, more research, better attitude?

5. Do I look at everything emotionally instead of making some well-thought-out plans?

6. When did I last read a book pertaining to a job I'd like to hold?

7. Do I continually think of myself as a secretary, as a helper, as a crutch instead of being the actual person doing the higher-level job?

8. Do I pass the blame for not having a good job off on someone else—my parents, the boss, the school I attended, and so on?

9. Am I willing to do the hard work necessary to hold a responsible job?

10. Am I willing to work as a member of a team to accomplish a worthwhile project?

11. Am I willing to help others on the way up, particularly women?

12. Am I willing to fight for my rights on equal ground and on the basis of what I have done and can do in the future?

b. *See how well you know yourself.* To find out your pluses and minuses, you must analyze your experiences, not just work experiences but things that have happened to you at home, school, and in the community.

JOB PROFILE QUIZ

Fill out the answers to the following quiz in your Female Assertiveness Notebook.

1. What are ten success experiences that you have had in your life—things you have done that have left you with a sense of accomplishment? Next to each "success experience" explain why you enjoyed it and the skill you used. For instance, if you won the senior debate contest in high school, the skill would be public speaking. The only stipulation: You, not someone else, must consider this accomplishment important. Note: Thinking this through takes time but it's worth it.

2. What are five to ten experiences that you have *not* enjoyed, ones that left you feeling confused, dissatisfied, or even with a sense of failure? Think through what it actually was that you didn't enjoy.

3. List the jobs you have held (paid or voluntary). Then note which aspects of each job were the most pleasurable for you (for instance, working with people, type of work, etc.) and which aspects gave you the most trouble.

4. How do you get along with fellow employees?

5. What has bothered you most about fellow employees?

6. How have you gotten along with your supervisors?

7. What has bothered you most about your supervisors?

8. How much anxiety do you feel in the following job situations (this item is adapted from a questionaire used by Dr. Patricia Wisocki at the University of Massachusetts):

The first day on the job	Being criticized by a peer
Being supervised	Making mistakes
Shifting job	Being ignored
Being alone	Looking foolish
Presenting a work report	Being absent from work
Failing at an assignment	Giving people orders
Being late to work	Telling someone he/she is
Traveling on a job	doing a poor job
Sudden emergencies	Firing someone
Being watched working	Feeling rejected
Being criticized by a superior	

Rate yourself on the following scale:
   1=not at all   4=much
   2=a little   5=very much
   3=a fair amount

9. What would you like to be earning in five years? In ten years?

10. What would you like to be doing in five years? In ten years?

11. What fantasies do you have relating to the work area?

If you really put effort into filling out this job profile, when you go over it you will discover some common links. For instance, I found out that all my "success experiences" took place in the morning or evening—never in the afternoon, when, for some physiological reason, I am always terribly tired. I also discovered that I'm a sprinter, not a "marathon man"; I like to work hard for days and then collapse; I don't like to pace myself for a long, even run. You may find you like solving problems but hate detail work, or that you're happy only when working with people and don't like to be alone.

3. *Make sure your personal job goals are based on reality—not your personal neuroses.* No one says you have to go to work if you're completely happy as a homemaker, or that you have to move out of your current dead-end position. Job goals can run the gamut. Your goal may be to make a huge amount of money, gain fame and prestige, face unusual challenges, help the downtrodden, have complete tenure and job security. You can also have the goal of having a low-key job where you do only what you have to do and receive your satisfactions from out-of-the-office activities.

However, many women have neurotic job goals. In all those years at *Seventeen* I never once thought of promotion, switching jobs, or asking for a raise. Instead I craved approval from my boss, co-workers, and contacts. It was crazy. On one occasion I had pulled off a virtually impossible public relations feat. My boss called and said, "Good job. Now send me a memo on your future plans." Instead of responding with, "I'd like some tangible recognition of the job I just did" (which, incidentally, she would have respected me for), I said a heartfelt, "Thank you" to the meager praise and felt good all day. Mama loved me!

Avoid such neurotic goals as winning approval and having everyone love you, being indispensable (the "If-I-leave, everything-will-collapse" syndrome) or setting up such impossible working situations that everyone says, "poor you." Getting attention this way may win you plaudits and sympathy but won't advance your professional interests.

Evaluate your job goals the way you do other assertive acts. Will the goal move you toward the direction you want? Will it increase your self-respect?

4. *Have a self-development plan.*

a. *Pinpoint some areas of interest.* The Job Profile Quiz should be of help. A close friend or your spouse can also be of assistance. For instance, while on vacation in Vienna, one forty-two-year-old woman, mother of three, with a background in theater, found herself thinking, "I'll die if I don't go back to work and do something challenging." Her husband, a psychologist, suggested, "What about getting into behavioral counseling as a career?" Her first answer was, "Maybe I should get behavioral counseling for my anxiety." He responded, "You must do something. It's not life or death if you don't do the right thing." So she applied to take a graduate degree in the counseling psychology program of a major western university, discovered it was "the right thing," and now teaches at three colleges!

b. *Find out what your chosen work field entails*—how the jobs within it are sorted out, who does what, what areas of knowledge are involved, what current and future problems confront leaders in the field. To do this, read books on the subject, more specific literature from professional organizations, trade magazines, want ads. Two excellent books are *Women & Success*, edited by Ruth B. Kundsin, Sc.D., and *Everything a Woman Needs to Know to Get Paid What She's Worth* by Caroline Bird.

c. *You should also seek out knowledgeable people in the field.* Interview people who actually hold the jobs. If you want to learn about advertising copy, talk to someone who does it. If you don't know anyone in advertising, ask your friends, parents, or husband to introduce you.

d. *Ask yourself, "What do I have to do to become the best candidate for the job when it becomes available?"* What's the interim step? It may involve taking a course, switching to a low-girl-on-the-totem-pole position to get a start in a new field, moonlighting. Planning and preparation now will pay off in the future. In one of my Assertiveness Training groups for women, one member, a nurse, has put herself on a spartan economy to save money toward getting a Ph.D. in psychology. In the meantime she works weekends at the hospital so she can take graduate courses on her midweek days off.

Plan a Job Campaign

Reading want ads is not enough. You have to take the assertive approach to getting the job that is right for you.

1. *Write a masterful résumé.* If you're not good with words, ask a friend to help you with it or go to a résumé-writing service. Tailor it to the specific job you want; don't make it a chronological catch-all. A prospective employer isn't really interested in where you were born. If you're a reentry woman, don't negate some of the community activities you've done along with being wife, mother, hostess, chauffeur and cook. One woman ran an amateur theater group in a Chicago suburb. She incorporated this experience into a résumé paragraph headed, "Experience in developing and managing talent." She cited the growth of her theater from 15 participants to 240, her initiation and production of a brochure that played an important part in selling "the season" of four plays, the part she played in picking casts and plays, the financial success of the operation. With this résumé she managed to land a job as a booking agent for a national lecture bureau.

2. *Make a list of companies that offer the kind of job you want.* Make a list of your contacts. Let everyone know you're looking. A friend just might hear about a job where the needs match yours. I would have been perfectly willing to leave *Seventeen* but I never divulged this to any of my highly placed contacts. At lunch they would say, "You've stayed so long; you must love it there." I would just nod. This is known as missing-the-chance-to-speak-up department. Investigate employment agencies and listen to what the counselors tell you. Get in touch with appropriate professional and trade associations; they frequently have inside knowledge of specialized openings. NOW may be of help.

3. *Write letters to people you don't know and would like to know.* Say just that. Do not write to a peer. Try the president of a company or the vice-president in charge of the specific area to which you think you can contribute something. Be sure to spell his/her name correctly and that you have his/her title right. In your letter explain briefly your accomplishments, point out that you realize that there may be nothing available at this moment but that you would like to *meet* him/her. The last is the most important. You want to get your foot in the door. When I was a junior at Cornell I wrote such a letter to a woman who was an NBC vice-president and

a Cornell graduate. We met at Easter and liked each other. That June she offered me a four-week summer job.

4. *Prepare for the interview.* With a friend or your husband, role-play the possible problem questions that may arise ("Why haven't you worked for a year?" ... "Supposing a deadline assignment comes up. Who will take care of your children?" ... "Why have you had three jobs in five years?" ... "Why are you unhappy with your present job?"). You should also rehearse the response-to-put-downs techniques I outlined in Chapter 5 just in case you get that "I'll train you and then you'll get pregnant" routine. If married, be prepared to answer the question, "If your husband gets transferred, what will you do?" You can say, "There is little chance of that happening" or do as one woman did and say, "We've made the decision that if I get this job, which means so much to me, and this situation comes up, Bill will get another job here."

5. *Perform well at the interview.* Think of it as selling yourself as a product. What will make you sell yourself well? This is not the time to come on disinterested and shy. Be capable and assertive.

Look good (part of selling a product is packaging). When I switched to free-lance writing and was going around calling on editors, I bought a sweater, scarf and skirt right from the cover of *Vogue.* As a magazine veteran I knew the effort that goes into picking cover clothes. And without exception the first words of every editor were, "I like your outfit." I made a good impression before I opened my mouth.

While you're being interviewed, be specific ("I can do this job because————," not, "I'm good with people") and positive. Don't use words or phrases like "perhaps," "maybe," or, "I'm not an expert in that area." Don't apologize for anything (like lack of college). Stress your special experience and expertise.

Your research should enable you to know going rates for the job you're after, but always wait at least eight seconds before responding to any salary offer made to you. The interviewer may say, "Oh, well, we knew we couldn't get you for that" and offer higher.

Don't forget you have the right to ask the interviewer about his company. Be prepared with a list of your own questions. These should not be of the "How long will it be before I get promoted?" variety (that's up to you when and if you get the job) but should relate to the objectives of the company and what you would actually be doing on this specific job.

If you haven't heard from the interviewer in a week, follow up and find out the decision.

Comments David McLaughlin, "It's easy today for a woman to sell herself—particularly for a job not previously held by a woman. Businesses today are conscious of their vulnerability in not tapping women."

Act Assertively on the Job

To do this, you will need the same skills you require in social situations—the ability to say no, make requests, express positive and negative feelings appropriately. But again, remember your aim is different: you are not seeking closer or deeper personal relationships with other human beings (although they may develop); you want to do your job well and in a way that makes you like yourself.

1. *Be competent.* Let someone else quote the Peter Principle or get away with reading the *Times* all morning and the *Post* all afternoon. When it gets down to basics, before anyone is promoted in an organization, the prospective boss will ask your current superior, "How well did she perform for you?" Even if you are expert at office politics, you still have to exhibit job competence to be assigned more responsibility.

2. *Make sure you have the skills needed to keep your present job.* Mary Joan Glynn, general manager and operating head of the Borghese Division of Revlon Inc., recalls that she painstakingly taught herself a new skill at each step up because she could not have performed each new job without it. "I was vice-president for product development at Doyle Dane Bernbach [the Manhattan advertising agency] before I learned how to prepare a budget," she says. "I sat down with the accountant and studied how."

a. *If you want to move on to a higher job, acquire the skills that will help you accomplish this aim.* You can learn them on the job, from research or taking courses. Be sure to let people know you possess these new skills.

b. *Make your working environment pleasant so that you can operate at maximum efficiency.* Don't be afraid to ask for a better lamp, typewriter, or chair. I work in our bedroom and, until recently, walking across the book-piled floor was like negotiating an obstacle course. The file cabinet and one bookcase already in the room just didn't hold enough working equipment. So I went to an unpainted furniture store, bought two cabinets (one with sliding doors) and a bookcase, had them hinged together and, presto, for an investment of $315 changed my working life. Now I can be neat and thus get more done.

3. *Don't let bad habits like procrastination, lateness, and lack of concentration interfere with your work.* To be assertive you must be in control of yourself. You must realize that it's up to you to modify, control, and change your own behavior. I outlined some of these rules for behavioral change in the goals section of Chapter 4.

To overcome your bad business habits:

a. Identify the habit you want to change (for example, lateness to work).

b. Prepare a specific program for changing these behaviors. You write down a contract of intention in which you outline the specific actions you will take to change.

c. Set as your goal something you can reasonably accomplish right now (you do not use, "I will get to work every day on time"; you do use, "I will be at my desk by 9 A.M. tomorrow"). You want a series of successes.

d. Examine the situation to see if you can make the unwanted act harder to perform and the desired act easier to perform. For example, I have telephonitis. Few things give me more pleasure than a series of hour-long conversations. But morning is my working time. If I chit-chat on the phone all morning, I'm good for nothing in the afternoon. So, every morning I *turn my phone off* until 1 P.M. In that way I remove temptation and make it easier for myself to perform my stint at the typewriter.

e. Establish the desired habit. And that's where the rewards come in. I repeat, you can give yourself presents or get them from others in the form of attention and plaudits ("How quickly you did that job. Your work certainly has improved"). Ask your friends to praise you as you work to overcome your job block.

f. Monitor yourself. Keep charts. It will make you feel good if you see you're performing the wanted behavior more and the unwanted behavior less. When I write, I try to do twelve pages a day. I make little lists that read "page 1 ... 2 ... 3 ... 4 ... 12." As I write each page, I make an appropriate cross check on the list. It helps me do my stint.

4. *Stand up for yourself.* In office situations you constantly deal with other people. How you handle yourself affects your relations with them, your work, standing in the company, and your opinion of yourself. How would you handle the following situations which were used in an Assertiveness Training pilot study of professional women at the University of Wisconsin?

EXAMPLE ONE: You are one of five assistants in an office, but you are the only one who is a woman. One of the secretaries of the supervisor just above you is about to leave on vacation and asks you to do some of her typing chores during her absence. What do you do?

Wrong way: You agree to do it or else give an overapologetic defensive excuse like, "I'd like to but I'm just so overloaded. I'm sure Mr. Smith will understand that I really can't."

Right way: "You know I can't do this. I suggest you take it up with personnel. I'm surprised you asked me; you know very well it isn't my work."

EXAMPLE TWO: One of your subordinates has not been handing in his work on time. In the past you've chastised him in a nice calm way. What do you do now?

Wrong way: Say nothing (thinking to yourself, "If I keep on criticizing him, he won't like me") or make the same nice, calm speech you've made before.

Right way: Call on your skills of supervision. You may want to bawl him out ("This kind of lateness isn't acceptable"), threaten ("This is absolutely your last chance") or try the "We have a problem" approach.

EXAMPLE THREE: Your supervisor tells you that your recent work has not been satisfactory. What do you say?

Wrong way: "But you told me that I handled the Graham project very well."

Right way: "You told me that I handled the Graham project very well so it can't be that. I'd appreciate it if you would tell me what is bothering you about my work."

EXAMPLE FOUR: You are at a meeting with your co-workers and are discussing a topic that you feel very strongly about. The majority of your peers are on the opposite side of the argument. The director comments that they are running out of time and calls for a vote before you've spoken about your views. What do you do?

In responding to this situation, it would be wrong to consider only that you "feel strongly" about the topic. You have to make a tactical decision based on your goals within the company. This is something only you can decide. Depending on your goal, it might be best to fight on the spot ("Before the vote I'd like to present my views"), take a delaying action ("There's much to be said on the other side, and I would like to send a memo to everyone present"), or to conclude that creating a fuss may not be worth the effort and the antagonism you'd arouse in the power hierarchy.

A Guide to Speaking Up on the Job

a. *Don't let other people take credit for your ideas*. If you ignore this kind of behavior, you encourage its repetition. Confront the person. Say something like, "You damn well know that the idea you gave at the presentation this morning was mine. Don't let it happen again."

Nip idea-stealing in the bud. Preventive device: If your boss takes credit for all your bright thoughts, put them in writing. Send a memo to your boss with a copy to his/her boss. Remember, your aim is to get credit. Refusing to talk to the culprit won't get you anywhere but limbo.

However, in refusing to let other people take credit for your ideas, there is a caveat: There may be times when the tactical situation—for one reason or another—calls for you to suffer the idea-stealing and not make an issue out of it.

Whatever action you take, make sure you do it out of deliberate choice.

b. *Express your feelings to the office pest.* You don't have to let someone else sit at your desk when you're not there, riffle your papers, go through your files on the pretext of "I need————," or tear pages of pretty clothes and recipes out of your magazines. As public relations director of *Seventeen*, I used to get daily copies of the *Times* and *Post*. Suddenly, I noticed that the *Post* would disappear overnight. This went on for months. I made it my business to find out who was stealing the paper and one day said to the offender, "You've been stealing my *Post*. I need it. Please stop." She laughed and said, "I've been playing a joke. I wondered how long it would take you to find out." The joke was over. She stopped stealing.

c. *Learn to say no to superiors, subordinates, and peers.* It is difficult to refuse a request made by the boss who controls your paycheck and promotions. You have to evaluate the risk. At the same time, not all bosses are ogres. Rule: In saying no in the job situation you cannot offer a vague answer like, "I just don't feel like it" as you might to a friend's suggestion that you go to the movies together. You must tell the reason why ("No, I'm sorry, but I can't stay late. I have an appointment for the evening and there's no way of getting in touch with the person").

You can also say no to a subordinate when the request is unreasonable. "No, you cannot take your vacation in June; that's our busiest season" ... "No, you cannot leave early on Friday afternoon. You're way behind in your work" ... "No, you cannot keep on making dental appointments for 9:30 A.M. Go at lunchtime the way I do." Remember, subordinates don't have to love you. They do have to respect you.

d. *Ask for what you want—whether promotion, raises, or favor.* If you don't get it, at least you'll know where you stand with the company. Make it as simple as possible for the boss to give you what you want. Don't ask him/her on a bad day or in the midst of frenzy.

In asking for a raise:

• Be sure you're familiar with office policies. If it's Standard Operating Procedure to review salary increases in January and June, don't ask in February or July.

• Be prepared with documentation as to why you deserve an increase. Don't use lines like, "I can't afford to live on my salary" or, "I need more money because I'm worth it." You do use lines like, "In the past six months I have taken over all the duties previously handled by a full-time employee" or, "I have just discovered that you are paying my male peer $2,000 a year more than I get—even though he has five years' less experience and does less work. Is it because he's male and I'm female? I'd like this inequity straightened out."

• Consider whether a face-to-face confrontation is the best way of getting what you want. Would it be wiser to send a memo detailing your accomplishments and what they have meant to the company? Should you send the memo and then ask for an appointment? Would it be better to see the boss alone or flanked by a backup subsidiary boss to talk up for you? If you do have the meeting, make sure you've marshaled your arguments—not just the content but how you'll present them.

• Reduce your anxiety. Role-play at home with your spouse or friend, anticipating all the possible answers the boss might give to your raise request ("Well, we've been cutting back and no one is getting a raise" ... "Come back in six months," etc.), and the answers you might give to various statements. Or try this Assertiveness Training exercise in Covert Reinforcement, designed to reduce your fears. In Covert Reinforcement, a technique developed by Dr. Joseph R. Cautela, professor of psychology at Boston College and past president of the Association for the Advancement of Behavior Therapy, you take the behavior you want to perform; you *imagine* doing it; you reinforce your performance of that act *through imagery*.

EXERCISE IN COVERT REINFORCEMENT

STEP ONE: Take the act you want to perform—in this case asking for a raise.

STEP TWO: Break the act down into specific parts. You should write them down. For example:

• At the office you calmly think, "I will call the boss's secretary now and ask for an appointment."

- You pick up the phone. Again you feel relaxed.
- Dial the extension in a calm way.
- Make the appointment. Again, you are calm.
- At the designated time walk into the boss's office.
- You hear the boss say, "What's on your mind, Jill?" Again notice you are calm and relaxed.
- You state your case. Again, you are calm and relaxed.

STEP THREE: Select a reinforcing image. It can be anything that provides you with a sensation of pleasure. Dr. Cautela used "skiing down a mountain feeling exhilarated," but it can also be eating a pound of chocolates at one sitting, meeting a gorgeous man, winning the lottery, or hearing your husband say, "I'm really proud of you."

STEP FOUR: Read the first item on your list and imagine it. Be sure that you imagine it the way you would like it to be: performing the act calmly. Do not practice failures. When you have the image the way you want it to be, then say to yourself "Reinforcement" and switch to your pleasurable image. Do this ten times and go on to the next item on the list. Do this exercise every day until you feel less anxious and able to go in and actually ask for the raise. Note: Don't get discouraged. You may have to do this many, many times before it works.

STEP FIVE: When you feel ready, perform the act in step-by-step fashion just as you did in imagery.

Whatever you ask for, you must:
- Be prepared so that your words come out right. In one instance, a resident wanted permission to carry out some unusual projects at a Manhattan hospital. She says, "Once I would have just gone in and asked the director of training. But this time I worked out my whole talk with pencil and paper and then role-played it with my husband. I was sure the boss would say no. But I was so well documented that when I got through with my presentation, he said simply, 'Sounds like a good idea to me.' "
- Realize that bosses aren't mind readers. If you don't ask for what you want, they can't know you want it.

e. *Learn to make points at meetings.* You don't sit there

like the proverbial dummy (unassertive), nor do you hog the show (aggressive), but you are positive ("I believe" ... "I think————") and prepared. Some people keep brainwashing themselves with, "I'm no good at business meetings" or, "Supposing I suggest something and everyone laughs" or, "I will fail miserably." You can train yourself to control this sort of obsessive dithering with the behavioral technique of Thought Stoppage.

EXERCISE IN THOUGHT STOPPAGE

STEP ONE: Sit down in a comfortable chair and place in your mind the thought you want to control: "I'm no good at business meetings—if I speak up, they'll laugh." As soon as you have the thought firmly in your mind, say out loud STOP!, then to yourself "Calm," and very deliberately relax your muscles for about five to ten seconds. You want to get at least *a momentary break in the thought* you want to control! If you don't get the break, do the exercise again and say STOP! much more loudly. Then go on to the next step—for instance, the suggestion you'd like to make at the meeting.

STEP TWO: Repeat the exercise, but say the STOP! to yourself instead of aloud. If you have trouble in getting the break, try snapping a rubber band against your wrist as you say it.

You should perform this STOP!-Calm-Relax routine on every possible occasion before the meeting. Do it *as soon as* and *every time* you have an anxious thought about it. Keep repeating the procedure, because if you give the anxiety a chance to build up, it becomes harder to control. Always aim at getting that momentary break in thought.

f. *Speak up when a fellow worker keeps you from doing your job.* This is not tattletaling but self-protection. Go to the boss but be prepared with a solution.

g. *If you're a supervisor, act like one.* Learn the skills of being a supervisor. This means:

• Learn how to get your subordinates to do their own work. This means you plan, give orders and follow through. At the same time *let them do their work*. This has always been one of my problems. I couldn't let go of the reins. I wanted to do everything, so I'd come in at 8 A.M. to do someone else's work. At the end of the day I was exhausted. She felt fine.

• Give feedback. Employees want to know when they've done a good job. Tell them.

• Learn how to fire an employee. No one likes doing this but, again, your aim on the job is performance, not filial love. You can give a warning ("Shape up or ship out") or offer a choice of firing or resigning, or just do it—directly and definitely. If it's reorganization, try the line, "I couldn't feel worse. I do hope we can hire you back." With the crybaby type, you can try, "Everybody has been fired at some time—you're not a failure, you're just in the wrong job." Even if the person has been a total loss, be pleasant and never fire when you're angry; that will lead to counteraccusations. You want to be in control of yourself, the situation, the person.

h. *If you're in business for yourself, you must learn to speak up for the money your services are worth.* Don't sell yourself short. Make a realistic appraisal of the cost to you, the expenses, and a preset figure of profit. You have to know your worth and be able to state it in financial terms. If you can't, you should not be in your own business. I can't and that's why I have an agent.

i. *Sleep with the boss—or not?* According to a survey, conducted by Edith M. Lynch for her book *The Executive Suite—Feminine Style,* most respondents said a resounding "No." The reasons offered varied from, "I'm afraid that if I slept with him, we'd lose our boss-subordinate relationship and neither of us would like to be around the other in the office" to, "Keep in mind you may have to work with the guy when the romance is dead. Can you?" One woman offered what I thought an intelligent and assertive response: "If I were in a position to become romantically involved, I certainly would not let the fact that someone is my colleague or my boss stand in the way. Of necessity, however, they should be of a certain caliber, someone who would not discuss it or cause gossip among other colleagues. Nor would I expect to be told things about work situations which were none of my business. Each individual should know herself and the other person well enough to decide whether or not she can handle any situation which would occur."

Rise Up the Ladder

To reach the executive suite or even the upper echelons of middle management, you have to succeed and survive as a person—not because you're a woman or because you act like a man. The same types of assertive techniques help both men and women move up the ladder.

A Guide to Climbing Up the Ladder

1. *Act confident.* Says David McLaughlin, "Men lead from strength. But even very successful women carry their cultural conditioning with them. They constantly worry, 'Someone will take the job away,' and thus they violate the basic rule of negotiation—come on sure of yourself."

Sally Quinn, who wrote the book *We're Going to Make You a Star* about her fiasco as hostess on a TV show, told me, "When I was twenty-one and just graduated from Smith College, I had no self-confidence. I didn't know what I was going to do. And then I met a great guy, an athlete who, at twenty-two, was an assistant professor. A week later I learned he was impotent. I couldn't understand how, with his handicap, he was so confident, so I asked him.

"He told me, 'Self-confidence is a matter of the image you present to the world. If you think you're a winner, people will treat you that way. Stop saying you're a loser. You've got to act like a winner.' "

Sally did. She made a success of a job on *The Washington Post,* when she'd never written a word in her life. She got the chance to be anchorwoman on the CBS "Morning News," blew it, and proceeded, in her own words, to become "the laughingstock of television." She says, "Finally, I had to quit, but I pulled myself up from a nervous breakdown and got on my feet. I got a job on *The New York Times* and now I'm a feature writer on *The Washington Post.* That traumatic situation changed me. Some months ago Governor Harriman gave a party to honor Senator Frank Church as a candidate. I went as a reporter. At the end they sent the ladies upstairs.

I wouldn't go, and I left. I wouldn't have done this before the CBS experience. It's my own personal stand."

Whatever "personal stand" you choose to take, you must do it from a base of confidence.

2. *Don't get stuck in a dead-end job.* Don't say to yourself, "My boss's job is the only one above me and he'll be here until the millennium"; prepare yourself for your boss's job even if you have to find its counterpart in another company. Or see if you can't slough off some of the menial parts of your present work while assuming the more creative duties of what is now another job. I know one food editor who, when the job of equipment editor opened up at her magazine, went to the boss and said, "I can do both jobs if you let me have one more assistant." She got the assistant, the new job and a raise—and got rid of the food-testing chore.

Wherever you now work, look around for a job that is not being done or need that is not being met, figure out why you're the best person to perform the service involved, and then approach the boss with a well-thought-out proposal. Even if he shoots your idea down, he'll be impressed. If there is any one failing that holds women back, it is their tendency to get lost in the job. Men want money, position, the power to get things done from the job. Women are often too agreeable, afraid of disappointing someone, and become doormats on the job.

3. *Find a powerful advocate.* This is also known as "get yourself a rabbi" (you'll hang on to his coattails), the "Godfather technique," and "hitch your wagon to a star." You don't have to pick the very top boss but someone ahead of you in the power hierarchy who's impressed by you and is good at moving people along. By allying yourself with a person in power you may not only move up in the company but often may move along with him/her when he takes off for a more challenging job.

4. *Take calculated risks.* The more risks you take, the more you learn about yourself. When you've risked enough times, you feel confident. It's hard to be strong if you never take risks. That's one of the many things I did wrong at *Seventeen*. I never left because I rationalized, "Another job might not be any better" . . . "This one is at least secure" . . . "I get free trips—I might not get them anywhere else." By risking, I

might have doubled my own salary and had plenty of cash to pay for my own expeditions.

5. *Be visible.* To get ahead, you can't just have the objective to "do a good job for the company." You want to apply your efforts to consequential tasks, working in an area where there's the chance of recognition, not on minor but necessary matters in a back room. Look for special projects. Create them or go to the boss of another department and say, "I'm totally turned on by————project and I'd like to be considered for work on something similar." You can also seek out special outside projects that will bring you professional attention—for instance, writing an article for a trade magazine. Remember, it takes just as much energy to work at a job with limited potential as it does to work at one with big.

6. *Choose your subordinates carefully.* Competent ones will help *you* move up the ladder.

7. *When negotiating situations occur, speak up assertively.*

• *Acceptance of assignments.* For example, out-of-town top management suggests a proposal for your area that you know is a bad idea. Counter with another suggestion or slant theirs differently ("That's right on target with something I was thinking about. What would you think if we did it in this way————?"). On many occasions I have used the sentence, "I think the most *professional* way of handling it would be to————."

• *Who'll be at meetings.* If you aren't included in the line-up for a specific conference and feel you should be, act. You can write a memo, "I understand there will be a meeting on the subject of————on January 19. I've got some ideas on this and would like to be present. O.K.?"

• *Who's to make certain trips.* Again, ask, if you feel you're the one to make the trip and provide documentation as to why your on-the-spot presence will help the company. This is one area in which I was strong. I would think up story ideas involving how teens lived in out-of-the-way locations and, in this way, traveled everywhere from Lima, Peru, to the USSR. I got to go because I had the idea.

• *Selling yourself for an upward move within the company.* Says David McLaughlin, "All the best negotiating starts with a knowledge of things. Men are able to get more information—in the locker room they hear, 'Joe is moving

into another department'—but they also do a better job of
research. Women are cautious and sometimes obsessed with
being a woman. They worry, 'How should I dress for the
meeting?' ... 'Supposing he asks me what I'll do if my husband gets transferred?' They should spend their time finding
out about the possible new boss, his history, the nature of the
problems in the company, the competitors for the job."

• *When it looks as if you're going to be fired unjustly.*
Make your boss *show cause.* If he can't, go to his boss and
say, "I'm being fired without cause." Be smart. Tote along
with you the complete file of ideas you've given to your boss.
Sometimes you can backstop the dismissal. It also helps if
you've built up a *heroine file* where bosses and contacts have
written laudatory memos and letters to top management
about you.

8. *Recognize the importance of sports.* Men do a lot of
business on the golf course and tennis court. "I've yet to meet
any woman who has figured this out and used it as a technique for herself," says McLaughlin.

9. *Learn about money and taxes.* Says David McLaughlin,
"An unfair proportion of firms pay women what they can get
away with. And leaping from the secretarial ghetto into management is no automatic guarantee of equitable salaries and
fringe benefits. Women are particularly disadvantaged because there are complex cultural processes that discourage
them from understanding taxes." His pointers:

• Make sure your base salary is competitive and fair because most other forms of compensation are keyed to salary.
Also, don't let your present salary control a new salary offer
when accepting a promotion or making a job change.

• Recognize that the key to pay progress is rapid promotion. Too many women executives let companies change their
titles and responsibilities without a proper pay boost. The key
to real pay progress is to beat the averages. This means pro-
motional increases that, in most well-run organizations, are
double the merit increases. After five years' work experience,
women executives should start to make at least $1,000 for ev-
ery year of their lives ($27,000 annually if twenty-seven,
$30,000 if thirty) if they're going to be in the upper half of
the executive population.

• Recognize that salary is just the tip of the iceberg in

managerial pay. You should know the amount of your life insurance coverage, how much salary continuance there would be in case of long-term disability, after sick pay runs out, and what the maximum is under group major medical plan. In the executive ranks salary accounts for only 40 to 50 percent of total pay. When you move, negotiate a total pay package including a leveraged bonus, some form of stock equity, if possible, and if the risks are high, an employment contract.

• Focus on plans that build your personal net worth. Stock options are very valuable, especially the new nonqualified type which runs for ten years. Don't ignore retirement plans. You can build net worth savings through a variety of corporate pay schemes—a qualified profit-sharing plan, a savings or thrift plan, a qualified stock purchase plan, stock option or deferred compensation in addition to the pension. You can utilize most of these techniques if you have your own business.

• Adopt a tax minimization strategy. Take advantage of deductions. Many forms of pay are tax free. Others can create tax shelters. Owning a house or apartment can offer tax advantages as opposed to renting.

10. *Think through how you're going to handle sticky situations.*

• *On the road.* When you travel with a male peer or boss, know his style. If you're going to Los Angeles, and he's the go-getter type who starts with breakfast with some contact at 7 A.M. and finishes with a business dinner that ends at midnight, don't interpret this as, "He doesn't want me with him—I'm being left out of the club" and sit in your hotel room sulking. Find out *beforehand* what is expected of you. Ask, "Should I make my own evening plans?" ... "Will I go along on your appointments?" If you find out that he wants his own company and not yours, set up your own schedule.

• *If you travel with a barfly or married man on the make.* Take the initiative and say, "I'm going to the theater this evening and then directly back to the hotel for an early night. Would you like me to get an extra ticket for you?" If he refuses, you're off the hook and he's free.

• *When a man automatically assumes you're a secretary.* Do what makes you feel right. You can shrug it off or correct him. A thirty-year-old bank vice-president says, "I've been to meetings and parties with magnates. When I'm introduced, they just look through me. They make the assumption I'm a secretary. Sometimes, just for fun, I tell them at parties that I am."

• *Awkward social situations.* When do you start to call your boss by his first name? What do you do when, at a meeting, someone uses a dirty word and all the males stare at you, awaiting your reaction? What do you do when you're refused admission to an exclusive male club? You have to be prepared for these situations, always realizing that you walk the executive tightrope. For example, you may be at an out-of-town restaurant with a group of male peers and a stacked waitress walks by. One man makes a crack. If you make a crack too, you're not sharing a joke; you're putting her down. If you say, "poor joke" or, "How well hung are you?" you're classified as a "Women's libber—stay away from her or she'll castrate you." Any reaction may make you stereotypable, so you walk the tightrope. Sometimes it may be best to do nothing right then and speak up to the offender later. Remember, the higher you rise the more men will categorize: "bitch," "earth mother," "sexist woman."

11. *Learn something in depth.* You move up in a company on the basis of contribution. You must keep current and avoid "technological obsolescence"; someone can come from behind who's twice as good. It also helps if you make a big impact on the job at the front end. Overkill at the beginning. This doesn't mean loud bragging. You don't talk yourself up until you get a feel for the situation. You delve in and work—fast, well, and extra. "This will establish you as a unique talent," says McLaughlin.

12. *Be mobile.* Don't stay in one job too long. For advancement you need depth of experience. Sometimes you can make all the necessary moves within one company. Usually you have to switch. Remember, if you're indispensable where you are, you may be unpromotable. Your boss may say, "We could never replace anyone like you"—and give the job you want to someone else.

13. *Be prepared to quit.* The supposed immobility of women is their most serious handicap. Companies move a promising young man around; they expect him to develop and change. A woman who wants to move out of the female

job ghetto must fight the preconceived ideas of people who have her indexed as an underling. She may have to quit to get away from a male chauvinist employer or from the patronizing boss who calls her "our bright girl." She may have to quit to advance or to maintain her self-respect.

Along with her "Be a lady" routine, my mother used to say, "Everything always works out for the best." From hindsight, I now know this isn't true. A lot of good things have happened to me even though I stuck for so long in a dead-end job, but how many wonderful things might have happened if I had just *once* asked myself, "Where do I want to be in five years?"

In operating assertively in the business world, follow three basics:

- Be a person rather than a woman or a man. Do a good job.
- Know where you want to go.
- Go after what you want.

Chapter 12

Conclusion

I backslid yesterday.

My work had not gone well. In the middle of the morning our downstairs neighbor called to complain about the lack of heat, which we control for the house from our apartment. Meekly, I accepted the blame, but when I checked the steam pipes, I discovered that no heat was coming up. I had reverted to my old pattern of apologizing for something that wasn't my fault. Then I took a cartoon for framing and let the shop proprietor talk me into a $25 pewter frame when I really wanted a simple black $10 frame. He looked so tired that I couldn't say no.

These two incidents started me on an anxiety whirlpool. For the rest of the day my anxiety and tension mounted. What book should I do next? Did I dare try my novel? Supposing I failed? Should I opt for the security of a nonfiction book where I'd have a proven technique? And there was the silver problem. What should I do about the family silver, which my mother had left in her will to my sister and me? My stepmother had been using *my* silver for twenty-two years. I needed a bread tray. Why should I go buy one when I really had one—in my stepmother's breakfront? Then my thoughts focused on my stepdaughter. Through the court's order, my husband now saw Ann every Saturday for lunch. But he never brought her home nor did he invite me to join them. What was I—the outcast, good enough to make a working woman's contribution to the household expenses but kept, in seclusion like an Indian woman in purdah, out of contact with the child?

That night I couldn't sleep.

Before Assertiveness Training, I would have stayed passive and helpless in the face of these anxieties, letting them build and build until I had a feeling of no control. Now it was different. After my restless night, I woke up and said to myself, "It's your life. Do something about it." This is what I did.

I knocked on my neighbor's door, and when he answered, I explained that the heat wasn't working and that he should please speak to the landlord about it.

I called the framer to ask if I could please have the plain black frame instead of the pewter. "No," he replied. "I've already started work on it." Well, I tried. So I'd be $15 poorer.

I telephoned my agent and discussed the next book problem with her. "Do outlines for the fiction and the nonfiction," she counseled. "Let's see the reaction. Then you can decide. Why worry about it now?" This was smart advice. I took it.

Gathering my courage, I called my stepmother and made a little speech about my right to the silver. Before I had completed it, she interrupted with, "Of course, you and Lee should divide it—I've been waiting for you to say something. I'm tired of polishing it."

Over coffee at night I spoke to Herb. This time I didn't nag or cry but said simply, "It doesn't seem right that you don't bring Ann to our home. Can you just ask her if she would like to come here for lunch on Saturday? Tell her I'd like very much to see her again. Whatever it is, I'll accept her decision."

This was a very different approach from my previous "You treat me like a nonperson" one. Giving me a pleased look, Herb said, "Of course."

Suddenly I felt like a winner—not because I had beaten anyone else but because I had had the courage to take a stand on several things and had accepted responsibility for my own decisions. I liked myself.

You too can become an assertive woman. This will not be an overnight process. It is something that you must work on continually as you try to banish from your brain the conditioning of Mama and society.

Society cannot change unless you change. You can do it if you try.

Appendix I

Full Relaxation Exercise

The following is the text of a tape recording made during a relaxation session and given to patients to take home. Readers who wish to record it for their own use should have it read by a person whose voice can on demand assume a lulling quality. The passages referring to the tensing of the muscles should be read briskly. Those calling for relaxation are read in a slow, soothing, almost musical cadence that carries some element of hypnotism.*

Lie down. Your eyes are closed. Your arms are at your sides, your fingers open. Get yourself good and comfortable. If stray thoughts enter your mind, say to yourself, STOP. Push them away and concentrate on what you are doing—

The first thing to do is tighten the muscles in the lower part of your body. Turn your feet inward, pigeon-toed, heels slightly apart. Curl your toes tightly, bend your feet downward away from you—now upward toward you—this tightens the muscles along your shins and in your calves—At

---

* From *Help Without Psychoanalysis*, Herbert Fensterheim, Ph.D., New York, Stein and Day, 1971.

the same time, tighten up your thighs, tighten up the muscles of your buttocks, and the muscles around your anus—not so tight that they are strained, but tight enough to feel the tension—Study it, study the tension—Tense, tense, tense— *(Five-second pause)*

Now relax—just feel the tension flow out—Concentrate on relaxing the muscles of your toes—Relax the muscles of your legs—Relax the muscles of your thighs—Relax your buttocks, the muscles around your anus—Now concentrate on each part of your body as I name it—Toes relaxed—legs relaxed—thighs relaxed—muscles of your buttocks relaxed —All the tension out—*(Ten-second pause)*

Now tighten up the muscles of your abdomen. Make the muscles of your abdomen as taut as if a child were going to shove a football into your stomach—Get them good and tight—Study the tension—Feel where the tension is—Hold it for ten seconds—Hold it—Tense—tense—tense—

And now relax—Relax the muscles of your abdomen—Let them go—Try to relax the muscles deep inside your abdomen—the muscles of your gut—Let them go—You are more and more and more relaxed—*(Ten-second pause)*

And now the muscles of your back—Arch your back— arch the small of your back until you feel the tension build—Try to locate the tension—There are two long muscle columns alongside your spine—You may feel the tension there—Wherever it is get to know the feel of tension—Your back is tense—tense—tense—

And now relax—Relax the muscles of your back—Let them go—Let all the tension out—Your back feels limp and heavy—Let it stay that way—More and more and more relaxed—*(Ten-second pause)*

And now the muscles of your chest—Take a deep breath and hold it—Just keep on holding it—Five seconds—Notice as you hold your breath the tension starts to build up—Note the tension in your chest muscles—Study where it is—Ten seconds—Keep holding your breath—Recognize the feeling of tension—Fifteen seconds—Now slowly, as slowly as you can, let your breath out—Slowly—Now breathe easily and comfortably, as in a deep sleep—*(Pause)*—Keep on relaxing the muscles of your chest—Let them go—Let the tension out— *(Ten-second pause)*

Now concentrate on each part as I mention it—Abdomen relaxed—Back relaxed—Chest relaxed—All the tension out—*(Pause)*

And now the muscles of your fingers, arms, and shoulders—Make a tight fist with each hand—Keep your elbows stiff and straight—Elbows stiff and straight as rods—Raise your arms from the shoulders to a forty-five-degree angle— The angle of your arms is halfway between the couch and vertical—Now feel the tension—Study the tension—Study the tension in your fingers—in your forearms—in your arms and your shoulders—Hold the tension for ten seconds—Hold it—Hold it—Tense—tense—tense—

And now relax—Fingers open—Arms down to sides—Just relax—Relax the muscles of your fingers—Let them go— Relax the muscles of your upper arms—Let them go—And now the muscles of your shoulders—Let them go— *(Pause)*—Fingers relaxed—Arms relaxed—Shoulders relaxed—Let your arms feel limp and heavy—Just keep letting go— *(Ten-second pause)*

And now the muscles between the shoulder blades and the muscles of your neck—Pull your shoulders back until your shoulder blades are almost touching—At the same time arch your neck until your chin points to the ceiling—These are areas very sensitive to nervous tension—Many people feel most of their tension here—Feel the tension—Not so tight that it hurts—Study the tension—Let it build up—

Now relax—Relax the muscles between your shoulder blades—Let the tension flow out—Let it go—And relax the muscles of your neck—Let them go—Your neck muscles are not supporting your head—Your head is falling limply against the pillow—All the tension out—Feel it flowing out—*(Ten-second pause)*

And now the muscles of the upper part of the face—Make a grimace with the top part of your face—Squeeze your eyes tight shut—Wrinkle your nose—Frown—Notice where you feel the tension—Study it—Note that you feel the tension in the forehead, between the eyebrows, in the cheeks below the eyes—

Now relax—Let all the tension out—Just concentrate on relaxing the muscles of your forehead—Let them go—Relax your eyelids—As they relax, you note they begin to feel heavy—They make you feel drowsy, but you're not going to sleep—You must stay alert—Relax the muscles at the bridge of your nose—Let them go—Relax the muscles of your cheeks—Remember where they felt tight—Let them go— *(Ten-second pause)*

And now the muscles of your jaws and tongue—Bite hard with your back teeth, press them together until your jaws are tight—Feel the tension at your temples, by your ears—Wherever you feel the tension—Study it—Push your tongue against the back of your lower front teeth—Your jaws are tight—Your tongue is tight—Study the tension—Get to know it—Learn the feel of the tension—Hold it, hold it—

Now relax—Relax the muscles of your jaws—Let them go—Relax your tongue—Your teeth should be slightly parted—Your jaw is hanging slack—More and more relaxed— *(Ten-second pause)*

Now the muscles around the lower part of your face— Tense the muscles around your mouth and chin—The best way to make them tense is to grin—A big grin, a grimace— Draw back your lips to show your teeth, upper and lower teeth—Draw the corners of your mouth wide, pull them back and down—Feel the tension in your lips, around your mouth, in your chin—Let the tension build up—Hold it—feel it— study it—Tense—tense—tense—

Now relax—Relax the muscles around your mouth and chin—Let them go—Get all the tension out—*(Ten-second pause)*—Now try to relax the muscles of your throat—Relax the soft part of your throat where you swallow—Relax the muscles of your voice box—Just try to get all the tension out of there—*(Ten-second pause)* That's the end of the first part of the exercise—Keep your eyes closed; you're still relaxing.

Now for the second part. Just ask yourself: Is there any tension in my legs, my thighs, in my buttocks? If there is, let it go—Try to get all the tension out—More and more relaxed—*(Ten-second pause)* Then ask yourself: Is there any tension in my abdomen, my back, or my chest? If there is, let it go—Breathe easily and comfortably, the way you do in a deep sleep—All the tension out—*(Ten-second pause)* And now ask yourself: Is there any tension in my fingers, my arms, or my shoulders?—If there is, let it go—Let your arms get limp and heavy—*(Ten-second pause)* Now ask yourself:

Is there any tension in my shoulder blades or in my neck? If there is, let it go—Your head is falling limply back to the pillow—*(Pause)*—And now ask yourself: Is there any tension in my face, my jaws, or my throat? If there is let it go—All the tension out—Just keep letting go—*(Pause)*

And now the third part of the exercise. Picture your pleasant scene, the scene we discussed before, or if you have trouble with that, picture the word CALM—Get a good clear picture, not just the sight, but the sounds, the smells, and the feel—If your mind wanders, always bring it back to the pleasant scene. And while you hold that picture in your mind, concentrate on relaxing the muscles of your toes—Let them go—*(Pause)*—Relax the muscles of your thighs—Let them go—*(Pause)*—Relax the muscles of your buttocks—Let them go—*(Pause)*—Keep picturing your pleasant scene. If stray thoughts come into your mind, just tell yourself STOP. Put them away, just concentrate on the muscles of your abdomen—Let them go—Relax—*(Pause)*—Relax the muscles of your back—*(Pause)*—Relax the muscles of your chest—Breathe easily and comfortably—Keep picturing your pleasant scene—*(Pause)*—Relax the muscles of your fingers—Let them go—*(Pause)*—Relax your forearms—(Pause)—Relax the muscles of your shoulders—Let them go—*(Pause)*—Relax the muscles of your shoulder blades—Let them go—*(Pause)*—Relax the muscles of your neck—Let them go—*(Pause)*—Keep picturing the pleasant scene—Relax the muscles of your forehead—Let them go—*(Pause)*—Relax your eyelids—*(Pause)*—Relax the muscles at the bridge of your nose—Let them go—*(Pause)*—Relax your jaw muscles—Relax your tongue—Relax the muscles around your mouth and chin—Let them go—*(Pause)*—Relax the muscles of your throat—All the tension out—Let yourself feel limp and heavy all over—Now keep picturing the pleasant scene—Calm and relaxed—Calm and relaxed—*(Ten-second pause)*—If you feel tension anywhere—just let it go—*(Thirty-second pause)*—Now I'm going to count from three to one. At the count of one, you will sit up and open your eyes. You'll be alert and wide awake and very refreshed—Three—two—one.

Moon Game Answer Sheet*

RATIONALE:	CORRECT NUMBER:	
No oxygen	15	Box of matches
Can live quite a while without food	4	Food concentrate
For travel over rough terrain	6	Fifty feet of nylon rope
Carrying	8	Parachute silk
Lighted side of moon is hot	13	Portable heating unit
Some use for propulsion	11	Two .45-caliber pistols
Needs H_2O to work	12	One case dehydrated Pet milk
No air on moon	1	Two 100-lb. tanks of oxygen
Needed for navigation	3	Stellar map (of moon's constellation)
Some value for shelter or carrying	9	Life raft
Moon's magnetic field is different from earth's	14	Magnetic compass
You can't live long without this	2	Five gallons of water
No oxygen	10	Signal flares
First-aid kit might be needed but needles are useless	7	First-aid kit containing injection needles
Communication	5	Solar-powered FM receiver-transmitter

Bibliography

Adams, Margaret. "The Compassion Trap." In *Woman in Sexist Society*, edited by Vivian Gornick, and Barbara K. Moran, New York: New American Library, 1972.

Alberti, Robert E. and Emmons, Michael L. *Your Perfect Right*. San Luis Obispo, Calif.: Impact, 1970.

American Psychological Association, "Report of the Task Force on Sex Bias and Sex-Role Stereotyping in Psychotherapeutic Practice." *American Psychologist*, December, 1975.

Aristophanes. *The Eleven Comedies*. New York: Liveright Publishing Corporation, 1943.

Bach, George R. and Deutsch, Ronald M. *Pairing*. New York: Peter H. Wyden, Inc., 1970.

Bach, George R. and Goldberg, Herbert. *Creative Aggression*. Garden City, New York: Doubleday and Company, 1974.

Bach, George R. and Wyden, Peter H. *The Intimate Enemy*. New York: William Morrow and Company, 1968.

Bach, George R. with Bernard, Yetta. "*Aggression Lab*." Dubuque, Iowa: Kendall/Hunt Publishing Company, 1971.

Bach, Lydia. *Awake! Aware! Alive! Exercises for a Vital Body*. New York: Random House, 1973.

Baer, Jean. *The Second Wife*. Garden City, New York: Doubleday and Co., 1972.

————. *The Single Girl Goes to Town*. New York: Macmillan, 1968.

Bardwick, Judith M.; Douvan, Elizabeth; Horner, Matina S.; Gutmann, David, *Feminine Personality and Conflict*. Belmont, Calif.: Brooks/Cole Publishing Company, 1970.

Beier, Ernst C. "Nonverbal Communication: How We Send Emotional Messages." *Psychology Today,* October, 1974.

Bem, Sandra Lipsitz. "Beyond Androgyny: Some Presumptuous Prescriptions for a Liberated Sexual Identity," to be published in J. Sherman and F. Denmark (eds.) *Psychology of Women: Future Directions of Research*. New York: Psychological Dimensions, in press.

————. "Fluffy Women and Chesty Men." *Psychology Today,* September, 1975.

Berne, Eric. *Sex in Human Loving*. New York: Pocket Books, 1971.

Bird, Caroline. *Everything a Woman Needs to Know to Get Paid What She's Worth*. New York: David McKay Company, Inc., 1973.

Block, Jeanne Humphrey. "Conceptions of Sex Role." *American Psychologist,* June, 1973.

Bloom, Lynn Z.; Coburn, Karen; Pearlman, Joan. *The New Assertive Woman*. New York: Delacorte Press, 1975.

Bower, Sharon and Bower, Gordon. *Asserting Yourself—A Practical Guide for Positive Action*. Reading, Mass: Addison-Wesley, 1976.

Brenton, Myron. *Sex Talk*. New York: Fawcett Crest Books, 1972.

Brockway, Barbara Stephens. "Assertive Training with Professional Women." Paper presented at the ninth annual meeting of the Association for Advancement of Behavior Therapy, San Francisco, Calif., December, 1975

Constantinople, Ann. "Masculinity-Femininity: An Exception to a Famous Dictum." *Psychological Bulletin,* No. 5, November, 1973.

DeRisi, William J. and Butz, George. *Writing Behavioral Contracts*. Champaign, Illinois: Research Press Co., 1975.

Dodgson, Charles Lutwidge. *The Complete Works of Lewis Carroll*. New York: The Modern Library (Random House), 1936.

Eisler, Richard M. and Hersen, Michel. "Behavioral Techniques in Family-Oriented Crisis Interventions." *Archives of General Psychiatry* 28 (1973): 111-116.

Eisler, Richard M.; Hersen, Michel; and Miller, Peter M. "Situational Determinants of Assertive Behaviors." *Journal of Consulting and Clinical Psychology,* Vol. 43, no. 3 (1975): 330-340.

Ellis, Albert. "Rational-Emotive Therapy." In *Direct Psychother-*

apy, edited by Ratibor-Ray M. Jurjevich. Coral Gables, Florida: University of Miami Press, 1975.

———. "The No-Cop-Out Therapy." *Psychology Today*, July, 1973.

———. *The Intelligent Woman's Guide to Man-Hunting.* New York: Lyle Stuart, 1963.

Ellis, Albert and Harper, Robert A. *A Guide to Rational Living,* North Hollywood, Calif.: Wilshire Book Company, 1973.

Fensterheim, Herbert and Baer, Jean. *Don't Say Yes When You Want to Say No.* New York: David McKay Company, Inc., 1975.

Fensterheim, Herbert. *Help Without Psychoanalysis.* New York: Stein and Day, 1971.

———. "Assertive Methods and Marital Problems." *Advances in Behavior Therapy,* edited by Richard P. Rubin, Herbert Fensterheim, John Henderson, Leonard P. Ullmann. New York: Academic Press, 1972.

Flexner, Eleanor. *Mary Wollstonecraft.* Baltimore, Maryland: Penguin Books Inc. 1973.

Fodor, Iris Goldstein. "The Phobic Syndrome in Women: Implications for Treatment." *Women in Therapy,* edited by Violet Franks and Vasanti Burtle. New York: Brunner/Mazel, 1974.

Ford, Clellan S. and Beach, Frank A. *Patterns of Sexual Behavior.* New York: Harper & Brothers, Publishers, and Paul B. Hoeber, Inc., Medical Books, 1951.

Franklin, Benjamin. *The Autobiography of Benjamin Franklin.* New York: The Century Co., 1901.

Franks, Violet and Burtle, Vasanti. *Women in Therapy.* New York: Brunner/Mazel, 1974.

Friedman, Philip H. "The Effects of Modeling and Role-Playing on Assertive Behavior." *Advances in Behavior Therapy,* edited by Richard D. Rubin, Herbert Fensterheim, Arnold A. Lazarus, Cyril M. Franks. New York: Academic Press, 1971.

Gambrill, Eileen D. and Richey, Cheryl A. "An Assertion Inventory for Use in Assessment and Research." *Behavior Therapy,* July, 1975.

———. *It's Up to You: The Development of Assertive Social Skills.* Millbrae, Calif.: Les Femmes, 1976.

Garskof, Michele Hoffnung (ed.). *Roles Women Play: Readings Toward Women's Liberation.* Belmont, Calif.: Brooks/Cole Publishing Company, 1971.

Gornick, Vivian. "Why Radcliffe Women Are Afraid of Success." *The New York Times,* January 14, 1973.

Gornick, Vivian and Moran, Barbara K., *Woman in Sexist Society.* New York: Basic Books, Inc., 1971.

Gutride, Martin E. and Goldstein, Arnold P. "The Use of Model-ing and Role-Playing to Increase Social Interaction Among Asocial Psychiatric Patients. *Journal of Consulting and Clinical Psychology*, Vol. 40, no. 3, 1973.

Higginson, Margaret V. and Quick, Thomas L., *The Ambitious Woman's Guide to a Successful Career*. New York: American Management Associations, 1975.

"J." *The Sensuous Woman*. New York: Dell Publishing Company, Inc., 1971.

Jacobson, Edmund. *Self-Operations Control*. Philadelphia: J. P. Lippincott Company, 1964.

Jakubowski-Spector, Patricia. "Facilitating the Growth of Women Through Assertive Training." *The Counseling Psychologist* 4 (1973): 75-86.

Johnson, Paula. "Antecedents and Consequences of Non-Stereo-typic Power Use." Paper presented at the annual meeting of the American Psychological Association, Chicago, 1975.

Kaplan, Helen Singer. *The New Sex Therapy*. New York: Brun-ner/Mazel, 1974.

————. *The Illustrated Manual of Sex Therapy*. New York: Quad-rangle/The New York Times Book Co., 1975.

Kazdin, Alan E. "Covert Modeling, Imagery Assessment and As-sertive Behavior." *Journal of Consulting and Clinical Psychology*, Vol. 43, no. 5, October, 1975.

Kline-Graber, Georgia and Graber, Benjamin. *Woman's Orgasm*. Indianapolis/New York: The Bobbs-Merrill Company, 1975.

Korda, Michael. *Male Chauvinism! How It Works*. New York: Berkeley Medallion Books, 1974.

————. *Power! How to Get It. How to Use It*. New York: Ran-dom House, Inc., 1975.

Kundsin, Ruth B. *Women & Success*. New York: William Morrow and Company, 1974.

Lawson, Donna. "The Art of Assertiveness." *Viva*, September, 1975.

Lazarus, Arnold A. *Behavior Therapy and Beyond*. New York: McGraw-Hill Book Company, 1971.

————. "Women in Therapy." From *Women in Therapy: New Psychotherapies for a Changing Society*, edited by Violet Franks and Vasanti Burtle. New York: Brunner/Mazel, 1974.

Lazarus, Arnold A. and Fay, Allen. *I Can If I Want To*. New York: William Morrow and Company, 1975.

Liberman, Robert; King, Larry W., DeRisi, William J.; McCann, Michael. *Personal Effectiveness*. Champaign, Illinois: Research Press, 1975.

LoPiccolo, Joseph and Miller, Vinnie H. "Procedural Outline Sexual Enrichment Groups." *The Counseling Psychologist*, Vol. 5, no. 1, 1975.

————. "A Program for Enhancing the Sexual Relationship of Normal Couples." *The Counseling Psychologist*, Vol. 5, no. 1, 1975.

LoPiccolo, Joseph and Lobitz, W. Charles. "The Role of Masturbation in the Treatment of Orgasmic Dysfunction." *Archives of Sexual Behavior*, Vol. 2, no. 2, December, 1972.

Lynch, Edith M. *The Executive Suite—Feminine Style*. New York: AMACOM, 1973.

Maccoby, Eleanor Emmons and Jacklin, Carol Nagy. *The Psychology of Sex Differences*. Stanford, Calif.: Stanford University Press, 1974.

MacDonald, Charlotte. "Stop Putting Yourself Down." *Woman's Day*, April, 1975.

Maier, Norman R. F. *Psychology in Industrial Organizations*. Boston: Houghton Mifflin Company, 1973.

Maslow, A. H. *The Farther Reaches of Human Nature*. New York: The Viking Press, 1971.

Masters, William H. and Johnson, Virginia E. *Human Sexual Inadequacy*. Boston: Little, Brown and Company, 1970.

McFall, Richard M. and Lillesand, Diane V. Bridges. "Behavior Rehearsal with Modeling and Coaching in Assertion Training." *Journal of Abnormal Psychology*, Vol. 77, no. 3, June, 1971.

McLaughlin, David. *The Executive Money Map*. New York: McGraw-Hill Book Company, 1975.

Meichenbaum, Donald and Turk, Dennis. "The Cognitive-Behavioral Management of Anxiety, Anger and Pain." Paper presented at the Seventh Banff International Conference on Behavior Modification, 1975.

Meredith, Scott. *George S. Kaufman and His Friends*. New York: Doubleday and Company, Inc., 1974.

Mill, John Stuart. *On the Subjection of Women*. Greenwich, Conn.: Fawcett Publications, Inc., 1971.

Mintz, Elizabeth E. "What Do We Owe Today's Woman?" *International Journal of Group Psychotherapy*, Vol. XXIV, no. 3, July, 1974.

Morgan, Marabel. *The Total Woman*. Old Tappan, New Jersey: Fleming H. Revell Company, 1973.

Osborn, Susan M. and Harris, Gloria G. *Assertive Training for Women*. Springfield, Illinois: Charles C. Thomas, 1975.

Phelps, Stanlee and Austin, Nancy. *The Assertive Woman*. San Luis Obispo, Calif.: Impact, 1975.

Phillips, Debora. "The Family Council: A Segment of Adolescent

Treatment." *Journal of Behavior Therapy and Experimental Psychiatry* 6 (1975): 93-100.

Pogrebin, Letty Cottin. "Rap Groups." *Ms.*, March, 1973.

Quinn, Sally. *We're Going to Make You a Star.* New York: Simon and Schuster, 1975.

Rosenthal, Robert; Archer, Dane; DiMatteo, M. Robin; Koivumaki, Judith Hall; Rogers, Peter L. "Body Talk and Tone of Voice: The Language Without Words." *Psychology Today*, September, 1974.

Richey, Cheryl A. "Increased Female Assertiveness Through Self-Reinforcement." Unpublished doctoral dissertation, University of California at Berkeley, 1974.

Riencourt, Amaury de. *Sex and Power in History.* New York: David McKay Company, Inc., 1974.

Salter, Andrew. *Conditioned Reflex Therapy.* New York: Farrar, Straus & Giroux, Inc., 1949; Capricorn Books Edition, 1961.

Serber, Michael. "Teaching the Nonverbal Components of Assertive Training." *Journal of Behavior Therapy and Experimental Psychology*, Vol. 3, no. 3, September, 1972. New York: Pergamon Press.

Serbin, Lisa A. and O'Leary, K. Daniel. "How Nursery Schools Teach Girls to Shut Up." *Psychology Today*, December, 1975.

Sherfey, Mary Jane. *The Nature and Evolution of Female Sexuality.* New York: Random House, 1972.

Staines, Graham; Tavris, Carol; and Jayaratne, Toby Epstein. "The Queen Bee Syndrome." *Psychology Today*, January, 1974.

Stuart, Richard B. and Stuart, Freida. *Marital Pre-Counseling Inventory.* Champaign, Illinois: Research Press, 1973.

Stuart, Freida; Stuart, Richard B.; Maurice, William L.; and Szasz, George. *Sexual Adjustment Inventory*, Champaign, Illinois: Research Press Company, 1975.

Susskind, Dorothy. "The Idealized Self-Image (ISI): A New Technique in Confidence Training." *Behavior Therapy*, Vol. 1, no. 4, November, 1970.

Tuffill, S. G. *Sexual Stimulation: Games Lovers Play.* New York: Grove Press, Inc., 1973.

Weathers, Lawrence and Liberman, Robert Paul. "The Family Contracting Exercise." *Journal of Behavior Therapy and Experimental Psychiatry*, Vol. 6, no. 3, October, 1975.

Wolpe, Joseph. *The Practice of Behavior Therapy*, 2nd ed. Elmsford, New York: Pergamon Press, Inc., 1973.

Wolpe, Joseph and Lazarus, Arnold A. *Behavior Therapy Techniques.* Long Island City, New York: Pergamon Press, Inc., 1966.

Index

305

About the Author

Daughter of a newspaperman, Jean Baer grew up in Mount Vernon, New York, and was graduated from Cornell University. She has worked for the Mutual Broadcasting Company, the United States Information Agency, and spent many years as senior editor and special projects director at *Seventeen* magazine. She is the author of four previous books: *Follow Me!, The Single Girl Goes to Town, The Second Wife,* and *Don't Say Yes When You Want to Say No* (co-authored with husband, Dr. Herbert Fensterheim, this book won an award from the American Psychological Association for "a noteworthy contribution to the public's understanding of psychology"). In addition, she is a frequent contributor to major magazines and newspapers on contemporary problems of women.

27 million Americans can't read a bedtime story to a child.

It's because 27 million adults in this country simply can't read.

Functional illiteracy has reached one out of five Americans. It robs them of even the simplest of human pleasures, like reading a fairy tale to a child.

You can change all this by joining the fight against illiteracy.

Call the Coalition for Literacy at toll-free **1-800-228-8813** and volunteer.

Volunteer Against Illiteracy. The only degree you need is a degree of caring.